CLOSE-UP ■ 01

First published in Great Britain in 2006 by
Wallflower Press
6a Middleton Place, Langham Street, London W1W 7TE
www.wallflowerpress.co.uk

A catalogue for this publication is available from the British Library.

ISBN 1-904764-57-6 (pbk)
ISBN 1-904764-66-5 (hbk)

Design by Elsa Mathern

Printed by Replika Press Pvt Ltd., India

CLOSE-UP ■ 01

FILMMAKERS' CHOICES John Gibbs

THE POP SONG IN FILM Ian Garwood

READING BUFFY Deborah Thomas

WALLFLOWER
LONDON & NEW YORK

CONTENTS

Editors' introduction

The title of this series signals its major intentions: to engage with the detail of films and television programmes and to make analysis of detailed decision-making central to the arguments being advanced in each individual study. These are modest objectives at one level, since it should be self-evident that any worthwhile study of the arts must engage closely with its objects. But even with the widespread institutionalisation of film and media studies and with a plurality of approaches to the subject being made available through an ever-expanding literature, studies that genuinely focus on the material complexity of films, and make this detail fundamental to their enquiries, are rare. The magnetic field of powerful concepts and approaches that dominated film theory from the early 1970s, and which often seemed to discourage engagement with the individual and specific, has weakened but it is still common to find, especially in texts designed for students, films being presented as little more than illustrations of wider concepts or approaches. 'Top-down' ways of thinking, in which the general framework takes precedence over the particular text, still pervade the literature and much teaching about film. Yet, if 'top-down' approaches can become programmatic, too often finding only examples of their own paradigms, the corrective cannot be to abandon informing frameworks. Theory and concept are required to channel and focus analysis, but investigation of the texture of filmmaking and of the dramatised world, informed by awareness of history and convention, must be able to question and re-shape concept and theory. There is still a huge challenge in understanding what films are and how they work to create meaning and affect. The objective of the *Close-Up* series comes to seem less modest when we begin to wrestle with the rich intersection of material elements in any moment of a film or television drama, attempting to find ways of capturing in language the nuances of action, performance and setting, the degrees of emphasis created by the selection of light, framing and editing, the grading of music, dialogue and other sound. *Close-Up* will engage with many different areas of cinema and television drama and individual contributions will be written from a variety of critical and theoretical positions. Each annual volume will reflect this variety by presenting three contrasting studies. What they will all share is a strong sense of the particular, the choices that make films distinctive and on which arguments for significance and value must rest.

John Gibbs and Douglas Pye
Close-Up series editors
February 2006

1.1 FILMMAKERS' CHOICES
John Gibbs

ACKNOWLEDGEMENTS

My first expression of gratitude is due to my colleagues in the Film and Television Division at the London College of Communication (LCC), part of the University of the Arts London, who have been extremely supportive during the writing of this project, and from whom I have learnt a great deal about the complex processes of filmmaking; the second is owed to the remarkable and resourceful students with whom we are lucky enough to work.

I am grateful to Wallflower Press for recognising the potential of the *Close-Up* series, and creating a new home for detailed criticism. I am indebted to the LCC Research Fund for facilitating the research and writing of *Filmmakers' Choices*. Thank you to Murray Smith for inviting me to the University of Kent to give a paper around the material in chapter one of this study, to Aoife Monks for encouraging me to give a research seminar at the University of Reading, and to those who took part in the discussions on both occasions.

My thanks to Uncle William for some important initial inspiration, to Emma Ramsden for her insights into Benigno's case, to the members of the Quilting B for discussing another recent Almodóvar film – *Live Flesh* – and for stimulating conversation on other occasions. I would particularly like to thank Douglas Pye, not just for his expert editorial work, but for the pleasures and insights provided by working with him more generally. To my wife Rebecca I want to express my love and gratitude for her support during the writing – *Filmmakers' Choices* is dedicated to our daughter Morgan, who was born as it neared completion.

INTRODUCTION

Making a film involves a myriad of choices. Every frame, every cut, every element of performance and every note on the soundtrack results from pursuing one option and refusing many others. When investigating a film, a valuable approach is to identify a decision, or a group of decisions, and ask 'what is gained by doing it this way?' Of all the thousands of ways of opening this film, say, what are the consequences of the particular approach employed? To think in such terms is to consider the crux of the artistic process: the relationship between decisions taken and a work's meanings.

Placing emphasis on the detail of decisions made and their consequences is not novel. The kind of enquiry I am describing here is similar to what Stanley Cavell has called 'the critical question – "Why is this as it is?" – which may be directed toward any acts and works of human beings and their societies' (1979: 187). Cavell was writing in 'More of The World Viewed', an essay reflecting on responses to his extraordinary book, *The World Viewed*, and the question is bound up with his approach to human intentionality more generally. For Cavell 'every gesture of the camera may or may not mean something, and every cut and every rhythm of cuts, and every framing and every inflection within a frame – something determined by the nature of film and by the specific context in which the gesture occurs in a particular film' (1979: 186–7). By giving these gestures – these decisions – appropriate weight we discover what they might mean.

Another important and related point of reference is the writing of V. F. Perkins. All of Perkins' work is rooted in reflection on the significance of detailed decision-making but his short, relatively little-known article, 'Moments of Choice' (1981), provided direct impetus for this study, and the *Close-Up* series more generally. 'Moments of Choice' examines instances of expressive choices in different aspects of film production. Moving from a discussion of décor into one of performance, this paragraph draws a generally applicable conclusion:

> Physical aspects of production like décor and dress can help the actors to feel themselves into their roles. But the detail of performance that brings the characters to life – movement, gesture, intonation, rhythm – has to be established on set. Here the director's job is, particularly, to hold each and every moment of performance within a vision of the scene as a whole so that the impact and effectiveness of *today's* scene is not achieved at the expense of what was filmed last week or what remains to be shot. [...] The pacing of a scene may seem just right in itself, but how will it look when the audience reaches it halfway through the film? Directors work in the knowledge that nothing is right 'in itself' but only in relation to the developing design. Balance and proportion are crucial. (1981: 1143)

This passage shares with Cavell an emphasis on the importance of considering elements of a film, and different kinds of decision, in relation to one another. It also demonstrates an additional interest of Perkins' criticism – a belief that the complex and interacting decisions can imaginatively and usefully be engaged with from the perspective of the filmmakers. Shifting from the audience's side of the equation to the makers' reminds us that 'What is gained by doing it this way?' is just as valuable a question for artist as for critic, and that the artist, as Perkins remarks elsewhere, is always a work's first audience (1990: 64).

Unfortunately, these emphases have had a marginal presence in academic film studies. To date, many subjects in the field are well served with theoretical and contextual approaches, yet few are well provided with a substantive criticism that examines how and what films mean. *Close-Up* is conceived as a forum for detailed analysis – it will ask 'the critical question' of films from a variety of movements, periods, genres and directors, and in relation to key concepts within the study of film and of television drama.

Filmmakers' Choices introduces the series by examining different areas of decision-making in a range of films. It begins with a comparison of two closely-related films, juxtaposing various decisions and considering their different effects, and then each chapter in the study examines a single film and a specific area of choice. In an earlier Wallflower Press book, *Mise-en-scène: Film Style and Interpretation* (2002), I argued that it is very difficult to consider a single stylistic area of choice without making reference to others. This is because – as the passages quoted above imply – decisions in one area are complexly integrated with other elements, both within a moment and across the length of the film. For this reason, and because I was keen to bring a detailed approach to other areas with which filmmakers are engaged, this book is concerned with what might be called *composite* areas of decision-making: ones that themselves interact with and imply a range of other areas of choice.

Investigating composite decisions involves balancing broader perspectives with an engagement at the most detailed level of the films' organisation. So chapter four, which addresses point of view, examines the realisation of particular sequences in order to discuss the complex relationship to its action which *Talk to Her* (*Hable con Ella*, Pedro Almodóvar, 2002) invites its audience to adopt. Chapter two, which looks at choices made in relation to generic conventions, pursues its theme quite broadly across *Unforgiven* (Clint Eastwood, 1992), but it begins with a particular decision in the presentation of a group of characters and seeks out a pattern of related strategies. Chapter three engages with choices of narrative structure – and particularly the creative possibilities of coincidence – by moving between a close reading of a sequence from *Lured* (Douglas Sirk, 1947) and reflection on the design of the narrative more generally. In chapter five the focus is a decision in the architectural design of the film's world which has ramifications for a range of interconnected areas of choice, and which is central to the significance and achievement of *Candyman* (Bernard Rose, 1992). Chapter one approaches the complexity of interlocking decisions in another way: the chapter explores ten areas of choice in a comparison of *The Reckless Moment* (Max Ophuls, 1949) and its remake *The Deep End* (Scott McGehee & David Siegel, 2001).

The choices discussed in the following chapters resulted from the intersection of developing sets of intentions with the collaboration of actors and crew working together in particular times and at particular places, within certain material and financial constraints. Writing about decisions taken and others refused involves acknowledging that these decisions would have been made in relation to the conventions of a historical time and place (both conventions of film form and those of broader social interaction). The filmmakers whose work is discussed will have made choices which were shaped by common assumptions of their day but, equally, may have been interested in challenging assumptions bound up in the conventions with which, and the traditions within which, they worked. The decisions explored here would sometimes have been made with a full sense of the extent of their implications and other times, and at other stages of what is a long and varied process, would have been made because they 'felt right'; artists of this calibre have the ability be extraordinarily self-aware as well as to make decisions in the moment – and have found ways of working which enable effective movement between these states. That the guiding and coordinating role in making these choices would often have fallen to an individual – typically the director – is compatible with recognising that decisions emerge through the complex processes of collaboration that lie behind any movie.

1. Choices and their consequences: a comparative analysis of decisions made in the realisation of *The Reckless Moment* (1949) and *The Deep End* (2001)

One of the best ways of determining what has been gained by the decisions taken in the construction of an artwork is to imagine the consequences of changing a single element of the design. Taking the commutation test a step further – rather in the manner of the scientific practice of keeping as many elements in an experiment as possible constant so as to notice more effectively the significance of the one varied – this chapter compares two different attempts at telling the same story.[1] Looking at a film and its remake – adaptations of an intelligent novel – here we will follow a different pattern from the other chapters in this study: rather than beginning with one decision (and one area of choice) and building discussion from there, this chapter will take advantage of the opportunity for comparison and look at the range of differing decisions taken in original and remake.

When *The Deep End* (Scott McGehee & David Siegel, 2001) was released in cinemas it was presented not as a remake of *The Reckless Moment* (Max Ophuls, 1949) but purely as an adaptation of Elizabeth Sanxay Holding's book, *The Blank Wall* (1947).[2] According to Peter Matthews' review in *Sight and Sound*, the UK press pack did not even refer to the existence of the earlier movie. A brief comparison of the novel with the films tells a different story. To give two examples of many available: *The Deep End* follows *The Reckless Moment* in having the sympathetic blackmailer die as a result of losing control of a car on a corner while driving away from the family home with Nagle's body; in *The Blank Wall* Martin Donnelly is not involved in a car accident, but confesses to the police for the murders of Darby and Nagle, condemning himself to the electric chair. At exactly the same point in both films, interrupting the first confrontation between the central character (Mrs Harper/Mrs Hall) and her daughter/son over the relationship with Darby, the mother receives a telephone call from her absent husband. In *The Deep End* this call is taken on the mobile extension in the son's bedroom, in *The Reckless Moment* telephone calls have to be received in the public space of the foot of the stairs, but in both films the conversation follows a similar turn, with daughter/son having a guarded conversation under the watchful eye of the mother, both complicit in keeping the real state of affairs from the absent father. In *The Blank Wall*, however, Mr Holley is fighting the Second World War in the Pacific and can only communicate with the family by v-mail; both films have reason to change the technology, but the presence of two such similar scenes cannot be coincidence. On the basis of the evidence McGehee, Siegel and their collaborators need to be seen as remaking *The Reckless Moment* rather than simply adapting Holding's novel: in other words, their choices are not simply those of adaptation and invention, they involve decisions about whether or not to follow the approach of the earlier Columbia production.

The story of *The Blank Wall*, and both of the films, centres on a mother and housewife who, in the absence of her husband, has to bring her family through a complex crisis while meeting its considerable demands upon her. The novel is entirely told through the woman's consciousness. Neither film attempts this, but in each we are party to the mother's experiences much of the time, and both films are interested in vividly conveying the dilemmas she faces. However, our response to each is likely to be very different.

Découpage

A number of the reasons for this are concerned with broad decisions the respective filmmakers took about how to stage and capture this action, including choices in mise-en-scène, découpage and editing.

The Reckless Moment is characterised by its use of long takes, long- or medium-shots and camera movement. It also gives us most of the action in long sequences which preserve strict temporal continuity. Consider, for example, the first sequence that presents the life of the house, which begins with Lucia Harper (Joan Bennett) returning home, laden with shopping, from her trip to Los Angeles to confront Darby (Shepperd Strudwick). After the opening dissolve, she walks from the car to the mail box, as we watch from the other side of the trashcan, some foliage protruding into the frame between her and us. Having collected the mail, she walks down the path to the house and weaves through the garage talking to her son David Harper (David Blair); we pan to follow this movement, viewing Lucia over the car on which David is working.

David:	Hey mother, how come you went up to Los Angeles this morning and didn't tell any of us?
Lucia:	I had some things to attend to attend to.
David:	I'm going to put on a new bumper, mother.
Lucia:	I think you're too late, and put on your shirt, David.

In the second shot the camera is placed inside the house's utility room: we catch Lucia walking past the window outside, and then pan right to view her (through the windows which separate this space from the kitchen) as she enters the house. From this vantage point we see her talk to her father-in-law, Tom Harper (Henry O'Neill), who is in the depth of the frame, looking toward Lucia from the dining-room by means of a serving hatch.

Lucia:	Hello Father, how's everything?
Tom:	Why didn't you tell us you were going to LA this morning?
Lucia:	I, uh, err, wanted to get to the store before the crowds.
Tom:	Sybil, will you turn that vacuum cleaner off, I can't hear the race results...

As she goes through the door into the hall, the film cutting on her action, 'Father' quickly comes back into sight moving through the living room, which is divided from the dining room and the hall only by (open) screen doors. The camera cranes with Lucia as she passes Sybil (Frances Williams) vacuuming on the stairs, and then pans and tilts with

Lucia, pausing momentarily outside Bee Harper's (Geraldine Brooks) door, and on to her own bedroom to confront Bee who is using the shower.[3] Of a sequence that lasts for five minutes and 15 seconds, and contains 28 shots, these three shots take up 51 seconds.

The sequence continues through the argument with Bee which begins in Lucia's room and then, after Bee has scolded Sybil from the landing, continues in Bee's room, the camera panning with Lucia's movement. Much of the argument is shown to us through the reverse-field cutting of static shots – except when Lucia walks around Bee's room – and all stationary shots in the sequence happen here. The argument over Darby is eventually interrupted by Lucia's husband Tom calling long-distance, and we watch by means of another complex camera movement, this time travelling alongside Lucia on the landing and descending the stairs with her to the telephone at their foot. The shot

Fig. 1.1

continues after this movement for a further one minute and 25 seconds, until the end of the sequence, as the family respond in different ways to the telephone call. The long-shot, long take is composed in some depth and Sybil's actions in the next room are revealed in the background. The action, and this last shot, continue as the family join in and then withdraw from Lucia's call.

All the camera movement in this sequence is motivated by Lucia's movements. As we pan, track or crane with Lucia through the house we are able to share her momentum, perceive the ways she negotiates physical and social spaces, encounter the different members of the household with her, and are close enough to read the expressions on her face. All of this – coupled with the fact that we are aware of her recent encounter with Darby when the rest of the household, except Bee, are not, enabling us to perceive her difficulty in responding to their questions about her trip to Los Angeles – provides us with a powerful insight into her situation.

At the same time, the décor often intervenes between us and Lucia, the camera taking a slightly different path through the house. The film gives us a perspective on Lucia, surrounded by the objects of her world; the intervening elements between us and her tempering our involvement with simultaneous distance. Even in the static shots, such as those in the reverse-field cut conversation with Bee, there are almost always elements of the décor intruding between us and the characters: the doorframe and chest of drawers when Bee stands at the shower door, the writing table and the parcels Lucia has just bought in the reverse-shot, the easel at which Bee is very deliberately sitting when Lucia follows her daughter into Bee's own room; one arm over the back of the chair, one foot resting on a cross support of the

Fig. 1.2

easel, Bee's assertion of bohemian sophistication undermined by a nervous biting of the nails of her left hand. In such ways we are presented with views of the characters within dramatically significant spaces.

Additionally, the film's first movement through the house initiates a network of motifs and interrelationships which will become more demanding and more oppressive as the film progresses. Elements are introduced that both establish the texture of family life and are integral to the film's thematic concerns: Lucia telling David to dress properly, the demands of the other members of the family make of her (only Sybil asks nothing of her in this sequence), her attempts to shape Bee's behaviour, the first of the telephone calls, the first and second of the two crane shots around the stairwell/hall, Sybil's complex position in relation to the family she works for, and so on. We also get the first use of the banisters in the hall to create an image of entrapment, something that gains its most powerful expression in the last moments of the film, but even here significantly impeding our view of Lucia.

We can see the development of these patterns by remarking briefly on the sequence when Lucia returns home to find Donnelly waiting to see her. This runs for seven and a half minutes and contains 26 shots, 13 of which are moving (I have not included small adjustments in this number, only pronounced movements of the camera, most of them tracking or crane shots). During this sequence the camera is in motion literally for half of the time, an extraordinary statistic for a sequence set within the confines of a by-no-means-enormous family home.

The continuity of action and the way that continuity is presented to us are vital here. The interaction of Donnelly with the family members who keep interrupting the conversation between victim and blackmailer, and Lucia's unsuccessful attempts to keep both separate, are made the more vivid because of the impression of continuity, achieved through a series of long takes which not only preserve real time for long periods but which also begin to imply connections between the elements that they contain. The long takes in *The Reckless Moment* add to the awkward intermingling that Lucia is powerless to prevent taking place between Donnelly and her family.[4]

In contrast *The Deep End*'s general approach is to realise its sequences through the reverse-field cutting of close-ups, either showing us one actor in frame at a time or in an over-shoulder shot where we can only see the back of the other character. The scale of these shots is usually head and shoulders; sometimes the face fills the height of the screen, occasionally a view will show a character down as far as their waist. (There are some shots in the film when we see the full figure of the actors but they are infrequent and fleeting, especially during conversations.) As these shots are close-ups, and are shot on standard or long lenses, our view of the background is restricted and tends to be out of focus.

Although this is a widescreen image, the framing is such that we get very little sense of the behaviour of characters in relationship to one another in these sequences. The film focuses our attention on the facial expressions of one character at a time, rather than provide us a view which reveals both – a very deliberate step when a widescreen frame can so readily contain two actors simultaneously. Rather than the sense of how these people interrupt and interrelate with each other which is achieved in *The Reckless Moment*, the cumulative effect of these decisions in *The Deep End* is to abstract the characters from their environment, and from each other.

Comparing the number of shots in the respective sequences also makes a revealing comparison. In the scenes when Margaret Hall (Tilda Swinton) returns home and confronts Beau Hall (Jonathan Tucker) there are 61 shots in five minutes. As we saw, the equivalent action in *The Reckless Moment* takes a similar time, but contains 28 shots. The introduction of Alek Spera (Goran Visnjic, the sympathetic blackmailer of the remake) contains 105 shots and lasts seven minutes and 50 seconds approximately; the introduction of Martin Donnelly (James Mason) is seven and a half minutes long, and is comprised of only 26 shots. It would appear from the statistics that *The Deep End* eschews not only the long-shot but the long take as well.

Instead, the decisions in *The Deep End* create a picture of Margaret in relation to her family where the tenor is of separation and disjunction. Where camera movement in

Fig. 1.3

The Reckless Moment connected, here the editing separates. In addition, where Joan Bennett's Lucia is almost always on the move, Tilda Swinton's Margaret, in this sequence and in the film more generally, is frequently stationary, sometimes stunned into repose. One of the defining images of Margaret in this sequence is her dismayed response to the news, imparted by her departing daughter Paige Hall (Tamara Hope), that Beau 'took off in the boat, mad about something', viewed through the panes and woodwork of a door, and held for four seconds after Paige has left the frame.

Another important difference is that rather than creating the illusion of continuous time, as its predecessor does, *The Deep End* frequently abbreviates time, eliding parts of the action through cutting or dissolves. These jumps through time and space are often accompanied with a sound bridge. In the equivalent sequence to Lucia's returning home, *The Deep End* gives us four sequences, and five distinct periods of time – and this total includes, as one period, Margaret's flashbacks to Beau's car accident which are shown to us as she sits by the lake. Similarly, the equivalent scene to the introduction of Donnelly, the arrival of Alek Spera, is split into five distinct units of time and space: by a dissolve between Beau reading of Darby's death and his confronting Margaret, by the raucous cut to the computer fishing game, by the cut to the aquarium in the living room and by another small elision from the awkward conversation between Margaret, Alek and Jack (Peter Donat) to Alek and Margaret's further conversation outside the door of the house.

From this description one might imagine these short, often jarringly cut-together sequences make vivid a day in which demanding activities pile one on top of the other. However, the effect achieved is quite the opposite. Each of these breaks in continuity *lessens* the cumulative impact; the pressure is not allowed to build as it is in Ophuls' film, but dissipated. As well as the general effect, there are also specific occasions when the elisions let the characters and audience off the hook: the last break in Alek's first appearance gets Margaret out of the embarrassing encounter between herself, Alek and Jack. Jack's question – 'Spera? From the air station?' – is left hanging and we do not have to watch Margaret and Alek complicitly manoeuvre themselves outside.

There is some camera movement in these conversations in *The Deep End*, primarily adjustments in framing to accommodate such movements as the actors make. There are only two occasions, in the first scene in the house, when the camera tracks to evoke a character's movement: a three-second shot following Margaret, and another of the same length accompanying Paige, Margaret's daughter. More typically, if the camera tracks or cranes, the character is stationary and the camera moves, often in a slow, encircling motion.

A camera movement not motivated by the action of a character begins the part of Alek's introduction when he and Margaret encounter Jack, facilitating one of the many watery compositions in the film, with the aquarium filling half the frame before the camera tracks right to show Margaret and Alek entering the living room from the study. Unlike the intrusion of décor in *The Reckless Moment* which always happens when the camera is following the action, this is a camera movement and an inclusion of décor existing solely in order to create the image: there is no other reason to have the aquarium in the foreground at the start of the shot, and no reason to move the camera other than to remove it from view. More generally, the camera and character movement in these sequences does not attempt to create the sense of flow through the house that characterises the corresponding sequences in the earlier film.

Characters and their environment

The Deep End makes full use of the beauties of its location. The dawn of the second and third days are marked by views of the boathouse with the lake, the mountains and dramatic cloudscapes in the background. We see another of these shots at the beginning of the sequence when Margaret sits by the shore and thinks about Beau's accident, in the sequence of her return home. Even when the characters are engaged in distressing situations, we are always aware of the beauty within which the Hall family live, the size of their garden, the vista from the foreshore. Rhythmically, the shots of the boathouse even act a little like the transitional shots of an Ozu film, creating space for reflection or (in Paul Schrader's view, at least) an opportunity to register the transcendent qualities of a world beyond an in-

Fig. 1.4

dividual family's problems. As this comparison suggests, however, the effect of these views is to dissipate the intensity of the drama. Every time we get one of those achingly beautiful images its makes us relax, and marvel at how fortunate Margaret is.

Helicopter shots also figure significantly in this pattern of landscape images. When the characters are travelling (and even as Margaret sails up the lake with Darby's body) the film will suddenly adopt a massive vantage point to view the car or boat within the enormity of the landscape. These perspectives have the effect of reducing the scale of the problems with which the film is in other ways asking us to consider important. The emphasis on the grandeur of the landscape suggests the impermanence of the human characters, their insignificance in the face of nature. When all the problems of Margaret and her family are long forgotten, these mountains, this ice-cold water will endure. Such strategies have the potential to offer significant perspectives on a family's dilemmas but here they seem to contradict rather than complement the film's attempt to involve us in the drama. Instead of adding a meaningful dimension to the film's overall systems of point of view they become distractions.

Balboa, too, is an attractive place to live, but it is not presented in *The Reckless Moment* in a way to foreground this – not, anyway, after the opening shots. It becomes a raw, bleached, *overexposed* place. The tracking shots in the garden, sharing some of the same features as those indoors, help to make the immediate surroundings of the Harper house an extension of it. At night it becomes more threatening as the elements of noirish Los Angeles journey with Darby, Donnelly and Nagle to Balboa. In *The Reckless Moment* we find the family home and its surroundings an oppressive place; in *The Deep End* we want to live there.

Character and action

If cutting away to the overarching perspective or making the most of the location when it is not in the interests of dramatic intensity to do so might be considered evidence of a less than rigorous approach to the construction of point of view, so might some of the other choices made around access to the characters in *The Deep End*.

In *The Reckless Moment* we get to know Donnelly through his interaction with the family. In his first sequence there is only one view of him in the absence of the

other characters, a two-second shot which comes after he has told Lucia that he can wait while she talks to her daughter and the two have left the room, in which he shifts his weight from one foot to the other and glances to his left. It is a subtle performance element which suggests an awkwardness not apparent from the way he behaves toward the family, captured in a brief long-shot in the middle of a complicated sequence: telling, but not overstated. There are other occasions when we get to watch Donnelly's changing relationship

Fig. 1.5

to Lucia and the family, but they are all moments when he is interacting with family members, or others (such as the shopkeeper at the drugstore, or Nagle his partner).

The Deep End takes a different approach to making believable and apparent the blackmailer's change of heart. In his first scene Goran Visnjic plays the character edgily and without any suggestion of compassion, although Alek does not look like he is comfortable with what he has to do. There is nothing of the gentleness that begins to emerge from Martin Donnelly, even in his first appearance, in the way he talks to Father and David. Rather than the trip to the drugstore and the extended conversations that Lucia and Donnelly share on their second encounter, when Alek Spera arrives at the house after Margaret has failed to make their rendezvous, he helps revive old Mr Hall who has fallen to the floor with some form of heart attack. When the ambulance has carried away the patient, Margaret and Dylan (Margaret's youngest child, who does not correspond to any of the characters in the other stories), Alek is left in the driveway. He walks slowly back toward the house and, in a series of 11 shots, we see him wander around the living room and kitchen, examine a family photograph, even open the oven and contemplate the joint inside. The sequence ends with Beau returning home. On being challenged about what he is doing, Alek looks sheepish and says he was just going.

Having refused some of the ways that the earlier film gradually let the blackmailer get to know the family, *The Deep End* has him save the life of Margaret's father-in-law – an emphatic method of drawing from him behaviour which moves him out of his professional role and making him share an emotive experience with Margaret. Yet the subsequent sequence alone in the family home seems a very laboured way of trying to convey Alek's changing view of Margaret and her situation. Equally, staying with the blackmailer here seems false to the spirit and logic of the drama: if we are really engaged with Margaret's experience, surely we need to follow the journey with Grandfather to the emergency room, not potter around in the kitchen with Alek. Where *The Reckless Moment* gives us Donnelly's change of heart through complexly dramatised action which is simultaneously achieving other objectives, *The Deep End* gives us two minutes of business that exists solely to make plain Alek's changing feelings. This discrepancy between means and ends leaves Visnjic with an unenviable acting challenge.

In Ophuls' film, too, there are moments when we follow Donnelly rather than go with Lucia: the first of these, excepting the brief shot in the middle of the sequence of his first appearance and that we watch him walk into the night after Lucia has already gone inside, is the next morning when he assists David with the horn on the car. Then, in the drugstore scene, when Lucia is in the callbox, we accompany Donnelly and witness the purchase of the cigarette holder, even sharing his optical point of view in a shot of the gift of which Lucia will remain entirely ignorant. There are two other major departures from Lucia's experience. The first is the occasion when Donnelly telephones Lucia, where, once we have cut to Donnelly, we stay with him for the rest of the telephone call; this leads into the long take where he walks through the foyer of the hotel up to the counter where he has the conversation with Nagle. The second is after Donnelly has said goodbye to Lucia at the bus depot, having told her that she should now forget about the whole affair (someone else has been arrested for the murder); the camera stays with him tracking with him through two complex movements as he searches the hotel foyer and bar for Nagle. Soon after this, we are privileged over Lucia and Nagle in witnessing Donnelly's arrival at the house, and accompany him as he strides toward the boat house and Lucia's aid. Finally, we witness his attempts to remove the letters from Nagle's dead body and the resulting car crash.

All of these moments involve interaction with other characters and are part of on-going action. We do not need a separate sequence of Donnelly exploring the house to show his feelings. We can accept Donnelly having a generous side because we have already seen hints of it in his relations with Lucia's family: the way he talks to Mr Harper (even giving him racing tips), the way he accepts the generous welcome of David, that he is prepared to wait while Lucia consoles her daughter. When Alek enters the house, he encounters some of the members of the family – Paige, Jack and Dylan – but he does not interact with any of them, whereas in *The Reckless Moment* we can see Donnelly getting to know and appreciate the family, and appreciate their demands on Lucia.

Not cutting away from Donnelly during the telephone call

Let us take a look at one of these moments in more detail: the telephone call Donnelly makes to Lucia. The call interrupts a passage of action taking place at the house, but once the film cuts to Donnelly at the other end of the line it stays with him, the scale of shot changing to a close-up part-way through the conversation. In his excellent produc-tion history of *The Reckless Moment*, which forms part of *Max Ophuls in the Hollywood Studios*, Lutz Bacher records the prolonged resistance which Ophuls put up to pressure from B. B. Kahane, production vice-president at Columbia, to shoot footage of Lucia to intercut during this phone call (1996: 287, 311). Clearly, this was a very important point for the director. *The Deep End*, by contrast, cuts between Alek and Margaret during their telephone conversation.

What was gained in Ophuls' version? Why was he so ready to fight for the decision he had made? Donnelly is wearing a light jacket, in contrast to the dark overcoat which he has worn on all his previous appearances in the movie, and is standing in a well-lit telephone booth which fills the screen. At the point where Donnelly moves the conversa-tion away from the urgency of Nagle's demands for the money and onto the fact that he is not going to ask for his own share, the film cuts from a medium close-up to a close-up, filling the screen with Mason's head and offering us a three-quarter profile view of his face.[5] At this point, too, quietly plangent music comes in on the soundtrack, which plays on until it fades out halfway through the next shot, when Nagle begins to speak. Not only do we not see Lucia, we do not hear her voice on the other end of the line.

> I understand you can't talk. Look, now. I just called to tell you that he won't wait till Wednesday, he wants the money no later than Monday. And there is a Nagle, I'm afraid there's very much a Nagle. [Pause] You don't believe me. [Cut] Listen to me. Listen. If you can get half of it? You don't have to raise… I already told Nagle I wouldn't be wanting my

share. And I want you to know, too, that if I had the money I'd pay him off and that would be the end of it. [Pause] Are you there? [Pause] Did you hear what I said? [Pause] I wish you would believe me. I wish things could have been different in many ways. Only one good thing came of it – I met you. [Pause] Which way do you come into town? I'll meet you at the terminal.

Donnelly stands close to the receiver, speaking quietly but passionately. Because we can only hear one half of the conversation it almost becomes a monologue, almost a soliloquy. We might think, as Donnelly momentarily does, that Lucia has hung up, as he goes on to say things he would be much less likely say in person. If this seems fanciful, it is more prosaically the case that not cutting back to Lucia focuses all our attention on what Donnelly says, how he says it, and what it means to him.

He has separated himself from his surroundings in making this telephone call, and the telephone box is framed on its own, without giving us broader introduction to the space in which it is placed. We can see him unobserved by anyone else, and (after the cut) in an intimate view not equalled by any other shot of him in the film, even the close-up after the car crash, which is of a similar scale but which does not give us as clear a view of his face. The receiver links him to a sphere where he is increasingly keen to act differently to the ways in which he has become accustomed, and to which his energy is increasingly directed. (Contrast his delicate

Fig. 1.6

animation here with the way he talks to others in the following shot.) These elements contribute to evoking something of the sense of the confessional.

Above all, not cutting to Alicia, in conjunction with some of the other decisions described here, makes available to us a perspective that Donnelly is working out his own emotions, rather than fully communicating with another person who has different priorities. His extravagant claims – 'one good thing came of it – I met you' – are spoken into the ether, although we can conclude from the return of the conversation to practicalities, that this sentiment was not reciprocated. This sense that he is projecting qualities onto Lucia which may be rooted more in what she represents to him than in any objective reality, contributes to an important element of the film's portrayal of Donnelly. It connects to other elements of his characterisation and behaviour, evident in his romantic notions about Lucia's maternal role (Donnelly: 'She's lucky to have a mother like you.' Lucia: 'Everyone has a mother like me, you probably had one too.'), his recollections of his own mother's desire for him to be a priest and his ultimate self-sacrifice for Lucia and her family. The decisions made here, with the determination not to cut back to the house in Balboa at their centre, relate complexly to some of the key trajectories and interests of the film, which have been explored further by critics such as Andrew Britton (1976).

Revealing Nagle

At the end of the conversation Donnelly puts the telephone down, leaves the intimate space of the booth and walks through the very public foyer of the Midtown Hotel. Now the surroundings which have been withheld from us become all too apparent. A complex, tracking, long take follows him as he walks through the space, and a series of objects (two lampshades, a sofa, two pillars) and people (a man who asks where the game is tonight, to which he replies 'I don't know, I'm not playing') intervene between him and us. This shot, together with two as he searches for Nagle later in the film, offer a presentation of Donnelly within his environment which answers the ones of Lucia in hers.[6] The parallel that Donnelly makes between her relationship to her family and his to Nagle, angrily rejected by Lucia in the ferry scene, is supported by the film in this sense of their mutual constraint.[7]

Several of the areas of significance introduced during the telephone call are developed, in some instances by means of contrast, in the shot that follows. Donnelly picks up his dark overcoat as he walks through the foyer. He walks up to a counter at the opposite end of the space from the telephone booth, and leans against it next to another man, also dressed in dark clothes. Nagle (for it is he) says, 'Tell him the game will be held in room 420 tonight', and then, 'Talk to Her?'

Donnelly: Yes.
Nagle: She'll have the money Monday?
Donnelly: She'll try.
Nagle: What d'you give me that 'she'll try' business for? I told you what to tell her, let's cut out the horsing around. Maybe I'd better go down there and talk to her?
Donnelly: I'm handling this. You lay off. You're not going near her.
Nagle: I'm not, huh?
Donnelly: No you're not.
Nagle: You know this lady's not in your class, Martin. I often think you get mad at me because I remind you of what you are. You're not respectable, Martin. Relax, take it easy.

Fig. 1.7

During this conversation we can see Nagle behind Donnelly. Nagle is standing straight and Donnelly leaning forward on the counter, so when Nagle speaks it is from the back of Donnelly's head. During the conversation, Donnelly never turns to look at Nagle, although he does incline himself more in his partner's direction when he becomes more heated.

This is the first time we have met Nagle in the film, and there has been repeated speculation as to whether he actually exists. Lucia has on more than one occasion accused Donnelly of inventing his partner – in the manner of Smallweed in *Bleak House* (1852–53) – and Donnelly has protested strongly that he does exist, and that she really does not want to deal with him: 'There is a Nagle, I give you my word', was the line with which the ferry scene concluded; the first part of the telephone call continued this trajectory.

The staging of this sequence plays further with the status of Nagle, not perhaps as a figment of Donnelly's imagination but as an aspect of himself which he is keen to disavow. The way in which Donnelly does not need to acknowledge his partner intimates a close relationship of longstanding; the way in which Nagle's voice comes from behind Donnelly's head suggests an internal voice. Certainly, Nagle claims kinship with Donnelly, and a damning connection with him. A moment ago we had Donnelly's confession, now we meet his bad conscience.

The Deep End, by contrast, makes it clear that Nagle is a real person from Alek's very first appearance: at the end of the scene Margaret can see him standing by a car in her driveway making calls on his cellphone. Not only does the decision to reveal him on this occasion prevent the film from developing any of the possibilities exploited by Ophuls, but having Margaret (and the audience) uncertain of Nagle's veracity would be a useful element for the exchanges between the two characters even if it had no additional meta-phorical weight.[8] Certainly, nothing is gained by having him show himself, neither does it seem true to character to have him travel all the way out to Tahoe and wait around by the car for his partner to conduct their business.

Making Bee into Beau

Some major changes to the family in *The Deep End* may have been designed to give the film a contemporary feel. In *The Deep End* it is a young daughter, Paige, who is handy with cars, rather than *The Reckless Moment*'s David. The elder sibling has also under-gone a change of sex, and a change of sexuality. In *The Deep End*, it is not Bee, Lucia's daughter, who has been involved with Ted Darby but Beau, Margaret's son, who has been having an affair with Darby Reese. An immediate problem with which this decision presents the film is a series of representational pitfalls around predatory gay men. Darby Reese is loathsome, and the film does not make much of an attempt to distinguish bet-ween Margaret's concern at her son's sexuality and her concern at the circles in which he has found himself moving. The film moves toward restoring Beau's innocence (he never learns about his mother's efforts to safeguard his liberty and reputation) and he finally becomes a supportive, but desexualised, son.

More crucially, in making the change the film loses the opportunity for play on the relationship between Mother and Daughter which is so significant, in differing ways, in the novel and the 1949 film. In *The Blank Wall*, Bee initially defines herself in op-position to the domestic role in which she sees Lucia; their relationship forms part of a broader structure of parental/child relationships – in Holding's novel the grandparent about the house is Lucia's father, rather than her father-in-law. *The Reckless Moment* is also interested in Bee's rejection of the role of wife and mother, although, as critics have pointed out, one of the elements that contribute to the bleak 'happy' ending of the film is that events and Lucia have succeeded in re-making the rebellious art-student in Lucia's own image, wearing the fur coat, and going out to the pictures with the boy next door. David, too, has finally been encouraged to dress properly, a sign of his socialisation. By making Bee into Beau, *The Deep End* has ruled out any possibility of developing this theme.

The easel (and the world of the art school which Bee aspires to, and which has drawn her into contact with Darby) works very differently to the music practice which *The Deep End* substitutes, and not just because it enables Bee to take a defiant and knowing pose during her conversation with her mother, where music practice is a way for Beau to escape his mother that has to be abandoned once she comes into the room. Their chosen pursuits shape the characters in particular directions: Bee is condescendingly combative to her mother, albeit naïvely so; Beau is always lip-tremblingly on the defensive to his, with whom he refuses to discuss his sexuality. Beau's practice, and later the tape he needs to record in order to get into Wesleyan, embody for *The Deep End* the academic future which Margaret must protect from the association with Darby. These are highly respectable activities which any middle-class parent would be proud of: Beau does not play Jazz in a shady bar, he plays mournful classical solos. Where for Bee, art school is (at the beginning) her route out of Balboa and her mother's lifestyle, Beau's music is the route toward a university future that is not offered as a promising time and space for self-definition – the dynamic of its presentation is all about how a threat to his respectability might jeopardise his place. Bee's engagement with art school is her attempt at non-conformity, Beau's music scholarship must not be jeopardised by his.

What *The Deep End* constructs instead of the regeneration of Lucia in Bee is a more developed parallel between the sexual repression of Margaret and of Beau. In both films, the child's encounter with their lover in the boathouse, and the mother's attempt to suppress the bodily evidence, is answered later in the story. Firstly, by the appearance of the blackmailer in the family home, threatening exposure, who then develops a relationship, of sorts, with the mother. Secondly, by an answering scene in the boathouse, between the mother and the blackmailers, on both occasions the death of Nagle prompting Lucia and Margaret to offer to go to the police – in effect to make public everything they have been attempting to bury for the sake of the family: the child's involvement with Darby, the disposal of his body, their own entanglement with Donnelly/Spera. These elements (with the exception of the offer to go to the police) are inventions of Holding's novel, as is the extension of the respectability/repressed motif to the relationship between small town and city.[9] In *The Deep End*, the parallel between mother and child's tentative movement outside of family-sanctioned forms of affection is taken further. Both Beau and Margaret are slapped across the face in the boathouse (by Darby and Nagle respectively), the injuries being commented on by the other. More significantly, each has a role in effecting the other's repression: Margaret by trying to protect her son from Darby and Beau by his disapproval at what he takes to be an affair between his mother and Alek (Margaret: 'It's not what you think.' Beau: 'How do you know what I think?'). Then the family's irregularity which came to light with Beau's car accident is concealed again by Alek's. In the final scene in the bedroom there is a rapprochement, with a restating of filial and maternal affection, but Margaret is in tears and Beau now deliberate in his innocence: 'I don't need to know. It's not important.' Mother and son are returned to a repressed state – mutually supporting but defined by an ongoing breakdown of communication and a refusal to acknowledge their experiences. This emphasis of *The Deep End* is not served, however, by the film's attempts to dramatise Margaret's repression more generally, as will be argued in the course of examining the next area of choice.

The change of period

The Reckless Moment is a film concerned with what a middle-class wife and mother cannot do, or has difficulty doing. Lucia is constrained on every side by the demands of her role in relation to the family, yet has no financial independence of her husband – her unsuccessful movement from bank to loan company to pawnbrokers is a vital and complexly realised part of the movie, as Robin Wood (1976) and Andrew Britton (1976) have eloquently discussed. This is a film which is interested in exploring the limitations on movement and behaviour for a woman in the society it presents.

Where Lucia has to dispose of Darby while wearing a full-length overcoat and scarf, Margaret Hall is already wearing tennis shoes, trousers and a waxed jacket when she finds the late Darby Reese. In *The Deep End* Margaret's inability to raise the money (which has been inflated by ten times in the intervening years) is more of the order of an inconvenience than a reflection of her disenfranchisement: it is because her husband is the co-signatory on the mortgage that she cannot raise any money on it, and her attempts to secure a loan seem to be damaged more by the lack of time available rather than anything else.

Second-wave feminism should have had some kind of influence on Margaret's understanding of her social situation. Indeed, she marshals a list of her domestic duties as ammunition in the conversation when Alek accuses her of not trying hard enough to raise the money. In the equivalent conversation in *The Reckless Moment*, Lucia talks not of her own labour – I am not sure she would describe what she does in these terms – but David's summer work selling hamburgers. When Donnelly responds by asking her if she ever gets away from her family, she looks up sharply, clearly taken aback.

Much of *The Reckless Moment*'s power comes from the convincing way in which it dramatises the *process* by which Lucia develops a perspective on her entrapment within the family. In moments like this, building on the foundations provided by the earlier scenes in the house, the film encourages us to see the two kinds of pressure on Lucia in awkward relationship, and to make vivid for us one of the main structures and interests of the film – that it is through the experience of blackmail, and her interaction with Donnelly, that Lucia comes to see the limitations of her role as wife and mother. However, when Alek, in *The Deep End*, asks Margaret the same question, the fact that she has just listed all of her domestic chores makes nonsense of her shocked reaction.

Fig. 1.8

Fig. 1.9

Margaret's response to this question is one of the weakest moments of characterisation and performance in the film; characterisation because of the illogicality just discussed, performance not least because Swinton's reaction is caught in close-up, whereas Bennett's is captured in an ongoing wider shot which includes both her and Mason, and in which her sharp glance and turn of the head is significant but not insisted upon by the emphasis that a closer shot would have provided. Moreover, Bennett is looking in front of her when the question is posed, and then looks across at Mason, *away* from the camera; Swinton is already looking past the camera (toward Alek in the world constructed by the reverse-field cutting, but narrowly off-screen right for the spectator) and this is held for three seconds, as we see the movement of her eyelids and the quiver of her lip, before she turns to look away.

Having Margaret tell Alek about her domestic tasks actually has the effect of diminishing their weight and importance; *experiencing* the family's demands is so much more effective than hearing them listed. Attempts to show the audience the domestic pressures on Margaret are further undermined by the fact that she spends several moments in the early part of the film sitting around. In the sequence of her returning home, we saw her on the bench by the dock thinking about Beau's accident – after one of the shots of the boathouse with a cloudscape over the lake, to compound matters – and then doing the crossword while waiting for him to come home. Lucia is always on the move, except when the rest of the house has gone to bed, when she does the accounts or writes to her husband.

As so often, the decisions taken in one area have consequences in others. Changing the period without really engaging with the effect of changing social perceptions also causes a problem for *The Deep End* in the way we are likely to respond to the members of the family. As a result of his complaints about broken remote controls and dry cleaning, and his expectations of being served lunch at the time of his own convenience, Jack, the father-in-law, comes across as a selfish curmudgeon. More damagingly, Margaret's acceptance of this behaviour, offering to bring the lunch up to him in his room, renders her cowed and feeble. The father-in-law in *The Reckless Moment* is also demanding and impotent, and does not distinguish himself in the way he behaves toward Sybil, but he has redeeming features. There is the touching moment when he offers to help Lucia – replaced in the later film by the scene where Jack lends Margaret $80 – and if he is too easily satisfied by Lucia's response, his latter-day counterpart is entirely unable to perceive anything wrong. Typically of Ophuls' film, one can see the ways in which Lucia's relationship to the family might be sensibly compared by Donnelly to his with Nagle, and yet can see something of value within the people who make up that family.

The Deep End does not create an impression of the family as an integrated and complex set of human relationships. In fact, we never see them all together. You believe that Margaret cares for the individuals and for the future prospects of her son, but the sense of the family as living entity, something the mother celebrates and makes sacrifices for, is quite absent here.

A change of season and location

The Reckless Moment changed the time of year when *The Blank Wall* is set from early May to Christmas. Christmas is intimately associated with the notion of the family, in its origins and in the way the festival is celebrated today. Setting the film in mid-December adds another level of pressure on Lucia: not least as the audience understands that the approach of Christmas piles a higher than average burden of work, expense and expectation on Lucia. Her husband's absence is accentuated by the time of year. Connected to this is the blue Christmas tree which has been offered to the husband and Father as the only problem that the family has to deal with in his absence, and covers the family's real predicaments with its symbolic growth.

The Deep End moves the time of year in which the story is set away from Christmas, perhaps because the decision to move the location to Lake Tahoe had already been made, and the weather conditions would not be suitable for the story's action. Lake Tahoe and Reno provide the requisite opposition between city and small town which is important to the earlier versions of the story (New York and a coastal town in the novel, Los Angeles and Balboa in *The Reckless Moment*). However, just as *The Deep End* does not effectively evoke the sense of the family as an entity, it never provides us with the sense of community that the others provide. (For a film which mostly takes place in the home or the city, *The Reckless Moment* very effectively evokes the small town through the drugstore scene, the post office and a handful of neighbours.)

No Sibyl

The most perceptive, and most sympathetic, person living in the Harper house is Sibyl. She has no equivalent in *The Deep End*, despite being one of the most important characters in the original film and the novel.[10] This decision may have resulted from practicalities: not many people have maids these days, and if they do that might be a bar to our readiness to sympathise with them. Andrew Britton's article in *Framework* is particularly strong on this aspect of *The Reckless Moment*'s complexity.

> The character of Sibyl is beautifully used in the film, the relationship with Mrs Harper gradually built up until, by the end, the outsider by race and status is the only member of the household with whom Mrs Harper can make open contact. [...] The other members

of the family either ignore Sybil, take her for granted, or treat her as an inferior: consider old Mr Harper's irritable 'Sybil, you *know* I drink tea,' or Bea's petulant anger when, trying to escape from the row with her mother, she finds that Sybil hasn't ironed her dress yet, to which Mrs Harper responds, 'You're not to talk like that to Sybil.' (One should note here the deeper complexity established by our awareness that Bea's 'repression' of Sybil – treating her as a slave – is a direct response to her mother's attempt to repress *her* – treating her as a child.)

Ophuls makes use of two devices to indicate Sybil's deep concern for the attachment to the family – specifically, to Mrs Harper. (1) The exploitation of long-take, deep-focus shots with a family group in the foreground, and Sybil watching and/or listening anxiously in the middle distance, as in the first telephone conversation with Mr Harper, and the conference between Mrs Harper and Bea in the kitchen during Donnelly's visit. (2) Sybil's demand if she can be of any help runs like a leitmotiv through the film. Mrs Harper constantly refuses it until the final sequence, which is introduced and interspersed by renewed offers of aid ('Would you like me to go with you? ... You call me if you need me... You'd better take your coat'), the total unselfishness and generosity thrown into relief by their polar opposite in Nagle's total self-interest ('I don't care about your daughter, your son, your husband or anybody else'). (1976: 23–4)

Britton does not point out, though it only strengthens his argument, that Father's line to Sybil is actually provoked by Sybil deliberately offering Mr Harper coffee in order to distract his attention from the awkward questions he is asking Lucia. To lose Sybil cuts out one of the story's major axes.

Conclusion

One conclusion that might be drawn from this discussion concerns the benefits of consistent patterns of decision-making. The full significance of the way Lucia moves through the house is achieved through the cumulative weight of the decisions, employed systematically as well as in a way which is true to the particular moments involved. The number of times we see Lucia get home to discover something unpleasant – the argument with Bee, Donnelly's visit, the recent departure of the police, Nagle – helps articulate the draining weight of the experience. The final movement through the house, the shadows and substance of the banisters oppressive as she descends the stairs to the telephone, gains force from our recollection earlier movements and earlier telephone calls; the desperation of the situation is compounded by the return of Bee and David in their new respectable attire, completing motifs which have been developing since we first saw Lucia at home.

The Deep End is consistent in its use of close-ups, as discussed earlier, but it therefore does not benefit from the emphasis of the occasional and carefully selected close-up. (Its extreme long-shots, although used less frequently, have, as argued above, rather unexpected consequences.) Moreover, the film's attempts to establish motifs seem pedestrian, particularly the use of watery and or blue imagery: the shots of aquariums, the ostentatious CGI water droplet hanging from the kitchen tap which begins one sequence. Here consistent becomes over-insistent; because these images are so assertively and so indiscriminately deployed they lose any potential significance.

One moment in *The Deep End*'s patterning of colour which does pay off is when Margaret, having disposed of Darby's body, and belatedly got the children off to school, notices for the first time Darby's car. It is a metallic blue corvette, with a suggestive number plate (6FT BLO, decorated with tags advertising Darby's eponymous night club: The Deep End – 'take the plunge'). This is not only a glaringly incriminating piece of evidence at the end of the drive, it also embodies everything about Darby which Margaret would rather not think about in relation to Beau. It is thrusting, conspicuous, lewd, designed for wasteful pleasure. After she has retrieved the keys from Darby's body in the lake, the car blasts dance music when she turns the ignition.

This success comes early in the film, before the pattern has become overdone and, importantly, in a context where there are good dramatic reasons for making the car blue. Having established the colour firmly in the nightclub scene, reintroduced it in the boathouse and during the disposal of the body, these associations are recaptured for us, pertinently. But the general shoehorning of aquariums, sharks on television and so on, into scenes, damages the motif both by their imprecision and the clumsiness with which they are levered into the movie. (Beau's bedroom is also predominantly blue, which seems fair enough, but so is Dylan's bedroom, Jack's bedclothes, Margaret's computer monitor when she writes email and the studio where Beau records for his music scholarship. The sequence after the credits begins with an extreme close-up of the water and gravel in Dylan's aquarium. All of these elements blur the motif.)

The decisions around the car do not have the assertive quality of so much of the motif because the symbolism is integrated into the action: it is logical that Darby would have driven over from Reno, and this is convincingly the kind of car he would drive. The tags on the number plate almost damage the effect by overplaying it, but with their exception the film creates an image that might be described by T. S. Eliot as an 'objective correlative', were he into this kind of thing, or by V. F. Perkins as a balance between action and image. Little in the rest of the movie would.

Another related characteristic which prevents *The Deep End* from being more effective is its inability to do more than one thing at a time. The scene with Alek home alone stands out because it exists for a single purpose. *The Deep End* finds the need to have scenes where Margaret sits introspectively, more than once with the assistance of flashbacks, or is shocked stationary in order to reveal her anxieties. The image of her held through the panes of the door actually follows a perfectly effective image earlier in the course of the same shot. While Paige is talking to her mother and before she has closed the door and left the frame, the shot presents us with a fragmented view of Margaret, separated from her daughter by the door frame, and constrained within a pane of the window. This lasts for a good five seconds before the door closes, and gives us plenty of time to consider the suggestive potential of the image while compre-

Fig. 1.10

hending the conversation and watching Margaret's reactions. If the shot had cut as the door closed, it would have enhanced the sense of separation and would not have obliged us to contemplate bewildered Margaret for a further four seconds. Similarly, to move the camera around a character who is stationary, as opposed to a camera movement which is motivated by the movement of the character, is a gesture which claims a lot of attention, and needs an appropriately significant conjunction of context and content to seem justified.

Again comparison favours *The Reckless Moment*, in which so many things are being achieved simultaneously so much of the time. I partly want to claim this for the extraordinary economy of the classical form, but the dramatic fluidity of *The Reckless Moment* takes things to a further degree. There is some fascinating material in *Max Ophuls in the Hollywood Studios* which makes clear how atypical was Ophuls' way of proceeding, largely disregarding the previously agreed shooting script, which promised a treatment based much more on analytical editing, and records the on-set efficiency and subtle negotiations with which Ophuls gained his way, including access to the studio's cranes. Bacher reveals the crew's initial suspicion at his working methods – 'why can't they stand still and say it' – and the discomfort of Columbia executives at the lack of coverage and close-ups that were shot. Apparently, the camera department presented Ophuls with a pair of roller skates at the wrap party so that he could 'keep up with the camera on his next', the party also the occasion of the first performance of James Mason's poem about Ophuls' passion for camera movement (1996: 281, 308).

Afterword: Choice 10 – casting

In the late stages of working on this chapter, I presented the material as a paper to research seminars at the universities of Kent and Reading. On both occasions the paper was followed by stimulating discussion, and I want to draw attention to comparison between a further choice which was drawn to my attention. In the discussion at Reading, Aoife Monks made a telling observation about the casting of Tilda Swinton as Margaret: Swinton, with her history in independent British films (particularly the work of Derek Jarman and her starring role in *Orlando* (Sally Potter, 1992)) is a surprising figure to choose to embody an American middle-class housewife.[11] (In 1949, the casting of Joan Bennett as Lucia also runs against type: although Bennett went on to play mothers in *Father of the Bride* (Vincente Minnelli, 1950) and *There's Always Tomorrow* (Douglas Sirk, 1956) her roles in films in the years preceding *The Reckless Moment* are very different – *Scarlet Street* and *The Woman in the Window* (both Fritz Lang, 1947), *The Woman on the Beach* (Jean Renoir, 1947), *The Secret Beyond the Door* (Fritz Lang, 1948).) In *The Deep End* the casting opens such a gap between performer and role as to suggest intent, rather than ineptitude. Monks' point, developed further by her and others taking part in the discussion, was that this could be considered part of a broader attempt to draw attention to the way in which the traditional mother's role Margaret is trying to inhabit no longer exists in the early twenty-first century. The argument could connect with other elements of the film: the sense of separation and disjuncture achieved by découpage and mise-en-scène, the fact that Margaret seems to have time on her hands, that the family seem perfectly capable of getting on without her. Could *The Deep End* be understood as a deliberate attempt to replay a form from the 1940s (with roots stretching deeper in the melodramatic tradition), the discussion considered, in order to examine how roles and certainties have changed?

Perhaps. It seems fair to say that there are impulses that carry *The Deep End* in these directions. My own response was, and remains, that these possible lines of inquiry do not bear the weight of a more comprehensive interpretation because there is not the structure, the matrix, necessary for individual elements to gain purchase. In another context, as my comparison with Ozu implies, the use of landscape could be an admirably effective strategy in establishing a contemplative perspective on the characters. Mise-en-scène and découpage might create a sense of distance between Margaret and the rest of her family in a film which had established family structures in other ways. Why did the filmmakers not invent a scene where Margaret cooks a meal for the family in the kitchen/dining room? It would have brought the family together for a moment, achieved a sense of interaction that could then have provided a context for the film's insistence on Margaret's separation, and could have been devised as a stressful activity to convey a sense of their demands on her – as a point of comparison think of the meal that Henry Hill (Ray Liotta) is trying to cook the day he is arrested in *GoodFellas* (Martin Scorsese, 1990). The housework that we actually see Margaret doing – running the washing machine and delivering the laundry to different parts of the house – is not the kind of task that would take precedence over raising blackmail money. An exercise in replaying earlier forms in a contemporary context would also have benefited from the film acknowledging its debt to its 1940s predecessor. Another point voiced in the discussion was the idea that perhaps the material of *The Blank Wall* and *The Reckless Moment* is so inherently about the relationship of the mother to her family, and constructed in such a way as to turn on a powerful involvement with her character, that it cannot harmoniously accommodate a project to create a central character of Antonioni-like remoteness.

I hope that looking at *The Deep End* has made it easier to see the effect of particular decisions in *The Reckless Moment* and vice versa, and helped demonstrate that each decision taken by the filmmakers has an impact on numerous others: period affects our way of understanding character, character development can be aided or hindered by colour scheme. In the evaluative element of the discussion I have favoured the original, but remaking a movie invites comparison, and choosing to remake a film as accomplished as *The Reckless Moment* creates quite a challenge.

2. Choices around generic conventions: *Unforgiven* (1992)

In the production draft of David Webb Peoples' script, *The William Munny Killings*, dated 23 April 1984, we find the following scene.

EXT. BIG WHISKEY HILL – DAY.

EXTREME CLOSE-UP ON DELILAH.

Delilah's face! The cut-whore. Skeins of criss-crossing raised flesh, a vicious web of scars dominated by her eyes that are deep and beautiful.

She's hanging clothes on a clothes line on Big Whiskey Hill, the gentle slope above the town. Alice, Little Sue, Silky, Kate and Faith are close by, hanging clothes or washing them in the gurgling stream.

Faith is the first to glance down the hill toward the town and to notice. She draws in her breath and turns to Alice and catches her eye and Alice looks down.

EXT. MUDDY NORTH ROAD.

The muddy North Road and the two riders, and they are Quick Mike and Davey Bunting leading their ponies in, passing a crudely painted sign that says:

'Ordinance 14. No firearms in Big Whiskey. Deposit them at County Office. By Order of Sheriff.'

EXT. BIG WHISKEY HILL – DAY.

The whores on the hill. One by one, with no words exchanged, they feel the silence and turn and exchange glances and they glance at Delilah. She winces and turns back to hanging clothes.

Readers familiar with *Unforgiven* (1992), the film made with this script, will immediately recognise ways in which the film's realisation of the scene differs from the script's suggestions. Some of these differences are minor – in the film we do not read the sign bearing 'Ordinance 14' until W. W. Beauchamp (Saul Rubinek) notices it as he and English Bob (Richard Harris) arrive in town. More significantly, where the script has Delilah horribly disfigured as a result of Quick Mike's attack, in the film her scars are much less pronounced. Thirdly, while the film, like the script, has Delilah (Anna Thomson) and the other prostitutes washing clothes and hanging them to dry, the setting is different. In the film, the laundry is being done behind a white picket fence attached to a white clapboard house. This house has a porch, equipped with a couple of rocking chairs, where one of the women sits, and another stands in a white apron, taking a few steps toward the riders as they pass. (The house is not high on Big Whiskey Hill, it is adjacent to the road into town along which the cowboys ride.)

Fig. 2.1

This chapter is concerned with choices made in organising generic conventions, and the investigation will begin with the unusual decision – initiated in the script, but taken much further in the finished film – to show the home life of the prostitutes of the town. We tend normally to think of the generic forebears of these women (the 'bar-girls' of so many westerns) inhabiting their place of work, and so even to show the women living together in a separate location is a significant decision, in terms of plot not strictly necessary. But the presentation of these women's lives outside of the brothel is even more striking. Although doing the washing or sitting on the porch are highly plausible activities for the characters, we are not often encouraged to think of prostitutes in westerns engaged in everyday domestic tasks; it is simply not a context in which we are invited to imagine them.

The appearance of the women is also surprising, perhaps not in terms of historical accuracy, but in generic association. As we can see more clearly a few moments later, when they throw clods of earth at the men, all the women are dressed in modest colours, browns, creams and blues. They wear their hair plainly, none of them are wearing make-up. Some, particularly Kate (Josie Smith) and Little Sue (Tara Dawn Frederick), seem more like girls than women. Their clothes are not showy dresses, with frilly undergarments and low-cut necklines, the familiar costume of the

Fig. 2.2

saloon entertainer, but instead garments which would not look out of place on the school mistress of Big Whiskey (although such a character does not appear in the film).

The setting, too, is perfectly credible but simultaneously rich in incongruous iconographic detail: the porch and the rocking chair are strongly associated with the pleasures and values of being a settler – *The Searchers* (John Ford, 1956), for example, trades heavily on this imagery – and we are all familiar with the white picket fence as a metonymic symbol of the American small town, past or present.

In short, these prostitutes inhabit the house, have the appearance of and perform the activities conventionally associated with settled women, their generic, social and (traditionally speaking) *moral* opposites. A group of socially-undesirable sex workers are found living in surroundings as resonant of American self-image as the White House lawn. What the film does here is to create a suggestive image by conflating two opposed traditions of generic representation. Moreover, in organising the conventions in this jarring and, within the terms of the debate, slightly sacrilegious way, the film draws attention to the conventions themselves – and what values they embody.

The collision of conventions that draws attention to what is bound up within those conventions might in another context be called a Brechtian strategy. If such a comparison seems far-fetched, compare *Unforgiven*'s image with Act Two, Scene Five of *The Threepenny Opera*. To quote from the stage directions: 'An afternoon like any other; the whores, mostly in their shifts, are ironing clothes, playing draughts or washing: a bourgeois idyll' (1979: 41). Brecht is striving for a similarly incongruous scene, where the prostitutes of Turnbridge are engaged in a range of housewifely tasks, as part of his dramatisation of the relationship between bourgeois and bandit. In either case, we might accurately call this a making of the familiar strange: setting against each other two opposed but well-known images, with the effect of making normally acceptable assumptions vivid, unnatural.[1]

More evidence of the film's awareness of its traditions of representation can be found at the end of the scene. As if to take the juxtaposition of different traditions of female representation further, the film cuts from the prostitutes silently standing in the street, having run the cowboys out of town, to a photograph of Claudia Feathers Munny. Claudia is one of only two wives that feature in the film's story, the other being Sally Two Trees (Cherrilene Cardina). One or two townswomen might be spied on the main street of Big Whiskey when English Bob is beaten up, but wives are mainly conspicuous by their absence.

Sally Two Trees is Native American, so she is rather unlike the 'settled woman' of our expectation. Indeed, a similar strategy is at work here: Sally seems the most successfully settled of all the characters in the film and for her to be the film's only living embodiment of the 'settled woman', given the genre's traditional association of Native Americans with erotic and dangerous heathenism, creates a composite character of comparable ideological paradox to the prostitutes.

Claudia, who has been dead for three years before the film's main action begins, is reported to us as having been a paragon of wifely virtue. We never see Claudia as

Fig. 2.3

she was in life, we only have evidence of how other characters refer to her, and the scraps of written narration that crawl up the screen in the film's opening and closing shots. Even her photograph is a standard nineteenth-century portrait, which reveals little of her character, beyond an imputed respectability. (The script suggests that the photograph portrays her 'smiling radiantly in her best dress' but these features, which might provide emotional and moral encouragement to her surviving husband, are absent from the muted realisation.) Yet William Munny (Clint Eastwood) looks to Claudia as a moral point of reference throughout, to the extent that her name becomes a watchword or even a mantra for him. There are a couple of remarks from Ned (Morgan Freeman) which support Munny's view of his wife – 'Course, you know Will, if Claudia was alive you wouldn't be doing this'– but for the most part we have only the insistence of Munny, and the film may encourage us to feel that he protests the moral worth of his children's 'dear departed Ma' rather too much. His repeated claims about his dead wife's character and, especially, the force of her moral reform on him – 'I'm just a fella now. I ain't no different than anyone else, no more' – betray concern about the precariousness of these values, particularly his moral conversion. Perhaps we should be as cautious about Claudia's goodness as the film encourages us to be about the heroism of the Duke of Death? The cut from prostitute to civilising wife could have articulated a striking moral contrast, but instead the movement is from a whore who is presented in ways which narrow the potential for contrast to an archetype which exists only as an image, and one already receding into a mythicised past.

Examination of *Unforgiven*'s male characters provides support for the case that the film invites a highly self-conscious reflection on the traditions of representation with which it works, and enlivens our broader investigation of the significant choices that generic conventions make possible for the filmmaker. William Munny, we know from the outset, is a man with a past and a reputation. Yet despite being played by the director-star, he begins the film not as a wandering hero but as a single parent and noticeably unsuccessful pig farmer. Munny is neither given the dignity of owning a ranch, nor even the more prosperous arable concern of Sally Two Trees and Ned Logan. Moreover, we soon discover that he cannot hit a tin at ten yards with a pistol, and his repeated failings to mount his horse become a dryly comic motif for the film. This

Fig. 2.4

is an extraordinary assault on our expectations of the protagonist of a western. As John Cawelti has written, 'The hero is a man with a horse and the horse is his direct tie to the freedom of the wilderness, for it embodies his ability to move freely across it and to dominate and control its spirit' (1970: 57). The off-screen voice of the Schofield Kid (Jaimz Woolvett) accurately summarises the situation, as he says to the mud-bespattered Munny, wallowing in the dirt of the pig sty, 'You don't look like no rootin'-tootin', son-of-a-bitchin', cold-blooded assassin!'

If Munny is not the wandering hero who settled down with the heroine – he was, after all, 'a known thief and murderer, a man of notoriously vicious and intemperate disposition' – then he was certainly an independent man of action who took the settled part. At the beginning of the film Munny has been through the experience that confronts the hero at the end of many westerns and, in a vivid illustration of the fear that seems to haunt so many western heroes, marriage has resulted in a loss of potency. In settling down, in being civilised by Claudia, Munny has lost the poise and power of the westerner.

Another of the film's major characters who has attempted to settle down is Little Bill (Gene Hackman). To phrase it again through the film's skilful deployment of conventions, this time quoting one of the first remarks English Bob makes on recognising the sheriff of Big Whiskey, Little Bill has 'shaved [his] chin whiskers off'. In his essay 'Why do cowboys wear their hats in the bath?', Martin Pumphrey argues that the absence of facial hair is one of the most consistent indicators of moral worth in the western. We expect our heroes to be clean cut, clean shaven: 'Unshavenness can signal exhaustion or illness, but until the spaghetti westerns of the 1960s began to play with the code, habitual stubble and moustaches were unmistakable signs of villainy' (1996: 53). Time and again the westerner will visit the barber's shop on his return to civilisation. (Pumphrey also points out that the barber's shop is a place in which the westerner is under threat, his masculinity challenged – it is no coincidence that English Bob is surrounded while receiving a shave.) Little Bill has become part of, and defender of, the community, although whether his new way of wearing his facial hair reveals a reformed character or merely the aspiration toward moral worth, is a subject of debate.

As was the case with Munny, Bill's settling down is not a straightforward or successful process. His penultimate words are: 'I don't deserve this. To die like this. I was building a house.' His bewilderment expresses the incongruity of being shot down despite having left the wandering life behind; being settled should guarantee protection against this kind of end. Earlier in the film we see him working on the house, and imagining the evenings he will spend on his porch once it is completed, but the stresses involved in his accommodation manifest themselves in the structure of the building which 'don't have a straight angle in … the whole house', and which leaks drastically when it rains.

Little Bill and William Munny end up antagonists in this film, though both, structurally speaking, could have claims to be the hero. Little Bill has the hero's traditional role of upholding law and order, keeping the town tame, yet goes about his job with a mixture of bravery, humour, pragmatism and cruelty. Munny is the avenging hero, and is played by Eastwood, but is also a bounty hunter and a criminal who brings terror to the town, destroying its legal structures. Nothing in this film presents a clear-cut moral opposition.

In *The Six-Gun Mystique* (1970) and its later reworking, *The Six-Gun Mystique Sequel* (1999), John Cawelti discusses the way in which the traditional western hero is a chivalric figure, not far removed from the heroes of Sir Walter Scott, and that this character is revealed in the hero's relationship to violence, especially as it is structured in the form of the showdown:

> Where the knight encountered his adversary in bloody hand-to-hand combat, the cowboy invariably meets his at a substantial distance and goes through the complex and rigid ritual of the 'draw' before finally consummating the fatal deed. The most important implication of this killing procedure seems to be the qualities of reluctance, control and elegance that it associates with the hero. Unlike the knight, the cowboy hero does not seek out combat for its own sake and he typically shows an aversion to the wanton shedding of blood. Killing is an act forced upon him and he carries it out with the precision and skill of a surgeon and the careful proportions of an artist. We might say that the six-gun is a weapon which enables the hero to show the largest measure of objectivity and detachment while yet engaging in individual combat. This controlled and aesthetic mode of

killing is particularly important as the supreme mark of differentiation between the hero and the savage. The Indian or outlaw as savage delights in slaughter, entering into combat with a kind of manic glee to fulfil an uncontrolled lust for blood. The hero rarely engages in violence until the last moment and he never kills until the savage's gun has already cleared his holster. Suddenly it is there and the villain crumples. (1970: 59)

W. W. Beauchamp's *The Duke of Death* clearly represents the duel between Corcoran and English Bob in such terms. As Little Bill renders it: '"You have insulted the honour of this beautiful woman, Corcoran," said the Duck. "You must apologise." But Two Gun Corcoran would have none of it and, cursing, he reached for his pistols and would have killed them but the Duck was faster and hot lead blazed from his smoking sixguns.' Yet the film's presentation of its central conflicts – and Little Bill's

Fig. 2.5

alternative account of the night in the Blue Bottle Saloon – could not be more different.

Even after the assaults on generic certainties perpetrated in 1960s and 1970s by directors such as Sam Peckinpah, Robert Aldrich and Eastwood himself, we still have a residual expectation of a showdown between morally-opposed forces. *Unforgiven* does not fulfil this expectation in any straightforward way. This is partly due to the ambivalence of characters: Delilah's attackers, the hired killers and the sheriff. The guilt of the cowboys has been tempered, particularly in the case of Davey (Rob Campbell), who is an accomplice to the crime rather its perpetrator – indeed, after initially holding Delilah, he actually tries to restrain Mike (David Mucci) – and is also clearly repentant for the action. From the moment Davey attempts to give Delilah a horse, a better horse than either of the two with which he is obliged to compensate Skinny (Anthony James), we can see that even the prostitutes have forcibly to renew their anger – as they are compelled to do since the news of the bounty has spread far and wide, and there is no going back. After they have driven off the cowboys, the camera watches the women as they watch them ride away, the uncertainty written on their faces underscored by the sombre music. Alice's words, with which she screws up her and the others' anger – 'She ain't got no face left, and all you can give her is a mangy pony!' – are manifestly an exaggeration in relation to the horse and, more importantly, Delilah.

The fact that Delilah's injuries are not as devastating as is reported, here and elsewhere, qualifies much of the action of the rest of the film, pointing up the way in which the story of the attack becomes a moral crutch grasped by the bounty hunters to justify their actions, and expressed through the repeated refrain 'they had it coming'. This is not to minimise the significance of the attack, nor the injustice which Little Bill dispenses in regarding the damage done to Delilah purely as an attack on Skinny's property. But what we can say is that the two cowboys are not unambiguously evil, that there is no honour in their deaths, and that their executioners are not supported in their actions by a clear moral foundation.

Given the way in which Little Bill has destroyed the image of the chivalrous Duke of Death, we may no longer be expecting a classic stand-off, but there is nothing romantic at all about the bounty killings. Davey is attacked without warning with a Spencer rifle from a protected position. The scene is agonisingly drawn out as he attempts to drag himself to safety with his broken leg, the first bullet having killed his horse, and then bleeds to death after being shot through the stomach. Davey's requests to be given a drink give us a vivid insight into his last experiences.

We are spared nothing as the scene plays out: placed close to Davey as he struggles to find cover, but also given an unsentimental view of the attackers. Ned cannot

Fig. 2.6

bring himself to shoot again after the first shot and Munny's attempts to land a second are gratingly interrupted by the short-sighted Kid's demands to know what is going on. At the same time, we are awkwardly affected by the tension arising from the fact that unless they shoot Davey quickly, he is going to make cover and they will have to go down to the valley floor to finish the job.

Fig. 2.7

After Davey has been shot, we wait to listen to his death with the killers. He cries out, 'I'm dying boys!' to his comrades and the Kid shouts back: 'Well, then you shouldn't have cut up no woman, you asshole!' Again the film is precise about the evidence, but the characters are interesting for their exaggeration and imprecision when justifying their actions. The second cowboy, Quick Mike, who did cut Delilah, is shot at point-blank range, unarmed, in the 'shit house' at the Bar T.

The treatment of these killings has something of what Cawelti describes, elsewhere, as 'a situation that we are ordinarily accustomed to seeing in rather romanticised terms [being] suddenly invested with a sense of reality' (1995: 236). Cawelti makes these remarks – in the context of the challenge presented to the traditional genres by films from the mid- to late 1960s and early 1970s – about what he calls the 'humourous burlesque' mode of generic transformation, although in *Unforgiven* the tactic has more in common

Fig. 2.8

with another of Cawelti's modes, that of 'demythologisation'. In terms of this chapter's argument we may, again, note that the similarities between this process and 'making strange' the familiar.

Adding a further level of complexity to the film's analysis, immediately after the shooting of Quick Mike we witness the beginning of a process of romanticising this most unromantic of acts. The kid's account – 'I shot that fucker three times. He was taking a shit and he went for his pistol and I blazed away. First shot… I got him right in the chest' – already contradicts what we have seen in its suggestion of a contest. But for once, the kid cannot keep up his bravado, and reveals the falseness, that we have long suspected, of his earlier claims to be a killer, eventually consoling himself with the thought that 'they had it coming'. In this way the film makes clear the relationship between the 'Chinese whispers' which spread concerning the extent of the injury inflicted on Delilah, and the parallel aggrandising of acts in the dime novels of Beauchamp.

Finally, there is Munny's eventual revenge on Little Bill and his deputies. A number of critics have accused the film of double standards in its last ten minutes. David Thomson, for example, asks of Eastwood's character: 'How does his understandable ineptness as a gunfighter suddenly and conveniently fall aside to reveal the old Leone-esque angel of death? (2002: 263). And we might want to give Thomson's objection some credence: after the way in which the film's violence has been stripped of any glamour, after the wittiness of the analysis of western conventions in the form of the dime novel, in the face of the ineptitude Munny has demonstrated throughout the film, and following that extraordinary line about death in the preceding scene – 'It's a hell of a thing, killing a man. You take away all he's got and all he's ever gonna have', delivered next to the lone pine tree in the cold light of late afternoon – the film now gives us an act of violence more accomplished than any W. W. Beauchamp could have hoped to witness.

Yet here too it is important to look at the way the film works with generic conventions, combined with the self-conscious setting of elements against one another. The turning point of the film is when Munny, on hearing about the death of Ned, takes the whiskey bottle with which the kid has been consoling himself, and which he has consistently refused hitherto, and starts to drink.

Whiskey, of course, has particular associations in the western. It is the hard man's drink, taken neat in shot glasses, banged down upon the bar. If coffee is associated with companionship and settling down – to take an example from the present film, what Little Bill intends to do with the porch he is constructing is to 'sit of an evening and smoke my pipe, drink coffee and watch the sunset' – whiskey's association is with raw masculinity.

Beyond the inherited associations of whiskey, the film develops its own significance for the drink. Will first mentions it when he declines the kid's invitation to ride with him: 'I ain't like that anymore, Kid. It was whiskey done it as much as anything else. I ain't had a drop of it in over ten years. My wife, she cured me of that, cured me of drink and wickedness.' He says something similar to Ned, during their conversation on their first night on the road. Later in the journey, when it comes on to rain, Ned offers Will a bottle of whiskey which he brought 'for when we have to kill them fellas'. After he has shot Quick Mike, the Kid drinks whiskey as fast as he can, and Will answers his question about whether he was ever scared in 'them days' by saying that he cannot remember because he was drunk most of the time. Munny throws away the empty bottle as he rides up the main street toward Greely's Saloon.

It seems that in order to shoot a man, it is necessary to be drunk. A vital element of the acts of violence which are referred to and take place in the film, with the exception of those committed by Little Bill, is that the perpetrators need to be intoxicated to carry them out at all.[2] All the behaviour that the Kid and W. W. Beauchamp are inspired by, all the great acts of masculine prowess, are the product of intoxication. To put the point the other way around, whiskey is associated with a definition of masculinity which is practically psychopathic. As Munny says to Ned by the campfire, before avowing how he has changed, 'You remember that drover I shot through the mouth and his teeth came out the back of his head? … I think about him now and again. He didn't do anything to deserve getting shot, at least, nothing I could remember when I sobered up.' So in one sense, Thomson's objection can be answered in relation to this motif. Certainly, Munny has regained his potency, a degree of accuracy, and the weight of the Eastwood persona. But it is the return to drinking whiskey – with everything that entails, including the death of six men – that has affected this transformation.[3]

Again, through careful choices, the film defines more precisely what was a potentiality of the script. In *The William Munny Killings*, Munny drinks from almost the beginning of the scene by the lone pine. The line where he responds to the kid's enquiry about the old days by saying that he cannot remember because he was drunk most of the time continues, in the production draft, with Munny saying to the kid, 'Give me a pull on that bottle, will you?' In the film, however, as Ed Gallafent has pointed out, the timing of Munny's first drink is precise and significant. Little Sue is describing how Little Bill has beaten the truth about their identities out of Ned and 'exactly as she speaks the words, "You was really William Munny out of Missouri", we see the character lift the bottle to his lips for the first time' (1994: 226). The return of William Munny – the restored westerner, rather than the man living in retired anonymity or beaten under the pseudonym Hendershot – corresponds exactly to his return to drinking whiskey.

There is a delicate balance, too, in the final minutes, because the film does not, in one sense, step outside the reality of the world it has presented. If we feel that Munny now has all the lines, the character earlier established had been tersely but eloquently short spoken. In the shoot-out Munny very methodically fires at his adversaries, whilst nerves get the better of them. There is nothing in this stand-off that contradicts Little Bill's dictums on what death and killing were really like in the old West. There is no fancy gunplay, no fast draw – just luck, and a comparatively cool head. The film plays its final act as an ironic coda which sets up awkward tensions in relation to our enjoyment of the film whilst also respecting the rules which it has earlier established.

At the same time, this careful articulation of Munny's transformation via the bottle, and the play on contrasting masculine images that it involves, achieves a further dimension of 'making strange' by implicating the spectator in the exhilaration of the climactic sequence as well as its horror. If we take pleasure in the belated appearance of the Eastwood persona, replete with growled pay-off lines, satisfying our desire to see Ned avenged, this pleasure is clearly at odds with all the work that the film has done so far to draw out the squalor of violence and the finality of death. Our awareness that this is an act more accomplished than any of those which W. W. Beauchamp has written about, and perhaps even our pride that Munny has accomplished it, sits uncomfortably with a range of other feelings which the film has set in play, including our sympathies with some of Munny's victims, and the views which the film had earlier encouraged us to side with. This is perhaps the film's boldest and most complexly worked of all its choices in the deployment of generic convention, not a 'making strange' which we can coolly observe but a set of contradictions which are played out in our affective responses as well as our judgement and moral sense. Like the killing of Davey, where our feelings were painfully mixed, the film creates a complex position for the audience, who are asked to balance compound and contradictory impulses and levels of understanding.

Conclusion

Unforgiven, in common with some other post-classical westerns, is interested in experiences which were not major concerns of the tradition. It begins by telling the story of the prostitutes of Big Whiskey, their collective response to their exclusion from the processes of law and order, after an original act of violence itself caused by a precarious masculinity – 'All she done, when she seen he has a teensy little pecker, is give a giggle. That's all. She didn't know no better.' In this context it seems highly appropriate that the film's way of dramatising such a story is to challenge, rather than unthinkingly accept, the genre's means of expression. A film that explores untold experience from the old West, it achieves its analysis through reflection on the traditions of representation themselves.

In the course of the chapter I have drawn attention to a number differences between film and script. Doing so is not intended to belittle David Webb Peoples' achievement: organising generic conventions is as much the job of writer as it is director and *The William Munny Killings* is a wonderful script which the film follows faithfully. *Unforgiven* does not include any scenes that do not appear in the script, its structural differences are those of excision – a final scene where Munny returns home is cut, for example, as is a feverish flashback to Munny's mistreatment of a horse in his former life.

What I hope the earlier discussion does reveal is how Eastwood and his on-set collaborators have developed and refined some of the impulses of the script. Our opening example examined the way the film exposed – iconographically – some of the values bound up in the character types with which it was working, but this is entirely in keeping with both the demythologising impulse of the whole film and its interest in the women's story. Instead of an extreme close-up of a face raised by 'a vicious web of scars', we encounter a less damagingly disfigured Delilah in a shot wide enough to admit the consolation of Strawberry Alice, which follows two long-shots introducing the domestic context and placing Delilah in the company of her comrades. The more modest injuries she bears counterpoint the exaggeration in the accounts of her

Fig. 2.9

wounding, undercutting the moral self-justification the bounty hunters, and making more effective the parallel between the different acts of mythologisation in the film. Similarly, making Claudia Munny's portrait entirely conventional gently undercuts the support a smiling portrait would give to the claims of woman's husband about her extraordinary qualities. With these changes in inflection the film extends our awareness of the mythic beyond the prowess of the westerner and identifies this tendency in the characters' relationship to the past more generally. Removing the delirious flashback to Munny's youth ensures that his history remains a matter of anecdote, rather than evidence, and cutting the scene of his return to the pig farm enables the film itself to end, in Gallafent's phrase, 'by fading into rumour and vague report' (1994: 228). What the film does in the playing, in its realisation, is to turn further from the expected, to qualify the broad statement, to make the generic familiar strange.

3. Choices around narrative structure: coincidences in *Lured* (1947)

'Coincidence. It's coincidence that you own a *Westminster* typewriter. It's coincidence that certain keys are out of alignment. It's *also* coincidence that you use *Victoria* paper. And of course, it's merely coincidence that pictures of missing girls were in your possession, and that letters they wrote in answer to personal column advertisements were found in your files!'

This chapter is concerned with choices made in narrative structure, with a particular focus on the effects that can be achieved through the juxtaposition of scenes and dramatic events – notably through the use of coincidence. The film under discussion is *Lured* (Douglas Sirk, 1947), a movie which has largely escaped critical attention, but which was a personal favourite of the director.[1]

Coincidence is often regarded rather dismissively when narratives are discussed. Historically, one of the reasons for attacking forms of melodrama, for example, has been the contrivance of plots and dramatic situations, as though exhibiting contrivance inevitably implied a failure of aesthetic judgement. Yet coincidence – which does have a particular association with melodrama – is often a vital strategy in the symbolic economy of narrative.

Thomas Elsaesser argues as much in 'Tales of Sound and Fury', the article which had such an important role for the study of film in championing melodrama, when he discusses the importance of coincidence, and other elements of melodramatic dramaturgy, to writers such as Collins, Dickens, Reade, Sue, Hugo and Balzac. Of these, he argues, the English writers 'relied heavily on melodramatic plots to sharpen social conflicts and portray an urban environment where chance encounters, coincidences and the side-by-side existence of extreme social and moral contrasts were the natural products of the very conditions of existence' (1972: 4). He also writes of Dickens using 'the element of chance' to 'feel his way towards a portrayal of existential insecurity and moral anguish which fiction had previously not encompassed' (ibid.). Coincidence makes available to filmmakers, and artists in other narrative traditions, a powerful opportunity for juxtaposition, for making connections or sharpening contrasts.

An example of an expressive juxtaposition of the connecting kind is identified by Charles Barr in his account of the first version of *The Man Who Knew Too Much* (Alfred Hitchcock, 1934). In a St Moritz setting, Louis Bernard (Pierre Fresnay) has established a 'warm holiday friendship' (1999: 135) with Jill and Bob Lawrence (Leslie Banks and Edna Best), and at the same time a relationship 'of weirdly exaggerated flirtation' with Jill, 'at which Bob, with equal exaggeration, connives':

We see Bob and Betty [Jill and Bob's daughter, played by Nova Pilbeam] sitting together in the restaurant, while Jill and Louis dance provocatively by, pausing at the table to tease him:

Louis: What do you think of the average Englishman?

Jill: Much too cold…

In revenge, with Betty's help, Bob takes the unfinished jumper that Jill is knitting for (of course) Louis, and hooks the end of it over the back button of Louis's dinner jacket. When he glides off again, this gradually disrupts the movement on the dance floor, as the knitting unravels and couples get comically tangled up by the wool. Another man attracts Louis's attention, to point out the wool snagged on his button. He stops and turns, and it is at this moment that he is shot dead.

If Bob had been the killer's accomplice, arranging for Louis to stop at the right moment by the window and present a sitting target, the manoeuvre could not have been more neatly calculated. The shot comes out of the blue, or rather the white of the snow, precisely *as if* willed by Bob, to punish Louis for his threat to the stability of the family, his exposure and exploitation of its internal tensions. (1999: 136–7)

Barr's discussion convincingly develops into an argument which establishes broader patterns in the film's organisation, in which public and private worlds are brought together and characters' desires find grotesque fulfilment. Although by no means the only filmmaker to use this kind of strategy, movies directed by Hitchcock frequently utilise the dramatic and thematic potential of the significant association of apparently unconnected elements. This reaches an extreme in *Rear Window* (1954), where the whole film is structured around juxtapositions between the activities that take place in L. B. Jeffries' (James Stewart) flat and the actions and experiences of his neighbours that take place simultaneously on the other side of the courtyard.

Rather than accept them unthinkingly or dismiss them hastily, we need to be ready to interrogate the connection between particular events or actions by means of narrative structure, recognising this as a part of a vital area of choice for filmmakers. In any movie worth watching a coincidence is unlikely to be only a coincidence. *Lured* provides a good example of how narrative juxtaposition can be organised to significant effect and the examination of a number of coincidences in the film's early scenes, and a series of parallels across the narrative more generally, enable us to move rapidly to the heart of the film's processes and concerns.

The scene I wish to consider begins in the thirteenth minute of the movie. We have, by this stage, already been introduced to Sandra Carpenter (Lucille Ball) and her friend Lucy Barnard (Tanis Chandler) at the taxi dance where they work. We have been given a partial view of Lucy's date with 'John', a man she has met through the personal columns, and heard about her intention to give up her work and go off with him. We have seen a shadowy figure dispatch a letter to Scotland Yard, and watched the reaction of the police to the appearance of the latest in a series of poems which have preceded the disappearance of a series of young women. We know that Lucy wears a bracelet of carved elephants as a good-luck charm, and that the latest poem refers to 'Elephants' which 'encircle her smooth white arm'. We have even been witness to the discussion between

Inspector Temple (Charles Coburn) and Professor Harkness (uncredited), a literary expert who has been able to identify the aspirational relationship between the verse of the 'poet-killer' and the poetry of Baudelaire, and their shared insistence on a correspondence between beauty and death.

This scene between Inspector Temple and Professor Harkness immediately precedes the action which we are about to consider, and the conversation between the men is fresh in our minds as our sequence begins. Professor Harkness has argued that:

> Baudelaire was obsessed with the notion that death is beautiful. Listen to this: 'A beauty, still more beautiful in death.' Your criminal has the same delusions: 'A beauty that only death can enhance.'

He goes on to describe the murderer in the following terms:

> ...if he's at all like Baudelaire, he'll be constantly in search of beauty, and courting it. A new lovely face will always appeal to him, or some unusual attractiveness will intrigue him, inspire him to a destructiveness. He'll delight in variety and never be quite content with what he finds.

This is summarised by Temple as 'sort of a modern Don Juan', a description which the literary expert partially accepts.

Back at the Broadway Palladium, Sandra has asked the manager of the taxi dance whether she can take time off to attend an audition for the prestigious Fleming and Wilde nightclub chain. Having been refused permission – 'Not unless you want to lose your job, girlie' – she storms out of his office and, after a moment's reflection, up to the telephone on the bar to cancel her audition and, hopefully, make another appointment.

The film cuts from the telephone on which Sandra is making her call to a tight shot of a second telephone on a desk, ringing. Behind it we can see the back of a photograph frame and, to the left, the side pocket, elbow and flank of a suit jacket. On the second ring, the forearm of the suited figure reaches down into the frame and picks up the receiver; the camera follows the movement of the hand toward the ear, but the tilt reveals that the man holding the receiver (George Sanders) is engaged in a passionate embrace with a woman wearing a fur coat (uncredited) (shot 1). Without breaking off the kiss, the woman takes the receiver and holds it behind her back, the camera tilting and panning to accommodate this movement as well. We can hear Sandra's voice – 'Hello? Hello? Fleming and Wilde Theatrical Enterprises?', and then

Fig. 3.1

again 'Hello?'. After a further period, the woman moves the telephone round to her face, the film cutting on this action to a wider shot, and the conversation continues as follows:

2. Match cut to wider view

Woman: Hello.

Sandra: Mr Fleming's secretary please.

Woman: Oh, just a moment.

Fleming: Who is it?

Woman: Darling, it's not for you, she wants your secretary.

Fleming: She? [He takes the receiver from her.] Hello?

3. Sandra in bar

Sandra: Mr Fleming's secretary?

Fleming: Yes.

Sandra: This is Sandra Carpenter.

Fleming: Who?

Sandra: Sandra Carpenter. I was due to come in tonight for an audition. Mr Milton gave me a card. But I can't possibly get away, the manager… Would you tell Mr Fleming for me?

4. Office, medium close-up

Fleming: Mr Fleming will be very disappointed, I'm sure: you have such a charming voice.

Fig. 3.2

Fig. 3.3

5. Bar, closer view, 30-degree change of angle.

Sandra: Oh, well I don't sing, you know, I dance.

6. Office, the same as 4

Fleming: I bet you do, and beautifully. Perhaps we can arrange a private interview.

Woman: You're intolerable. [As she says this, Woman turns to face away from Fleming, but remains standing next to him.]

Fleming: Hold the line, please, something's out of order here. [Covers receiver.] Jealousy's eyes are green, my dear. Don't let yours turn that dreadful colour.

Woman: You're incorrigible. [Woman starts to apply her lipstick.]

Fleming: Of course I am, I am an unmitigated cad. [Takes hand away from receiver.] Now carry on my dear, talk to me.

7. Bar, medium long-shot

Sandra: Look here, is it customary for Mr Fleming's secretary to pass judgement for his boss?

8. Office, wider shot, change of angle

Fleming: Mr Fleming never makes a move without me. In fact, he very frequently has me take his young ladies out to dinner, in order to talk things over.

9. Bar, same as 7

Sandra: Thanks, I'll go hungry.
Customer: Lemon squash, please.
Fleming: You're an American, aren't you?
Sandra: So?

10. Office, still wider view, wide-angle lens

Fleming: Mr Fleming is quite partial to American girls, they have an irresistible way of putting a man on the defensive.
Woman: Robert! You're im...
Fleming: ...possible. What were you saying?

11. Bar, same as 7

Sandra: Would it be against Mr Fleming's Anglo-American policy to tell a girl when the next audition is please?

12. Office, same as 10

Fleming: [Woman now standing in doorway looking challengingly at Fleming.] Tomorrow night at nine. Can you make it?
Sandra: I think so.
Fleming: I guarantee that you'll see Mr Fleming personally. [Looks round at Woman.] Now are you happy?
Sandra: I'm very happy. [Woman leaves, slamming door.]
Fleming: Then why don't you smile.

Fig. 3.4

13. Bar, similar scale and angle to 3

Sandra: Alright, I'm smiling. Any more instructions Mr Sec... [Sandra turns round, catches sight of a customer's newspaper, puts down telephone and grabs paper as camera tracks in on headline: 'Dancer Reported Missing', and the subheading: 'Lucy Barnard Feared Eighth Victim of "Poet-Killer"'. The score blares.]

Fig. 3.5

14. Office, similar scale and lens to 10, but 30-degree change in angle which reveals another doorway

Fleming: Miss Carpenter? Hello? [Fleming agitates the cradle of the telephone.] Hello? [Wilde enters through the newly revealed doorway behind Fleming and walks toward the desk; Fleming turns and sees him.] Oh, hello Julian. [He looks into the receiver, then puts it down.]

Wilde: Chapman has just delivered the architects drawings.

Fleming: I feel rather like Napoleon after Waterloo.

Wilde: You sound more like Romeo after Juliet closed the balcony window.

Fleming: That's the first girl whose hung up on me in years.

Wilde: It's well overdue. Take a look at these, Robert. I think the plans are perfect now. We shall have the finest nightclub in London.

The juxtaposition of Sandra's discovery of Lucy's disappearance and her first conversation with Fleming, followed by the appearance, immediately afterwards, of Fleming's business partner Julian Wilde (Cedric Hardwicke), is the nexus of coincidence from which I wish to launch this discussion. Why interrupt this telephone call with Sandra's discovery of Lucy's disappearance? Why then leave Sandra and stay with Fleming to witness the entrance of, and ensuing conversation with, Wilde?

A number of features of the sequence provide a context for thinking about these questions. One is the extraordinary introduction to Fleming: remarkable in its economy and efficiency – though characteristic of the best sequences of the film in this respect – and remarkable in the character thereby constructed. Fleming transforms himself from distracted lover to focused pursuer in a matter of seconds, and from intimate embrace to separation in less than two minutes.

The sequence moves from the surprising intimacy of the first shot, to views which make physical the growing distance between the couple. Each time we cut back to Fleming and his female companion, the tendency is for us to be given a wider view.[2] When Fleming compliments Sandra on her voice, the framing is less tight than the shot of the kiss. The set-up used for the shot in which the woman turns her back on Fleming is replaced, when we return from the bar, by a wider view of the two of them. By the time Fleming is telling Sandra when she can next attend an audition, the woman has moved to the door and stands looking haughtily and questioningly at Fleming, a wide-angle lens accentuating the space between them. The separation is completed when she slams the door: shot 12 is not a wider view than 10, but the action makes the emotional situation plain and neatly completes this trajectory of the scene.

The line 'happy now?' is directed by Fleming both to Sandra and to the woman standing in the open doorway. Such is the audacity of this man that he can advance his suit with one woman while using the same expression to finish with another. (If this is not the couple literally splitting up, it is as far as the film is concerned: the next time we meet the woman, at Fleming's nightclub, she is emphatically an 'ex'.) It is also worth noting that Fleming remains sitting through these events; through what could be a moving exchange (both in terms of the telephone call and the row) he has merely settled himself more comfortably on the desk, facing half away from the woman in the room. This is the behaviour of someone of great self-assurance. He only stands up when Sandra has put the telephone down on him, an action which consequently stands out, inviting us to wonder why Fleming is now so disturbed? It is not that he will not be able to make contact with Sandra again; she has just made an audition appointment for the following evening. Is it the fact that something is more important to her than him that agitates, or is it just the fact of a woman putting the telephone down on Robert Fleming? The scene began with Sandra speaking into an unanswered telephone – now it is Fleming.

The sequence makes it important to distinguish carefully between our own perspective and Sandra's. Sandra is certainly aware that she is in discussion with a rather dangerous character, romantically speaking, but she cannot be aware of the simultaneous dispatch of her potential predecessor. The audience, on the other hand, see and hear the duality of the telephone conversation and benefit from the perspectives on the action provided by framing and composition.

We are also privileged over Sandra in information and impressions achieved through the organisation of the film's narrative structure: particularly, we have been witness to the conversation between Temple and Harkness only moments (of screen-time) before. The sequence presents a somebody who most convincingly answers the pathology of character presented by Professor Harkness. Would it be possible to show more immediately a character whose romantic and sexual interest moves from woman to woman? In this short scene (just over two minutes long) he has ditched one for another or, at the least, been prepared to sacrifice his existing relationship, which seemed intense enough at the beginning of the telephone call, for the possibility of contact with Sandra. It is clear from the response of the woman, moreover – she calls him 'incorrigible' – that this is not atypical behaviour. In addition to this inconstancy, Fleming has displayed a marked tendency to be have his head turned by 'some unusual attractiveness', in this case Sandra's voice, which has 'inspire[d] him to … destructiveness' – if not, as Harkness means, against the possessor of the attractiveness, then certainly to the detriment of his previous relationship. Whether or not a ladykiller in the literal sense of the word, Fleming is undoubtedly one in the metaphorical.

One of the effects of the film's narrative structure, therefore, both through the organisation of scenes which precede the telephone call and by the abrupt introduction of the newspaper headline, is to suggest the possibility that Fleming is the poet-killer. Whether Fleming turns out to be the murderer – he does not – is not, ultimately, what is important here. What is of greater significance in the overall pattern of the film is how readily Fleming fits the profile presented by Professor Harkness, his relationship to the psychosexual behaviour described surviving Inspector Temple's later attempt to distinguish between the outgoing, socially skilful Fleming and the more retiring characteristics which he feels belong to the poet-killer.

'A beauty that only Death can enhance' – this is the line which is taken as reflecting the tenor of the poems, repeated several times in the dialogue. The outlook embodied in these words, the way of seeing which views the dead body as more attractive than the living, refuses independent volition or autonomy to the woman concerned. The author of these lines is not interested in the subjective experience of the person he is writing about, only her appearance. The poet-killer eradicates his victim's mind so that his appreciation of the body can be unalloyed. (It is not that his victims would not consent to a real relationship with him: Lucy clearly and joyfully consents to the proposal to go off with 'John', even if we suspect that there may be a pragmatic financial element to her attraction to him as well as a romantic one.) The murdered women are subjected to an extreme form of objectification.

If there is only one character who takes the process of objectification to this length, there are many others who practise it in less extreme forms. The film plays with the idea that not only Fleming but also a number of the other men we meet could be the murderer; importantly, all of them share key characteristics with the killer. Evidence to support this claim is provided in the first instance by the taxi dance: not only the sizing-up performed by its clientele – the sailor: 'Spin around, sweetheart'; and Oswald Pickering: 'Strike me pink! If you ain't the prettiest little girl in the whole place' – but the description by the promoter, whose patter introduces us to the Palladium:

> 'Fifty beautiful, ravishing, glamorous dance partners. Fifty girls of your dreams to hold in your arms: short dreams, tall dreams, blonde and brunette. Dance with one or dance with fifty. Only six pence a dance, gentlemen.'

Short, tall, blonde, brunette: immediately we witness a reduction of whole to part, person to appearance, and a commercial operation promising to fulfil desires predicated on 'some unusual attractiveness'. Then there is the succession of characters that Sandra meets in the course of her investigations. Van Druten (Boris Karloff), for example, is very particular in his choice of models, speaking approvingly of Sandra as possessing 'the van Druten figure'. We might refer to Maxwell (Alan Mowbray), the butler at 18 Kenilworth Square who looks Sandra up and down as part of the interview process, or to Sir Charles (Charles Coleman), his employer, who approves the advert specifying attractiveness in his search for a parlour maid. Remember, too, Mr Moryani (Joseph Calleia), the procurer, for whom Maxwell also works, who rejects Sandra on the grounds that she is too intelligent. Even Inspector Temple needs to be included in this list, his appraisal later paralleled by Maxwell's (both of them eye her figure; both of them, like Fleming in the telephone scene, sit on the edge of a table while considering her), and its implications pointed up at the time by Sandra's deadpan remarks ('Uh-Oh', 'Now it comes'). It is fair to say that Temple's action is designed to anticipate the response of the killer, and that he equally esteems Sandra's powers of observation, but the fact that he and the other detectives have feelings for her which exceed the usual regard between colleagues is made very clear in the film, not least through the series of shots which show their reaction to the news of her engagement (see opposite). These similarities in behaviour are not coincidences, but they are parallels within the narrative structure – correspondences between police and criminals, romantic lead and lascivious minor characters.

In addition to this widespread appearance of characteristics that relate to the pathology of the murderer, it is worth noting that Fleming, the film's male lead, frequently behaves in ways that invite comparison with the other male characters, including some of the most unsavoury. He also is a potential employer who mixes romantic interest with professional: at the audition that never happens, he would have subjected Sandra to similar scrutiny to that which she receives from Temple, van Druten, Maxwell and Moryani. In the telephone scene, and for a little while subsequently, he hides his identity from her by pretending to be his secretary: all of the men who have ads in the personal column, including, of course, the poet-killer, also employ pseudonyms. Are the lines of Oswald Pickering, the customer at the taxi dance so different to those – more sophisticated, more charming admittedly – of Robert Fleming?[3] Just as there was a financial transaction between Pickering and Sandra (he has paid for the dance, the Palladium pays her wages) so also there is the promise of one between 'Fleming's Secretary' and Sandra. Fleming's behaviour toward Sandra's voice on the telephone is in itself a form of blind date, the *modus operandi* of the poet-killer. Sandra subsequently has her own reasons for suspecting that Fleming might be the killer and he becomes one of the men she is investigating, but not until the evening of her trip to meet the 'music lover' at the Schubert recital. At present, he is merely one of the men she has to negotiate in life, work and play.[4]

Fig. 3.6

Fig. 3.7

Fig. 3.8

A primary structuring decision in the narrative of *Lured* is that once she has been taken on as a detective by Scotland Yard, we encounter most of the film's events and all of the film's suspects in Sandra's company. There are some short sequences at which Sandra is not present at all: the action which runs from Fleming talking to Milton through to Maxwell adapting Sir Charles' advertisement, for example, which introduces Kenilworth Square before Sandra gets there. Within sequences, too, we are sometimes privileged over her. This is true of the telephone call and it will be for moments in the dynamic of scenes again: we see plenty of Fleming's activities at the concert that she does not; in a later scene, that we see Mr Moryani covertly listening to her telephone call to Scotland Yard helps to build suspense; the audience can hear the commentary that Fleming's ex gives on his technique at the nightclub when Sandra cannot. But the general point is that as Sandra opens her investigation into the authors of a series of personal column ads, we scrutinise them with her. And because we do not know who is the killer, all of these men – with the exception of Temple but not, on his introduction, Barrett (George Zucco) – are possible psychosexual killers.

In addition to this structural alignment between our position and Sandra's in the film's mystery story, the film's success depends on our emotional relationship with Sandra. One of the major pleasures of the film, I would argue, is the way in which Sandra's character and, of course, Lucille Ball's performance enlist us on her side in an investigation, in which every man is suspect. This is not to say that we view all of the male characters with horror – Fleming can be a very charming cad – but we are invited to look at all of them sceptically, and are likely to respond to the way Sandra conducts herself through some difficult situations. For example, consider the way she deals with Fleming, in the telephone scene or at the nightclub where she is one step ahead of the moves which the commentary that accompanies their dance leads us to expect him to make. Or remember the way she extracts information from Maxwell. There is a wonderful disregard that Sandra shows in the physicalisation of Ball's performance: the way she puts her elbow on Oswald Pickering's shoulder at the taxi dance; the sigh she gives as she gathers that she must meet with 'Music Lover' at the Ionian Hall to 'share his ecstasy'; the way she walks to the bar to telephone Fleming and Wilde. And then there is Sandra's dry sense of humour: evinced by her responses to Temple as he asks her to lift her skirt above her knees, and later close her eyes when he is deciding whether she will make suitable material for the force. Sandra is a dynamic protagonist for the film, and if the procedural scenes after Fleming's arrest are the least interesting in the movie, it is because she is in so few of them.

The coincidence of the interrupted telephone call introduces a pattern in which the story of Sandra's investigation of Lucy's disappearance is continually entwined with a focus on her pursuit of a career and an interest in her chances of romantic happiness. These combined concerns are developed through the way in which many of the personal ads lead to job interviews: the first one she responds to, where the vacancy has already been 'adequately filled'; her short-lived role working as a model for van Druten; the job at Kenilworth Square, which has been advertised in the personal column. This is a world where men pay for the pleasure of a dance, you are hired by the police for your attractiveness, and an audition can become confused with a date. Everywhere Sandra turns, she encounters economic or professional activities that turn on the attractiveness of women; equally, many of the film's romantic relationships are shaped by a financial balance of power. The relationship between the economic and sexual are played out in many different variations in the film.

So, Fleming's behaviour is similar to a number of the other men in the film, in ways which I am arguing are also connected to the paradigm of the murderer. Yet while the film is deliberately structured to make all of these men potential suspects there is particular evidence that links Fleming to the crime or to the actual murderer, his business partner Julian Wilde.

The relationship between the two partners, as it is characterised in the rest of our scene, their first together, is an interesting mixture of contrast, parallel and mutual regard. Differences are quickly established: the complementary skills that they bring to the business, their comparatively different ways of relating to women. Similarities are also insisted upon: through the editing and framing of the reverse-field-cut-conversation which emphasises that the partners have taken up symmetrical positions, and opens up a visual parallel between them in both wider and closer shots in this sequence, a strategy that is repeated in the views we see of them in their last meeting in the prison interview room.

Fig. 3.9

The closeness of their intertwined lives is revealed as the story unfolds. They work together, they live in the same house, share the same housekeeper, are mistaken for each other, and are so closely related that Fleming can be convincingly framed with the mass of circumstantial evidence. There is also the intriguing coincidence at the Ionian Hall when

Fig. 3.10

Fleming and Wilde surprise each other on arrival, and the film makes it deliberately difficult – through a certain hesitation in each performance – for us to determine which of them might be 'music lover', subsequently playing further on this uncertainty. (The moment when Fleming, at the nightclub later in the same evening, asks Sandra whether she has considered the possibility that he might be 'Music Lover', unaware of the full implications of the question or her affirmative reply, is a skilful example of the way the film sides us with Sandra in her investigation, and of the way in which her investigation and her romance are dangerously interwoven.)

Is it possible to suggest that at a poetic level there is more to the relationship between the two men than the fact that they live out of each other's pockets? To be 'doubled' in the full dramatic, psychological sense, one character needs to enact the unacknowledged desires of the other. What we can certainly claim is that Wilde's behaviour is the corollary of Fleming's attitudes: Wilde takes to its logical extreme the tendency to objectify which is everywhere apparent in Fleming's behaviour. Perhaps, in this light, we can put a bit more pressure on the timing of Wilde's first entrance: does Julian appear in response to Robert's frustration? Is it a coincidence that Wilde appears just at the moment when the woman Fleming has been talking to fails to fit in with what he wants?

There is also some interesting evidence to consider in the conclusion of the scene. As Wilde reads aloud from the newspaper about the poet-killer, Fleming throws open a further door which leads directly on to the rehearsal room where 'the pretty little girls' are auditioning. (The decision to construct the set in this way was not a cheap one:

Fig. 3.11

the perspective which the film thereby achieves on Fleming was clearly important to Sirk and his collaborators.) While we are looking at Fleming standing in front of this setting we hear him dismiss Wilde's voiced concern at the fate of the eight women feared victims: 'You're too sentimental. The eight little darlings probably ran off with professional charmers who promised them the riches of the Orient. You don't understand women, old boy.' The film offers us an element of dramatic irony here, because we know that this is exactly the sort of promise that has lured Lucy Barnard to her demise. In retrospect, we can see that Wilde does – in these extremely limited terms – 'understand women': perhaps he has learnt his technique from Fleming after all.

Fig. 3.12

Behind Wilde, in the reverse-shot, we can see two of the framed photographs of young women which are such a feature of Fleming's surroundings. In a later scene it is possible to see eleven separate framed portraits in Fleming's office, while never gaining a view of the whole room. It is worth taking a moment to reflect on the extraordinary prevalence

of these 10 x 8 glossy prints, which we see in particular locations: Fleming's office and Fleming's den, but also the police station. Are all the poet-killer's victims trying to break into show business? That would be the main reason for their having photographic studio portraits readily to hand. The other partial explanation, one that would account for Fleming's collection, if not that of the murderer/police, and supported by

Fig. 3.13

evidence from elsewhere in the film, is that getting girlfriends through the theatrical business appears to be Fleming's *modus operandi*. The two purposes are condensed in the telephone call with Sandra and elsewhere: even when in the less familiar surroundings of the concert at the Ionian Hall, he talks about the women he is hoping to meet as 'talent'. (Perhaps also reflecting his own particular understanding of romance, Wilde replies by saying that the concert hall will provide no 'hunting ground' for Fleming.)

One of the two portraits in the shots of Wilde may well be of the woman who has slammed the door moments before – it is difficult to be sure because the plane of focus is on Wilde rather than the background – the woman in the picture certainly wears her hair in the same way. But it could equally be a photograph of Arlette Tomlinson, one of the murder victims whose strikingly similar portrait Temple shows Sandra in the next sequence. Whether this is another unlikely coincidence or not, we can reflect that the two women (or three, if the portrait is of yet another person) aspire to similar fashion ideals, and similar ways of presenting themselves.

All the film's men, tarred by the brush of the murderer, share a mind-set, and a way of seeing, and the women in the film largely accede to the ways of presenting themselves that this way of seeing dictates. Lucy calls herself 'Blue Eyes' in her correspondence with 'John'. The women in the portraits in Fleming's office and the women who have been murdered all seem to be inspired by the same styles of dress and coiffure. Even Sandra, despite her resilient wit and ability to hold her own amongst the various perils of the investigation, seems to know and pragmatically accept the rules of the game. Certainly, she is not overwhelmed by the romantic skeletons in Fleming's cupboard.

One of the film's first images, the taxi dance, provides a picture of masculine/feminine relationships which resonates through the rest. By its nature a taxi dance is analogous to, and only a couple of steps away from, prostitution, and the detail of the first scene at the Broadway Palladium does nothing to contradict this. The men's sense of their proprietary rights – what they have bought for their dance ticket – extends to the conversation of their dance partners, as is clearly revealed when Sandra and Lucy try and speak to one another. When Oswald Pickering asks 'whose paying for this dance, I'd like to know?' he is resisting behaviour which demonstrates the independent volition of his dance partners, and wishing to preserve a fantasy that does not acknowledge the true feelings, or identity, of the women. As argued earlier, Oswald Pickering and the organisation of which he is a customer are in important ways representative of the characters and society we subsequently encounter. All in all, this is a pretty bleak picture, and one that our pleasure in Sandra's individual successes, and the strong comedic element of the film's mode, cannot disguise.

The tone and precise generic identity of *Lured* present an interesting conundrum: it is amongst the jolliest serial-killer films one is likely to see, its comedic elements emanating from decisions around casting, and particularly from the character constructed by Lucille Ball.[5] Perhaps we can make headway by returning to thinking about narrative structure. On the one hand it is a crime movie, the story of an investigation, and a film where the heroine starts off investigating a crime (by means of investigating a series of men) and ends up investigating one man in particular. Many years before second-wave feminism inspired subsequent attempts to reconceptualise crime stories with women in the central investigative role – *Coma* (Michael Crichton, 1978), *Blue Steel* (Kathryn Bigelow, 1990) – *Lured* intelligently reworks the framework of this kind of narrative. But in terms of the broad structures of point of view, the film's narration does not share the typical structure of most detective stories, where we either experience the events of the film with the central character, or where the detective (perhaps because he is narrating the story) knows the outcome when we do not. Neither is it a crime story where the audience's greater knowledge than the characters is systematically used to generate suspense (there are a couple of moments, but this is not attempted in a sustained way). Rather than play the story wholeheartedly as a melodrama of action, the mystery is combined with other emphases which we tend to associate with the melodrama of passion: a female protagonist and a tendency to encourage us to look for the forces that may be shaping a character's behaviour.[6] At the same time, the film is unlike a melodrama of passion in that – perhaps partly because its heroine is able to take action – it does not share the participatory anxieties of the melodramatic mode. (The comedic elements of the film's construction also prevent the melodramatic from becoming too powerful, although a number of situations in the film could, with a little shift of register, push the film into a different mode. The gothic melodrama is never very far away, and at the point of Sandra's engagement, and in some of her earlier encounters with troubled patriarchs, the film almost heads into the territory of the 'persecuted wife' melodrama, where the heroine marries a man who subsequently turns out to have unnoticed and unwelcome depths or designs.) Perhaps what we have here is a crime film that has been combined with tropes of the melodrama of passion, including a female protagonist and a particular orientation of point of view.

For all her skill in interpersonal relationships and detective work, it is not suggested, I think, that Sandra is able to perceive the relationship between her fiancée and the other men in an ideological sense. Our broader perspective than Sandra's is achieved – as I hope the preceding discussion demonstrates – by means of mise-en-scène and through the film's narrative structure, both in the sense of its parallels and its juxtapositions. Even when directing a detective mystery, a comedy-thriller, Sirk is able to achieve a similar balance between the broader perspective of the audience and the narrower perspective of the character as we see in his earlier and later melodramas of passion.

Afterword on *Pièges*

Lured inherits some of the elements that make up this uncommon generic mix from the film of which it is a remake, *Pièges*, directed in France in 1939 by Robert Siodmak and starring Maurice Chevalier, Marie Déa and Pierre Renoir. In a number of respects the films are surprisingly similar. The score is by the same composer (Michel Michelet) and contains many of the same themes (including the song 'All for Love', 'Mon Amour' in the original). Major elements of the plot have been transferred to the new version, much of the dialogue and some of the character names are directly translated.[7] Even the title sequence – a series of signs picked out by the beam of a torch – strongly resembles the earlier film. However, in simple ways which are actually very significant, and very relevant to the discussion of this chapter, *Lured* differs from its predecessor. A number of these differences are to do with direction, casting and performance, but the ones I wish to draw brief attention to are concerned with narrative structure.[8]

In *Pièges* the story moves straight from the first (and, in this film, only) scene at the taxi dance, via a poster announcing the disappearance of her colleague, to Adrienne

Charpentier (Marie Déa) being interviewed at the police station. In other words there is no equivalent to our sequence in the original, no telephone call, no introduction to Fleming (called Robert Fleury, played by Maurice Chevalier) or Wilde (Brémontière – Pierre Renoir) until the scene at the concert. Nor is there any visit by the police to a literary expert, no analysis of the poem's Baudelairian qualities. In short, most of the elements of the film which I have been moved to write about are inventions of the remake.[9]

Among the changes effected in *Lured* is an increase in the degree of coincidence in the story, and not only as a result of the invention of the coincidences of the telephone scene. The encounter between Fleming and Sandra at the Ionian Hall becomes a coincidence as a result of the earlier telephone conversation – in *Pièges* the visit to the concert is the first contact between Adrienne and Fleury, and our introduction to the latter. The unexpected encounter between Fleming and Wilde in the foyer, which helps cultivate the ambiguity over which might be the 'Music Lover', is another coincidence made possible by having the earlier scene introducing the partners – in *Pièges* there is no suggestion that either was unaware that the other was attending, and we encounter them for the first time sitting next to each other in the auditorium. Again, I would argue that this is not evidence of a failing on *Lured*'s part, an excess of contrivance. The coincidence of Fleming turning up at the concert that evening and noticing Sandra allows him to become one of the suspects in the investigation with all the benefits previously described. Their chance encounter at Kenilworth Square – business associate of Sir Charles recognises maid as she serves him port – also helps the film to develop the image of a house where every social level shares a paradigm on heterosexual relationships. (This is not the only sense in which the film offers a peculiarly Dickensian vision of post-war London.) In these, and the other ways – such as the timing of Wilde's first entrance – coincidences work to bring together narrative elements and insist upon a variety of deeper and non-literal connections.

4. Looking, talking and understanding: subjectivity and point of view in *Talk to Her* (2002)

Talk to Her (*Hable con Ella*, Pedro Almodóvar, 2002) is a film of striking images and contentious actions; any serious account needs to consider the attitude toward these that the film encourages its audience to take. *Talk to Her*, moreover, is a film explicitly concerned with point of view, in that it makes subjective experience and identification part of its subject matter. It therefore seems a highly suitable film to explore in relation to point of view as an area of choice for the filmmaker.

Talk to Her has a central focus on the friendship between two men and, at the same time, is constructed around two 'love' triangles with Marco (Darío Grandinetti) at the point of intersection. This chapter follows the emphasis of the film in that it mainly addresses the triangle that also includes the friendship – Benigno (Javier Cámara), Marco and their relationships toward Alicia (Leonor Watling) – and will say relatively little about Lydia (Rosario Flores) and El Niño (Adolfo Fernández). My investigation will build from the moment when Marco sees Alicia in the dance studio: the sequence begins one hour 28 minutes and 29 seconds into the film and lasts for two minutes and 30 seconds.

1. Out-of-focus shot of orange wall, light fittings, a plant; medium close-up, once Marco has entered
   [A door opens from frame right and Marco enters in focus, in profile. He looks out of frame left. He closes the door.]

2. Wide-shot, Marco walks into room, from behind the camera off frame right
   [He looks around. Our view is from the hall and so our view of the living room is restricted.]

3. Medium-shot of wall with standard lamp and large print of Alicia's head on the pillow, photographed at the clinic
   [A point-of-view shot.]

4. Close-up of Marco looking out frame right; a shuttered window is behind him
   [Marco looks down, and then round at window. He walks to it and begins to draw the blind.]

5. Medium-shot; reverse from the street
   [Marco is already looking off frame lower right as the blind comes up. He steps onto balcony, continuing to look off lower right.]

6. Long-shot of dance studio, and on an angle consistent with Marco's gaze
   [Dancers dance.]

7. **Varies: medium close-up – medium-shot, camera within dance school**
[Close view of female dancer as she pirouettes, she and a male dancer further away from the camera (out of focus) dance, eventually out of frame left. The camera adjusts and refocuses to catch another five stepping into the space the others had filled.]

8. **Medium close-up of Marco on balcony; similar position to 5, but closer**
[He continues to look searchingly off frame right.]

9. **Same set up as 6**
[Foreground full of dancers, Alicia can (just) be seen on crutches making her way across the far wall of the studio.]

10. **Same set up as 6**
[Marco looks.]

11. **Closer shot on same axis as 6**
[Through the distortions of the glass we can see Alicia sitting in an orange plastic chair as a gaggle of dancers move from in front of her.]

Fig. 4.1

12. **Close-up of Marco: on similar axis to 8**
[He opens his eyes in surprise.]

13. **Close-up of Alicia; camera within the studio, much closer view than that available to Marco, front on to Alicia.**
[She watches the dancers with tears in her eyes.]

Fig. 4.2

14. **Begins as 12, but as Marco moves, the shot pulls focus to the picture on the far wall of the room**
[Marco leaps inside the room and puts his back to the window.]

15. **Close-up of Marco**
[He is looking off frame (slightly left) which I take to indicate he is looking at the picture which we see in the following (and preceding) shots. He is breathing heavily.]

Fig. 4.3

16. Close-up of photograph of Alicia

17. Long-shot of dancers in studio
   [Camera position and angle consistent with
   what can be deduced to be Alicia's viewpoint.]

18. Very similar, but not identical to 11
   [Alicia looks on.]

19. Long-shot, Alicia in studio
   [This is shot against the light and Alicia is almost in silhouette. It is some
   time later: all the other dancers have gone. Katerina (Geraldine Chaplin) speaks
   off-screen and enters carrying mat.]

20. Aerial view of mat
   [We can see the instructive images of exercises printed on blue matt. Alicia
   enters, after a pause, assisted by Katerina's hands. She looks past camera.]

21. Close-up view of Marco through window; not very different from 12, but he
   is in one half of the window
   [He looks off-frame right, but from inside the room.]

22. Not as long as 6, not as close as 9
   [Katerina exercises Alicia. We watch through the window.]

23. Same set up as 21
   [Marco continues to watch.]

The camera is inside the flat before Marco opens the door, but once he is inside, Marco
has the advantage over us as he walks through the hall and into the bedroom. (Our view
of the apartment remains restricted: the revelation that Benigno has replicated the bedroom he saw in the magazine in its entirety is kept back for a later sequence.) We rejoin
Marco in shot 3, by sharing his optical point of view, as he looks at the large photograph
of Alicia's head on the pillow, her eyes closed. As if following a train of thought, he turns
his head in one slow movement until he is looking at the window and then walks toward
it (shot 4). As we watch him pull up the shutter in shot 5, the camera now outside the
apartment facing back, he is already looking off-frame right, in the direction of the dance
studio on the other side of the street, a shadow in the reflection of the facing building
allowing us to see the direction of his gaze.

   Shot 6 is a view of the studio consistent with the perspective available from Benigno's apartment, but rather than cutting back to Marco looking, which would complete
a point-of-view figure, this is followed by a view of the dancers emphatically shot from

inside the dance school. Shots 8, 9 and 10 collectively create a point-of-view figure, as do 10, 11 and 12 – 11 being the point-of-view shot in which Alicia is revealed and 12 capturing Marco's surprise at seeing her. However, we cut from this close-up of Marco wide-eyed, starting backwards, to a close-up of Alicia herself (shot 13). This is not an angled view, shot on a long lens through the studio window, rather the camera is close to Alicia, squarely in front of her; we can see tears in her eyes.

We then cut to Marco (the same set up as the previous shot of him) who darts inside the flat and puts his back to the window, the camera pulling focus to the picture of Alicia on the far wall. This is followed by a reverse-field cut to show Marco, his back still to the balcony window, looking off-screen in a direction consistent with the framed photograph, followed itself by a close-up of the photograph, which shows us Alicia's image but not the frame or the surrounding wall.

Rather than complete a potential point-of-view figure by returning to Marco, the film now cuts to another shot categorically within the dance studio. It is a long-shot, showing a number of dancers at work, its backdrop one of the walls which we have not previously seen. This view of the studio is consistent with the view which Alicia must have from her chair. Indeed, the next shot is a close-up of Alicia, similar but not identical to shot 13, in which she looks past the camera, the reverse-field cut with eyeline match supporting the notion that the previous shot represents what she can see.

Shot 19 appears to be some time later: the room is now empty but for Alicia and the off-screen voice of Katerina. The only light comes from outside and the now distant figure of Alicia is almost in silhouette. It is another view categorically within the studio, and another angle on the space, looking back towards the windows through which Marco has looked in. Until this point the soundtrack had been dominated by the plaintive composition 'Alicia Vive', together with a few sounds specific to the space in which Marco inhabits (the door to the flat opening, the shutters going up, the clatter as he backs into the window). Now the music is combined with the conversation between Alicia and Katerina, who enters frame left with an exercise mat. This is subtitled as follows:

> Katerina: I was so thrilled to see you coming in alone today, just with canes, on your own.
> Alicia: Did you see?
> Katerina: How was rehab today?
> Alicia: Very good.
> Katerina: Are you tired?
> Alicia: Yes, very.
> Katerina: Doesn't matter. We'll do some additional exercises. We'll do some leg stretches.
> Alicia: I've done one hundred today already.
> Katerina: We'll just do a few more.

Shot 20, during which the end of this conversation takes place, is an aerial view of a blue exercise mat onto which, after a moment or two, Alicia lies down, on her back, assisted by the hands of Katerina. Alicia looks straight upwards. We then cut to a view of Marco looking through the window of Benigno's flat. This is followed by a shot of the studio from outside, similar to those earlier in the sequence, which preserves the angled view consistent with Marco's vantage point and through which we can see Katerina exercising Alicia's legs. Finally, shot 21 is the same set up as 19, and shows us more of Marco looking off-screen right. In these last three shots the only accompanying sound is the score.

We need to register the emotional power of this sequence, which can be lost in the dry forms of notation and description. Marco has just visited Benigno in prison, and arrived at his flat, which he is going to rent, for the first time. This in itself lends poignancy to the scene. Alicia's appearance is a breathtaking moment, coloured by the narrative situation, the actor's performances and Alberto Iglesias' emotive score, and the particular way in which her appearance is managed by the film.

The revelation of Alicia's miraculous recovery would be an important and potentially powerful moment in the film whichever way it was handled, but the decisions made by Almodóvar and his collaborators are particularly suggestive. Her entrance is carefully choreographed. In shot 9 Alicia, in a pale grey tracksuit top, can actually be seen making her way on crutches toward the seat on which she sits in shot 11, but she is difficult to make out, shielded by a cluster of dancers. When we return from the reverse of Marco, both shots tighter than the views previously available to us, the dancers launch into their routine and our view to Alicia sitting on a chair is suddenly cleared. The effect of the closer views is an increased intensity, that of the choreography an almost magical appearance.

One interpretation that the realisation of the sequence makes possible is that Alicia's appearance is in some respects a 'summoning up', a response to the wishes of Marco. What such a structure often implies is that the external world seems to be responding to the internal needs and desires of a character; it is an extreme dramatic form of wish fulfilment. The film has provided plenty of evidence to suggest that Marco does desire such an event. The first thing he did on discovering El Niño's relationship with Lydia, and therefore the truth about his own – 'splitting up', as Benigno puts it – is to walk into Alicia's room and tell her that he is alone, single, lonely. When impressing on Benigno the impossibility of his marriage plans, Marco admitted that he 'likes' Alicia. And here he stands in Benigno's flat, where he knows the nurse used to watch Alicia before her accident and, seemingly inspired by the giant photograph of Alicia on the wall, he goes to take up that old perspective at the window. The intensity of his scrutiny, perhaps our own hopes of seeing Alicia restored to health, the ethereal turn of the music, conspire to make this a singular moment.

The achievement of the sequence, however, is that this sense of a 'summoning up', with its powerful evocation of Marco's experience, is only one of a number of perspectives which it holds in balance. Shot 12 gives us Marco's reaction on seeing Alicia, but the shot which follows does not confirm his and our brief sighting with another point-of-view shot. Rather, we cut to a close-up of Alicia which provides a very different view to that available to Marco: one which gives an insight into Alicia's emotional response which would be impossible to perceive from a distance. The shot allows us close to the experience of a character who has spent all of the film, with the exception of one extended flashback, in a coma. The comatose Alicia has been credited with many thoughts and emotions during the narrative: this is a rare opportunity to consider the real person.

Alicia's appearance carries a sense of hopelessness. Not only her tears suggest this, but also the way in which she sits, slightly unevenly in her chair, a little like a rag doll; her hair hanging loose, awkwardly cut, which contrasts with the way in which she wore it when dancing, and the way in which the other women dancing in this sequence wear their hair, in the habitual manner of ballerinas. Are her tears delight at being back, or dismay at what to her is a sudden transformation from grace to helplessness? Four years of her life have disappeared without trace, and she has not even the compensatory delight which her father and friends must share at her recovery.

Even before the close-up of Alicia, the camera had demonstrated its independence of Marco by moving inside the studio for a shot of the dancers at work. While the sequence gives us a series of views which replicate the line of vision of Marco, and thus clearly evoke his perspective, it has a freedom to show us the scene from completely different positions. The film succeeds in the difficult balancing act of evoking something as intense as Marco's experience of seeing Alicia while at the same time giving the spectator perspectives entirely independent of him.

The close-up of Alicia cuts to the shot in which we see Marco jump back inside the room (14), followed by a shot of him from the inside with his back to the window and then a reverse-field cut to a close view of the photograph of Alicia on the far wall of the apartment. Marco's is an unusual response, even in circumstances of shock and bewilderment. Presumably his flight is governed by a reluctance to be seen: an innocent response would be to stay and look. Perhaps his astonishment is coloured by guilt? He is, after all, taking on Benigno's role in things, both in the sense of supporting his friend and in inheriting his view from the window. Additionally, in giving us this close-up of the photograph of the supine, supremely passive Alicia – which is clearly what Marco is looking at, our sense of his eyeline in the preceding shot (15) strengthened by the pull of focus in the one before that (14) – rather than the awkward, alive Alicia outside, the film might suggest a momentary preference in Marco for controllable fantasy over reality.[1] Has Marco failed to listen to the old injunction to be careful about what you wish for in case it comes true?

The next decision is again not an obvious one. Rather than cutting to another shot of Marco looking off-screen, completing a potential point-of-view figure, in the next shot (17) the camera is back in the dance academy providing a view, itself not a point-of-view shot in the strict sense, which corresponds to Alicia's perspective of the dancers in the studio. Shot 18 gives us Alicia looking off-screen, evoking without cementing 17 as her viewpoint.

The film makes repeated use of what we might call a truncated point-of-view figure, where the power of the conventions to definitively identify a shot as representing the optical point of view of a character is refused in favour of an approach which, while drawing on the power of the eyeline match, is nevertheless less emphatic. This is a vital component in the balancing of viewpoints which the sequence achieves. It reveals to us what a character is looking at without drawing us too fully into their point of view in the wider sense. It is never ambiguous, but allows us to jump from one extreme of the space depicted to the other, and from the perspective of the character with whom we have been travelling, to that of another who we have never properly met before.

The next view, later in the day, comes from the fourth point of the compass, showing the darkened studio with the buildings on Marco's side of the street in the background. This again establishes a perspective that is decidedly not Marco's (even though, as we soon see, he is watching), and further develops the spectator's sense of Alicia's experience through the soundtrack which places us in the room with the women. The halting movements of the two women in the empty studio contrast with the full, choreographed studio of moments of screen-time before. Rather than take her place in the waves of synchronised performers, Alicia can only practice therapeutic exercises when everyone else is gone. The void between where she is and where she would like to be is clear.

Then we are given another close shot of Alicia as she edges onto the mat. She can barely move herself, needing almost as much manipulation at this stage of her rehab as she did when in a coma. As well as the contrast with Alicia's earlier self as we observed her, through Benigno's eyes, going through her points at the bar, we are also made aware of the differences between Alicia now and when comatose – the aerial composition here reminiscent of one of the defining views of her time in hospital, and several other images from that part of the film. When she was in a coma there was a self-contained quality to her appearance. She needed assistance for basic functions, yet there was something assured about her nevertheless. This impression partly resulted from the contrast between her first appearance and the pained somnambulism of the dancers of *Café Muller*, but it also stemmed from the contrast between her passivity and the various human casualties that moved around her. Now, she has to face again the difficulties and possibilities of life, and from a position very different from where she left off.

The sequence finishes with a point-of-view figure: Marco watching from inside the apartment, the two women viewed through the angled glass wall of the studio. This makes it clear that Marco has returned to, and stayed, watching the real Alicia, but coming after the conversation between the women which is now denied us (we aurally are returned to Marco's space as well as visually) the limitations of his view are clear.

We can deepen our account of what is going on here by referring to the dimensions or axes of point of view identified by Douglas Pye (2000). In the sequences immediately prior to this one we have been closely aligned to Marco on the cognitive axis: since he made contact with Benigno we have experienced the film in the company of his character and before Alicia's appearance are united in our ignorance at her recovery. (This is not to say that we are entirely aligned with Marco in these terms even in this sequence – as mentioned above, the view we have of the flat is less than his, but we know Benigno's decorating plans when Marco does not.) In broad terms, in the part of this sequence before Alicia appears we are also placed closely to Marco on the spatial axis: we are in the flat with him or hovering in the street, in close proximity to the flat, watching him in the doorway of the french windows; we hear what he can hear; we share his optical point of view in a series of point-of-view figures. But in shots 13, 17 and 18 a shift on the spatial axis of point of view, moving us away from Marco into close physical proximity to Alicia, makes possible a shift on the cognitive axis: we are aware of Alicia's experiences and feelings in a way that Marco cannot be. Shots 19 and 20, later in the day, continue to place us closer to Alicia than Marco on the spatial and cognitive axes, which has the effect of distancing us from Marco's point of view in the most general sense. When we return to him for a point-of-view figure, and are realigned with him on the spatial axis, the evaluative dimension of our relationship with him may have shifted as we recognise the limits of his perspective. In short, the film's play with these variables should have an impact on how we view Marco in evaluative terms.

Another interest of the sequence is that it disrupts the structures of looking identified by Laura Mulvey in 'Visual Pleasure and Narrative Cinema' (1975), that have been such a feature of the academic discussion of film ever since. The process of drawing the spectator into identification with the hero, where we look with him at the female figure which is thereby objectified, is subtly challenged by the sequence.[2] The sequence breaks away from Marco twice: once immediately after the point-of-view figure which reveals Alicia's appearance and his reaction to it, to give us the closer view of Alicia (Shot 13) which evokes her feelings, her subjectivity, for the spectator and which privileges us over Marco, who is excluded from these perceptions; secondly when Marco retreats into Benigno's room to consider the passive image of Alicia and at the moment where the third shot of the point-of-view figure would cement our perspective with his, we cut to Alicia's view of the studio and then another close-up of Alicia (17 and 18). Instead of being sutured into the masculine process of looking, we leap away to the viewpoint, the space and, in the following shots, the hearing of the living person on the other side of the street. An invocation of Mulvey's argument here also helps to explain Marco's dash for privacy. The wished-for object of his gaze has suddenly proved – on her unexpected appearance – to have greater autonomy than he was wistfully anticipating.

The living Alicia is contrasted, therefore, with Benigno's image of Alicia, fixed in time, passive, framed. The photograph captures for the sequence the unchanging image of the suspended Alicia, and in a way which defines it explicitly as Benigno's view: his photograph (we presume), his enlargement, his bedroom wall. Benigno's problems partly arise from the fact that his obsession with Alicia was born from the limited perspective available from his apartment: he grew fascinated watching her dance from his window.[3]

Benigno's saving grace is that, unlike the poet-killer of *Lured* in his relations with women, Benigno does credit the comatose Alicia with personality and individuality. He is unaware that his view of Alicia is extremely limited and has imagined that his care for her is reciprocated, but he cherishes the few facts he knows about her interests, and not only finds ways of pursuing them on her behalf (the autographed print of Pina Bausch, for example) but has moulded himself in her image, and has thereby developed a fulfilling cultural life. His love may be profoundly unrequited, and predicated on fantasy rather than reality, but he credits her body with consciousness when nobody else does – a faith that is in part vindicated. To accuse him of being a psychopath, as Alicia's father and medical officer do, is to miss the point.

The film employs a number of strategies that ensure Benigno remains a sympathetic character despite his crime. One is the invention of *Amante Menguante* (*Shrinking Lover*), visualised for the audience as Benigno recounts the film to Alicia, which enables *Talk to Her* to avoid showing the impregnation. Another is his friendship with Marco: in the qualities of the relationship, in similarities between the men which make Benigno seem less extraordinary, and in comparisons between the two which sometimes work in his favour. Marco is charismatic, sensitive and attractive. He is something of an outsider (Argentinean, a travel writer often abroad) and we discover much about the world of the film in his company. All these factors are likely to encourage us to perceive him as a sympathetic character, and so the very fact of his friendship with Benigno benefits the latter by association.

Moreover, Benigno possesses qualities that are absent in Marco. The remoteness between Marco and Lydia is continually revealed in Marco's behaviour towards her at the clinic, most obviously his inability to touch or talk to her, and this is contrasted not only

Fig. 4.4

with El Niño but also Benigno, and reinforced through the composition of images which use the structuring shapes of the window frames of Lydia's room to dramatise the comparative distance between the characters. Benigno's characterisation of the Lydia/ Marco relationship on hearing of its demise – 'There was something in your relationship, forgive me, that didn't work' – seems to be confirmed by the evidence presented by the film, and perhaps so too is his earlier advice to 'talk to her'. In such ways the comparison between the two men, and their respective behaviour toward their sleeping 'lovers', sometimes tells against Marco and for Benigno. Following from this last point, there are qualities evident in Benigno's behaviour – caring, devoted, enthusiastic – which allow us to be generous toward his relationship with Alicia before we know of the rape and, in conjunction with the other elements discussed above, make us less likely to harshly judge him when we do.

In some ways Marco's behaviour might be felt to be the more perverse. Benigno at least had one conversation with Alicia before the accident. We spend a lot of the film considering Benigno's relationship to Alicia to be an imaginary one, both in the sense of the imagined reciprocation of love, and in his hopeful belief in the existence of feelings and human life in someone in a vegetative state. Yet Marco is in a similarly deluded situation: he believes Lydia is in love with him (and was too busy talking *at* her, when she was conscious, to hear that this was not, or no longer, the case). Marco's relationship with Lydia has further similarities to Benigno's imaginary one with Alicia. Both men admired the women from afar before speaking to them, and both won the confidence of the respective woman by performing a service for her: finding a wallet or killing a snake. The opening sequence, in retrospect, suggests a further parallel between Benigno and Marco in their relationships with women: Benigno goes to watch Pina Bausch so he can talk to Alicia about it; Marco cries because he cannot share the beauty of what he has seen with Angela (Elena Anaya). If Benigno is living in an imaginary relationship frozen in a conversation four years ago, Marco is dominated by his recollection of a relationship finished more than ten years before. The sequence of Alicia's return, with Marco explicitly walking in Benigno's footsteps, is therefore only one example of a number in the film in which Marco invests in ways of behaving we associate with Benigno.

The moment when Marco talks to the comatose Alicia takes place at the beginning of the longest take in the film. It begins with Marco coming into the room, sitting down by Alicia and telling her that he is alone. Only the lower half of Alicia's body is covered by a sheet and the room is otherwise empty; Marco has left the door open, but the propriety of his behaviour is certainly likely to be questioned by the audience. He admits as much himself by starting when Benigno suddenly comes into the room and the frame. Benigno says, 'Admit it, you were looking at her breasts', to which Marco replies, 'It's hard not to, they're getting bigger.' The steadicam shot, which contains considerable movement and reframing, goes on to capture Benigno and Marco discussing the end of Marco and Lydia's relationship, but also, when Rosa (Mariola Fuentes) has entered the room and Marco has left, the conversation about Alicia's late period. In linking the first action and the last, the shot draws on the inherent potential of the long take to imply a connection between the different elements it includes, suggesting a relationship between Marco's desires and Benigno's actions.

So, too, does the dramatic logic of the 'summoning up'. Marco may wish Alicia alive, but it is Benigno whose actions succeed, in a macabre version of *Sleeping Beauty*, in waking Alicia from her endless sleep in *El Bosque*. Marco, the film's ending suggests, is going to be a romantic beneficiary of this – not so Benigno. This is not to say that the film lets Marco get away unscathed, the film develops critical perspectives on his behaviour, as an examination of the scene in which Marco first claps eyes on Alicia – which bears intriguing similarities with the scene of her return – reveals.

Following his arousal from sleep, waking from dreaming about kissing Lydia, Marco is making his way down the corridor to visit Dr Vega (Roberto Álvarez), when he slows to look through a door that stands slightly ajar. We watch him through the opening as his face registers surprise and he pushes the door further open. We cut to share his optical point of view: the door continues to open revealing Alicia lying on the bed, partially naked, a blanket draped across her waist, its folds and her reclining pose evocative of a classical nude such as

Fig. 4.5

Lely's portrait of Nell Gwyne or Trutat's *Reclining Bacchante*.[4] Beyond Alicia's bed we can see Rosa, facing the wall, putting on some surgical gloves.

Marco is looking at the unconscious, naked woman when she opens her eyes. We cut to a shot of Marco starting at this, which closes the point-of-view figure, and he moves quickly away from the door. In the reverse that follows, which is the same set up as the point-of-view shot, we see and hear Benigno tell Rosa to shut the window-door because there is a draft, notice that Alicia has opened her eyes, close them and then close the door on our watching camera. We, but not Marco, are treated to their conversation:

> Benigno: She's opened her eyes.
> Rosa: That gives me the creeps.
> Benigno: And when she yawns?
> Rosa: I shit myself.

As Marco pushes the door, and leading up to and including the moment when Alicia opens her eyes, we can hear a sound that might be the wind. Indeed, Benigno notices the draught moments later, but the sound adds something preternatural and mysterious to the occasion. The rational explanation that we are presented with comes after Marco has left the scene; neither is he party to the earthy conversation about Alicia's unconscious bodily functions.

There are several correspondences between this sequence and the scene of Alicia's return. On both occasions we share a problematic (in this case, specifically voyeuristic) point-of-view shot with Marco. On both occasions Alicia might be said to respond to the gaze and desires of Marco but in ways which surprise both Marco and the spectator and which assert Alicia's aliveness, her lack of passivity and her independence of the perspective levelled at her. On both occasions Marco reacts by flight. On both occasions we are then given perspectives that are not available to him.

Our experience of this moment is likely to be uncomfortable: both anxiety lest Marco should get caught, and concern about the motives and ethics of his behaviour. In fact the episode is structured as a rebuke to Marco – and perhaps by extension us, as we join him in his looking – rather like the little dramas which sometimes rebuke L. B. Jeffries (James Stewart) and the spectator of *Rear Window* (such as the discomfort of the newly-wed couple at the presence of their landlord, and their closing of the blind, just before Stella (Thelma Ritter) accuses Jeff of being a 'window shopper'). If the surprise of Alicia opening her eyes is not challenge enough to his and our gaze, then he and we are rebuked a second time a few minutes later when Marco again pauses outside the door, on his return from Dr Vega, and this time Benigno looks back into the camera providing Marco's point-of-view shot and orders him into the room.

Notably, and in contrast to Marco, Benigno then displays behaviour in relation to Alicia that treats her as a subject rather than as an object, explaining to her that this is the man who cried at *Café Muller*. Just before he does this, he applies drops to Alicia's eyes while telling Marco that he remembers that he had cried watching the performance. Benigno talks about the crying just as he applies the eye drops, and the film gives us a close-up of the action, with liquid running down Alicia's face, at exactly this moment.

Fig. 4.6

In a sense Benigno is animating Alicia, and the film seems to collude with him in this, giving weight to this notion in the way the sequence is put together. As well as highlighting Alicia's 'tears', the film also triggers a sympathetic moistening of its spectators' eyes, the symptomatic response we give when watching someone else's eyes being made to water. (I suspect Benigno's actions have the same effect on the spectator in the room, Marco: Grandinetti does blink four times a few seconds of screen-time later.) This moment takes the film's play with identification a stage further, encouraging from its audience a physical act of sympathy with an unconscious character.

Benigno's complaint

When Marco visits Benigno in prison for the first time, Benigno tells him about how important his travel books have been to him. As the subtitles record it:

> I've read all your travel guides. It was like travelling for months with you at my side, telling me things no one tells you on journeys. My favourite is the one on Havana. I really identified with those people, who've got nothing and invent everything. When you describe that Cuban woman leaning out a window by the *Malecón* waiting uselessly, seeing how time passes and nothing happens ... I thought that woman was me.

Fig. 4.7

As Benigno is telling Marco this we are given a two-shot, but one which is so composed, with the reflections of the glass partitions in the visiting room so organised, as to superimpose the talking Benigno over the silent and still Marco.[5] The effect is almost that Benigno animates Marco's image: a suggestion that gains power by being juxtaposed with the conversation in which Ben-igno describes how he has imaginatively identified himself with the people described in the book, and imagined himself into the position of a protagonist in reading the travel guide. This is another example of Benigno identifying incorrectly, of writing himself into a story where no protagonist is required. In addition, Benigno identifies himself with a woman glimpsed by Marco on his travels: somebody fixed, viewed by his travelling protagonist. 'I thought that woman was me' – this last line is given greater emphasis by being the final action of the sequence.

Significantly, a copy of Marco's guide to Cuba (with a photograph of what might be the waiting woman on the cover) appears among the possessions we see in the sequence of images which accompany Benigno writing his last letter, which are shown to us as Marco reads it. The book is alongside a photograph of Benigno's mother and a smaller version of the photograph of Alicia's head on the pillow. The inclusion of this image in such company, among the women most important to him, is further evidence of what is emerging as Benigno's fatal flaw: that he is someone who identifies too much, too strongly; that his identification becomes almost completely a projection of himself.

A psychoanalytic reading would need to draw on the other element that is brought together in the sequence of images: his mother's wedding photograph, torn to remove the husband/father, and the wider elements of the film to which it refers. Such a reading might argue that the root cause of Benigno's problems is that he never fully achieved separation from his mother, and consequently cannot distinguish easily between where he ends and another begins. Benigno's behaviour, and much of the film's other imagery, would support such a diagnosis. Consider the relationship between Benigno and his dependent mother (her incapacity, the film suggests, psychological rather than physical) and how that relationship might then have been transferred to Benigno's ways of relating to Alicia, both by means of the mother's off-screen presence as he watches Alicia (from what is, after all, his mother's flat: even after her death the same photograph appearing prominently in shots of Benigno watching from the window), and by the transference of Benigno's role from housebound carer for his mother to carer for the now bedridden and supremely passive Alicia. Such an argument would help explain why Benigno finds *Amante Menguante* so disturbing, particularly the concluding action of the film (where the hero, having been rescued from miniature adult life at the home of a 'terrible' mother, climbs bodily into the vagina of his sleeping lover and stays inside her forever), which seems to trigger his attempt to make love to Alicia (it is not suggested that Benigno has behaved like this on other occasions). Pertinently to this chapter's broader discussion, a clinical diagnosis along these lines would account for Benigno's tendency to live vicariously, in this example of the travel guides, but also in the way he has adopted all his enthusiasms from Alicia. The failure to recognise the boundaries between himself and others might also explain why Benigno finds a world without Alicia so terrible to comprehend. Ultimately, Benigno takes his identification/projection not only to the extent of rape but also to suicide or, as he tells himself, to a coma in which he can be with Alicia.

Conclusion

The film's ending – in the title 'Marco y Alicia', in the imagery from the stage where a young couple in Pina Bausch's *Masurca* break off from the group and begin to get to know each other, and in Alicia's closing smile – suggests a new relationship will form from the desolation of the preceding action. What makes this a more promising prospect than the (pre)history of Marco's feelings for Alicia might suggest, is that this is a moment when Alicia and we are privileged over Marco. We see her notice Marco crying at *Masurca*. The sequence begins with a close-up of her looking past the camera, the eyeline match leading to a view of the back of Marco's head (the film then cuts to the action on stage, again refusing a point-of-view figure), and we subsequently see her looking with interest at Marco in the foyer, both events occurring before he realises she is in the theatre. Alicia herself, then, has the chance to desire, rather than merely be the desired object of others. And Marco, at least, is someone who likes both Pina Bausch and travel independently of knowing Alicia's interests – his views on silent cinema are never revealed.

This sequence not only evokes the opening, it also calls to our minds the two occasions when Benigno told Alicia about the crying man. When Alicia is attracted by Marco's tears, is she just struck by a sensitive, and handsome, man or is she unconsciously remembering Benigno's words from the time she spent in the coma? Does this suggest that she *could* hear things when in her vegetative state? The advice 'talk to her', given by Benigno to Marco and taken up by the film's title, is offered for the benefit of the person who will do the talking but perhaps, as Benigno believes, there is also a benefit for the listener. This is the crux of much of the film: where is the dividing line between a relationship which merely provides an opportunity for a person to work out his or her own feelings on someone else and one which is genuinely communicative? When you talk to somebody, do you talk with them or talk at them? Do you look at somebody without their knowledge, or do you look at each other?

Talk to Her is a film which constructs a sophisticated and challenging structure of point of view for its audience. Not every film has one of its main characters in a coma, not many encourage sympathetic understanding for a nurse who rapes an unconscious patient in his care. Above all, this is a film which asks us not to make snap judgements about its characters. The situation is always more complex than we or the characters might presume: Angela turns out to have a more complex past than a young woman in bridal white is supposed to have (the film is not overexcited about this, it just is a fact); a female bullfighter is frightened of snakes; talking to the builders and getting a photograph framed turn out not to be the typical activities of a young professional on his day off but elements of an extensive fantasy life; Marco's relationship with Lydia is revealed to be something other than he, and we, perceived it to be.

The generous perspective that the film encourages, slow to judge and quick to understand, is one of its key qualities. In the complex structure of narrative parallels, and as a result of the detailed organisation of the mise-en-scène, the film manages to be understanding toward its characters, and yet is able to be critical of them at the same time. Moreover, this is all in a context in which imaginative identification is a subject of the film itself. The organisation of point of view interacts with the subjects of the film: subjectivity, identification, the assumptions made as a result of a restricted viewpoint.

In discussing Marco's first encounter with Alicia at *El Bosque* I made a comparison with *Rear Window*, but it is also interesting to invoke Hitchcock's film in relation to the sequence of Alicia's return. Both films are structured around a tension between point-of-view shots from an apartment against independent views of who and what is looked at. Both achieve a complex play between the fantasy constructed from the limited view from the apartment and a reality which is indicated by deploying shots which are unmistakably views independent of the apartment and/or its inhabitants. A difference is that in *Rear Window* the fantasy is projected outside the window as a response to the pressing reality within, whereas in *Talk to Her* the fantasy is preserved inside the apartment (and on its walls), as though Benigno has collected impressions of the outside world and brought them back to the apartment to work over. If the apartment in *Rear Window* can be described as a projection box the one in *Talk to Her* is a camera obscura. Benigno is not just a man who projects himself imaginatively, he is simultaneously a *tabula rasa* or, perhaps better, a blank canvas, gradually coloured with selective details of Alicia's life and interests.

This comparison is also useful because it illustrates a shared interest in the tendency of a limited view – particularly in a character reduced to looking rather than taking part – being compensated for by the projection of the self onto the partial evidence available.[6] But while the characters suffer from limited perspectives, the audience is not restricted in this way. In *Talk to Her* this is true of the broad organisation of the narrative, but it is especially true in sequences such as Marco's first encounter with Alicia and the scene of Alicia's reappearance, in which the film vividly registers the experience of the limited viewer, but delicately provides us with other kinds of perspectives on the action.

5. What killed Ruthie Jean?: architectural design in *Candyman* (1992)

Kitty: Well all I know, there was some lady in the tub and she heard a noise.

Helen: Do you remember her name?

Kitty: I think her name was Ruthie Jean. And she heard this banging and smashing like somebody was trying to make a hole in the wall. So Ruthie called 911, and she said there's somebody coming through the walls. And they didn't believe her.

Henrietta: They thought the lady was crazy, right?

Kitty: Uh huh. So then she called 911 again, and they still didn't believe her. And when they finally got there she was dead.

Helen: Was she shot?

Kitty: No, um, she was killed with a hook. Tcshhhh! [Mimes ripping.]

Henrietta: It's true. Yeah it is. I read it in the papers. Candyman killed her.

Kitty: Yeah but, uh… [She winks, deadpan, at Helen.] I don't know nothing about that. [She looks meaningfully at Henrietta (off-screen) and gets up to leave.]

In a key scene from *Candyman* (Bernard Rose, 1992), Helen Lyle (Virginia Madsen) discusses the design of her apartment block with Bernadette (Kasi Lemmons), her collaborator in post-graduate research into urban legends. Following up the story told her by Kitty Culver (Sarina Grant) in the newspaper archives, Helen has discovered that 'Lincoln Village', the luxury apartment complex where she lives, was built as a housing project and that it follows the same template as the projects of Cabrini-Green, where Ruthie Jean lived and died. Before completion, the city planners, realising that this particular building was on the same side of the tracks as the more affluent parts of town, made some cosmetic improvements and sold the units off as condominiums. Whereas at Cabrini-Green, as Bernadette puts it, 'the highway and the L-train … keep the ghetto cut off'.

This means that the apartment which Helen shares with Trevor (Xander Berkeley), her lecturer husband, follows exactly the same floor plan as the one in which Ruthie Jean was murdered. And Helen is able to explain to Bernadette how the killer, or killers – 'they don't know which' – were deemed to have gained access. When the bathroom mirror/cabinet in these apartments is prised from the wall, the back of the corresponding unit in the neighbouring property is revealed. Helen even knocks out the cabinet from the (vacant) adjoining condominium to demonstrate her point. They both look through into the empty apartment. Bernadette teases Helen by pretending to have seen someone inside. The scene concludes

Fig. 5.1

with the two women repeating the name of Candyman while looking into the now re-instated bathroom mirror. Helen says it five times, the number which, when spoken while looking at one's own reflection, is supposed to summon the monster. Bernadette chickens out at four.

The decision to make an architectural parallel between the two apartments, between the floor-to-ceiling windowed luxury of Helen's apartment and the gutted, besmeared shell of Ruthie Jean's, is the one around which I want to structure this chapter's discussion. The connection between the two spaces is so central to the film's meanings that it may have been an 'informing' decision in the film's construction – it is fundamental to the film's organisation, development and significance, and it inspires a whole network or interrelated choices, from set design to dramatic structure.[1] I will outline some salient points about the connection, drawing on some of these interrelated choices, before going on to explore them in more detail.

1. The apartment which belongs to Helen and the one formerly occupied by Ruthie Jean correspond to the two social strata that appear in the film, which in ordinary circumstances would not coincide: on the one hand, the world of Lincoln Village condominiums, of the University; on the other Cabrini-Green, Anne-Marie (Vanessa Williams) and her baby, the terror of crack gangs and zero opportunities. Helen only learns about an association between Candyman and Cabrini-Green because Henrietta Mosely (Barbara Alston) happens to be cleaning the room in which Helen types up her interviews after academic hours and overhears the name – in ordinary life, these two would be unlikely to come into contact.

2. Obvious from the film, but not so far from this account, the difference between these two worlds is not merely one of class but also one of race. Henrietta and Kitty are black, as are all of the residents of Cabrini-Green that we meet, including Candyman (Tony Todd). The students and lecturers that we get to know are white, with the exception of Bernadette who appears to be mixed race. The film is keen to identify the colour bar which underlies the inequitable distribution of wealth and opportunity.

3. Contrary to appearances, these worlds are linked: this is what we can conclude from Helen's architectural research, and the relationship is developed by the film subsequently. The Gold Coast and the ghetto have been physically separated, but Lincoln Village both implies a social connection and embodies the historical and institutional act of establishing difference. The creation of an African-American underclass was an act of social repression, and Helen's apartment and its shadow, the apartment of Ruthie Jean, stand as the film's metaphor for this: parallel realities which co-exist, one 'repressing' the other.

4. In the scenes in the projects, the skyline of downtown Chicago is frequently present in the distance. The skyscrapers are always on the horizon but entirely out of reach to the inhabitants of Cabrini-Green, the wasteland between bearing out the effects of city planning discussed earlier in the film.[2]

5. These social concerns are interwoven with the legend of Candyman, in the way in which the inhabitants of Cabrini-Green attribute Ruthie Jean's murder to the monster, but also in this scene through Helen and Bernadette daring each other to repeat his name in the bathroom mirror. Candyman does not respond to Helen's summons on this occasion,

but later in the film he manifests himself in ways which turn on bathrooms and mirrors – and draw on the film's architectural parallel in their effect.

6. The social repression is answered by a return of the repressed: in the traditional manner of the horror film and in other ways. The architectural parallel serves to articulate connection between normality and monster.

7. Décor is an important element in the pattern of differences and relationships between the spaces on either side of the parallel. Helen and Trevor's condominium is characterised by white plastered walls and floor-to-ceiling windows but also by the decorative use of a series of artefacts from other cultures: masks and puppets from around the world, statues and objects of religious or other social purpose now divorced from their practical context. The flat formerly occupied by Ruthie Jean, however, is dark, gutted and indescribably filthy. Pushing further into the spaces of Cabrini-Green, we encounter graffiti and – much later in the film – murals in a different style which seem to have an active devotional purpose.

8. The Lincoln Village apartment is the setting for several scenes dramatising the deterioration of Helen's relationship with Trevor. These have a less direct relationship to the central axis of the film – one might describe them as a minor variation within the film's main theme – but are answered in the film's final scene which also takes place in the bathroom.

The next day, Helen and Bernadette's research takes them to Cabrini-Green, and the apartment formerly occupied by Ruthie Jean. Having gathered the courage to get past the gang of young men outside the building, who take them to be police offi-

cers, cautiously climbed two flights of stairs, and disturbed Anne-Marie, the next door neighbour, by photographing the graffiti sprayed across her front door, they reach the apartment. Once inside, Helen leads Bernadette through the layout, identifying features in common with her apartment. Additionally, similarities in framing and composition help to remind us of the earlier scene at Lincoln Village, and foreground the differences – where Helen's apartment is bright and airy, this is dark and oppressive. They debate the wisdom of going further and, in opposition to the wishes of Bernadette, Helen climbs through the mirror/cabinet of Ruthie Jean's bathroom, into the apartment from which the attacker(s) approached. Climbing through another hole, beaten roughly through the cinderblock, Helen discovers, shortly after the audience, that the opening she has just climbed through forms the mouth of a picture of

Fig. 5.2

Fig. 5.3

Candyman's head spray-painted on the other side of the wall. In the room Helen finds a pile of candy, a razor blade hidden within one of the pieces.

This is a sequence of extreme tension, both for characters and audience, but what is remarkable is that our disquiet is primarily generated not by the promise of the preternatural but by the vivid and disturbing realities of Cabrini-Green. 'What if someone's packing drugs in there? Are you just gonna apologise and give them your card?' asks Bernadette, trying to persuade Helen not to enter the space beyond the mirror. Even if – as viewers of a horror film and not characters within the narrative – we have a greater sense of the likelihood of a supernatural explanation to Ruthie Jean's murder than Helen or Bernadette, the main source of our anxiety is the everyday horror of life in the projects rather than the paranormal threat of Candyman.

Consistent with this emphasis on the social reality of the projects, the film's shocks at this stage are organised around the dynamic created by a pair of middle-class women intruding into a community that is not their own. A good example of this is Anne-Marie's first appearance, accompanied by her guard dog, while Helen tries to photograph the graffiti sprayed across her front door. Anne-Marie's second appearance is even more suggestive. After Helen has climbed back into Ruthie Jean's bathroom, the women, and the audience, are startled by a figure revealed behind them in the reflection as the cabinet door is closed – but it is not Candyman, it is Anne-Marie finding out what is going on. She then berates them: 'You don't belong here lady! You don't belong going through people's apartments and things!'

These frights – and we could list others including the dog jumping up at the window on Helen's next visit to Cabrini-Green, and her encounter with the overlords in the toilet block – are all material in nature and hinge on the presumptions of turning other people's lives into a subject for personally rewarding academic inquiry. Helen is delighted to discover 'Sweets to the sweet' decorating the exterior of Anne-Marie's apartment, oblivious to the fact that it is rather less than 'great' to have such interesting cultural phenomena sprayed across your front door. When Anne-Marie and her barking dog appear, the resulting surprise has the quality of pricking Helen's presumption. The second appearance of Anne-Marie contains a more explicit rebuke to Helen, and to the audience closely following her enquiries.

While drawing attention to these aspects of Helen's behaviour, it is important to remember that she remains a compelling protagonist. She is at the centre of every

Fig. 5.4

scene in the film, and the visit to Cabrini-Green is constructed in such a way as to engage us emotionally in her experience. We arrive in the car with the two women and our first views of the gang outside the entrance to the building are shot from inside the car on a long lens. We then track with Helen and Bernadette toward and through this hostile group, the majority of shots employing wide-angle lenses which allow us a good view of the women but which keep the men at a distance. In the exploration of the apartments, views restricted (she walks into the darkness in the corridor leading to the bathroom) and privileged (the zoom out to reveal the picture of Candyman as she unwittingly steps through its mouth) both work to make us concerned for her. The very fears generated by the sequence are likely to further bind audience and character. The decisions that structure the sequence so as to convey Helen and Bernadette's experiences during the investigation also have the consequence of restricting our viewpoint to that of the middle-class visitor: members of the audience are quite likely to accept some of Helen's assumptions and fail to anticipate her mistakes.

The encounters with Anne-Marie begin to challenge this limited view: in the admonishments already mentioned, but especially when Bernadette and Helen follow her into her own apartment, beyond the vandalised exterior and into the home she has built for her son. Only now do we get to know something about one of the inhabitants of Cabrini-Green. This is also a scene in which we have an opportunity to be sceptical of Helen, suspicious that her interest in baby Anthony is only to further her enquiries. We may be struck that despite having just clambered through the filth next door, and despite the fact that Anne-Marie is nursing

Fig. 5.5

her baby, Helen does not take off her gloves to shake hands. Bernadette is more respectful of Anne-Marie than Helen, as she is of the dangers of Cabrini-Green, and this contrast helps to draw attention to some of the limitations of Helen's way of conducting herself.

The gulf between life in the projects and in the milieu of the University is powerfully underlined by the way in which the film concludes the first visit to Cabrini-Green. We travel from the last words of Anne-Marie's account of hearing Ruthie Jean's screams through the walls, and her fears for her own safety and that of her child, straight into an opulent restaurant, the cut momentarily preceded by a sound bridge of Professor Purcell's abrasive and ungenerous laughter, the fleeting impression being that this is a response to what Anne-Marie's has been saying.

Purcell (Michael Culkin) is the supreme representative of the academic world. As junior figures in the department, Helen and Bernadette are condescended to by him: 'So how are our two most beautiful graduate students getting along, then?' The characterisation of Purcell, and Trevor's obsequious behaviour toward him, encourages us to see that there may be pressing reasons why Helen should want to gain a more elevated position within her profession, why 'burying' Purcell would not only be very satisfying but perhaps valuable. Yet we may increasingly conclude that it is these sorts of motives that lead her to Cabrini-Green, rather than a disinterested thirst for knowledge or social justice.

Knowledge leads to power and power, in the academic world presented, leads not just to privilege, but to smugness. Purcell, whose status in the department is such that Trevor placates him at the expense of his wife, sits bullishly in the position that having written a paper on the 'hookman' ten years ago affords him, and allows him to be supremely self-satisfied. In the lecture-room Trevor gets laughs at the expense of students who volunteer legends before revealing the phenomenon of urban folklore with a flourish. (Urban legends are a very well chosen subject of research for the film to centre itself on, not least because once the nature of such stories has been drawn to a person's attention, she or he is immediately placed in a very different relationship to the stories than when listening to or telling them uncritically – the awareness of an academic perspective immediately creates a superior position.) Even as graduate students, Helen and Bernadette share knowing winks and smirks at the expense of the credulous storytellers they interview.

Trevor clearly relishes the attention and respect that lecturing brings him – to the extent, we later discover, of having an affair with one of his most enthusiastic undergraduates. As Helen has become increasingly knowledgeable, and thereby increasingly empowered, it appears that Trevor has started a relationship with a younger woman, one who still has to look up at him. Helen's (and our) first introduction to the character of Stacey (Carolyn Lowery), the student concerned, coincides with Helen's discovery that Trevor has been teaching the freshman class about urban folklore before she and Bernadette have finished collecting legends from the students. Despite Trevor's appeals to his responsibility for the proper education of his students, we may suspect that he has organised his curriculum in order to hamper Helen's research, part of a broader resistance to his wife's growing status.

In the scene where Helen interviews Kitty Culver and Henrietta Mosely, the dialogue of which is transcribed at the beginning of the chapter, both the smugness and the presumptions that characterise the negative aspects of Helen's approach to sociological research are there to be observed. In particular, elements of Virginia Madsen's performance suggest a superior, humourous disbelief which Helen cannot quite hide from Henrietta, and she starts guiltily when Henrietta insists on the truth of the story. Helen's behaviour contrasts strongly with the powerful seriousness with which Henrietta listens to Kitty, and with which Kitty signals that she is not to be quoted. It is also significant that if Helen does not hide her tape-recorder, equally she does not ask for permission to record the conversation. She sets it up while the women are entering the room, and it is quite likely that Kitty does not realise she is being taped.

These are quite subtle elements of the scene: the action of starting the tape-recorder is not emphasised with a close-up (although it is not in any sense hidden), Helen's behaviour – which is nothing more than a look away and down and a movement of the tongue – may only be interpretable because Henrietta realises Kitty is not being believed. They are not likely to prevent us from building our relationship with Helen, a process which has been accelerated in the previous scene at the injustice of Trevor's behaviour with the freshman class. But in the manner of many a horror film, subsequent events may lead us to reflect on assumptions made by the central characters which we too readily accepted at the time. We might also reflect, after having met more senior members of the faculty who display such qualities to a greater degree, that Helen has learnt this way of seeing with her subject, in her institution.

Purcell tells the women, the rest of the table and the audience the historical story of Candyman:

The legend first appeared in 1890. Candyman was the son of a slave. His father had amassed a considerable fortune from designing a device for the mass-producing of shoes, after the Civil War. He had been sent to all the best schools and had grown up in polite society. He had a prodigious talent as an artist and was much sought after when it came to the documenting of one's wealth and position in society in a portrait. It was in this latter capacity he was commissioned by a wealthy landowner to capture his daughter's virginal beauty. Well, of course, they fell deeply in love and she became pregnant. Hmm. Poor Candyman! The father executed a terrible revenge. He paid a pack of brutal hooligans to do the deed. They chased Candyman through the town to Cabrini-Green, where they proceeded to saw off his right hand with a rusty blade. None of them came to his aid. But this was just the beginning of his ordeal. Nearby there was an apiary: dozens of hives filled with hungry bees. They smashed the hives and stole the honeycomb, and smeared it over his prone, naked body. Candyman was stung to death by the bees. They burned his body on a giant pyre, then scattered his ashes over Cabrini-Green.

Fig. 5.6

He tells it well, with some relish and no little skill, but from a distinctly knowing and self-satisfied narrational position – 'Poor Candyman!' This story of Candyman's origins is one of the elements that make the film's eponymous character sympathetic. Helen is certainly moved by the story, and the film encourages us to be as well. As Purcell begins to recount the violence inflicted on Candyman, the film cuts to a slow zoom in on Helen. The lighting in this set up is entirely different from the previous views of her in the sequence, and light falls softly across the middle section of her face, so that her eyes stand out from their surroundings. At the same time, Purcell's voice is joined on the soundtrack by the sounds of the attack, the victim's agony and by Philip Glass's score. The visual form of Helen's eyes is picked up in the next shot – the eyes of the Candyman graffiti mural, caught in the flash of Helen's camera. Although we are still listening to Purcell's tale, we have cut to Cabrini-Green on the occasion of Helen's next visit. Her eyes are again highlighted in the following shots as she looks over the top of her camera, and blinks away tears.[3]

Fig. 5.7

Fig. 5.8

In being sympathetic and, once we meet him, charismatic, Candyman embodies the characteristics Robin Wood finds central to monsters of the radical horror films of the 1970s. Wood argues that the central structure of the genre can be encapsulated in the phrase 'normal-

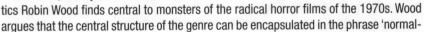

ity is threatened by the Monster', where normality describes a 'conformity to the dominant social norms', the monster embodies society's fears, and the relationship between the two is predicated on the fact that the monster is a product of normality (1986: 79):

> One might say that the true subject of the horror genre is the struggle for recognition of all that our civilisation represses or oppresses, its re-emergence dramatised, as in our nightmares, as an object of horror, a matter for terror, and the happy ending (when it exists) typically signifying the restoration of repression. (1986: 75)

As Wood argues, however, the central mechanism of the genre provides plenty of room for inflection in terms of where our allegiance is encouraged to lie in relation to the monster and the society which it threatens. Our relationship to both monster and society in *Candyman* is characterised by the vital ambivalence which Wood suggests is fundamental to progressive or radical horror movies: Candyman himself is genuinely monstrous, frightening and does some horrendous things (the murder of Bernadette is particularly shocking), and yet in other ways he is sympathetic, attractive, charismatic and *human*. As the viewer discovers, the film goes further in these terms than most horror films, in that it emphatically refuses a happy ending in which order is restored, and transforms its heroine into a monster herself.

Purcell's is the fourth of five Candyman tales which we will hear. All of the succeeding stories contrast strongly with the first, the version told to Helen by a student at the beginning of the film. For the white, middle-class university students, the Candyman story is an urban legend which turns on teenagers, particularly female teenagers, being punished for expressing their sexuality. In this context it has been transformed into a cautionary tale about the dangers of stopping being the good girl, told with the customary ending to the urban legend: 'My, uh, my roommate's boyfriend, knows him [Billy, the survivor].' The character of Candyman has become divorced from his roots and from the urban experience, and now appears to terrorise the world of the American small town, rather the city. In the student-told version of the story, which we see visualised as the first action of the film, it has acquired the bland texture of the teenie-kill pic/1980s slasher film. The world of this story is the white-picket-fenced affluence of the middle-American small town, 'near Moses Lake, in Indiana'. The monster described embodies a return of the repressed, but in the form of a monster we are neither invited to know or to understand. Here the film invokes what Wood has characterised as the reactionary horror films which came to dominate the genre in the 1980s, where the monster is evil incarnate, inhuman, its role to punish expressions of youthful sexuality. *Candyman* alludes to this cycle, and then goes on to become something much more interesting.

The fifth Candyman story, told to Helen by Jake (DeJuan Guy), is the story of the attack on the boy in the public toilets. That story shares with the murder of Ruthie Jean, as told by Kitty Culver and later by Anne-Marie, violence which has no obvious cause, that randomly terrorises the residents, and which the police are unable or unwilling to respond to. In Cabrini-Green people are reluctant to tell the story; it is something they are literally afraid of telling. Knowledge is connected to power in Cabrini-Green, too: the leader of the overlords is protected until Helen's arrival because of the reluctance of witnesses to speak out.

Helen's encounter with the gang in the toilet block brings the material trajectory of the film's horrors, and the first movement of the film, to a conclusion: following Jake's story and the graffiti trail into the intolerable stench and squalor of the toilet block, she meets a human, everyday version of Candyman – the leader of the overlords – who beats her senseless with the blunt side of a metal hook. Forty-three minutes into the film, however, after Helen has picked out the gang leader in an identity parade and recovered from the injuries he inflicted, the *real* Candyman begins to manifest himself,

and to do so in Helen's parts of the city. The first of these appearances is in the University car park, just as Helen's academic ambition has been revived by Bernadette's news that their work is going to be published, and as Helen gleefully looks at the transparencies she took at Cabrini-Green which Bernadette has had developed. Helen's rational, middle-class explanation of the murder of Ruthie Jean has sapped his potency: 'Your disbelief destroyed the

Fig. 5.9

faith of my congregation. Without them I am nothing. So I was obliged to come.' Helen wakes to find herself deposited in Anne-Marie's bathroom, in a bloody situation where she is the prime suspect.

Candyman's precise timing may be a response to the threat of publication – an academic, rational explanation of the folklore of Cabrini-Green will do further damage to his status as an entity that thrives on fear and belief – but it is simultaneously triggered by Helen's renewed interest in her career after a period of recuperation and domestic activity. The logic of the horror film is for the return of the repressed to respond to forms of behaviour which embody the assumptions of 'normality', of the dominant ideological patterns of the society depicted. Helen's glee at the thought of significant professional success precisely refers us toward the values that the film is calling into question, not least the confident claim to be able to understand and explain behaviour outside the waspish academic world. This is a suitably hubristic moment for the return of the repressed to announce itself.

After Helen's arrest at Anne-Marie's, and the indignities of her strip search, the shocking change in Detective Valento's (Gilbert Lewis) behaviour toward her confirms her movement from a witness who can speak because she is an outsider to Cabrini-Green – a middle-class woman who can provide rational evidence – to somebody involved, compromised, suspected and only able to provide a supernatural explanation of events. She moves from a situation where her worldview (and perhaps a sense of superiority over the inhabitants of Cabrini-Green) was confirmed by the detective and the identity parade, to one where this has collapsed and she is as irrational (from the police perspective) as any of the Cabrini-Green inhabitants. Helen begins as a tourist and ends up the object of others' intrusive investigation.[4] As an ethnographer might say, Helen's academic distance has collapsed.

The early scene in Helen's apartment is most emphatically answered when Candyman finally does smash his way through her bathroom cabinet. Helen is feeling particu-

Fig. 5.10

larly fragile: she has just been bundled out of the police station sheltering under an overcoat to avoid being photographed or filmed, having spent the night in the cells. Her confidence in her husband, who was not answering the telephone in the middle of the night, has been damaged. Into the shelter of her apartment, through the intimate space of the bathroom cabinet, is suddenly thrust the bleeding and lunging stump of Candyman's hooked arm: her world is invaded by Cabrini-Green, in a form which vividly conjures up a history of racial oppression.

Moments before this explosive entrance, Helen has been projecting the slides she took at Cabrini-Green on her apartment wall, and has noticed Candyman's reflection in one of them. He is caught behind Helen in a shot showing her reflected in Ruthie Jean's bathroom mirror. This conjunction forms an intriguing double parallel: Candyman's appearance reinforces the link between the mirrors in the respective parts of town – he has answered Helen's initial summons after all, but in the parallel bathroom mirror – but also makes a connection between Candyman and Anne-Marie, who was reflected in this mirror on the occasion of Helen's first investigation of Ruthie Jean's apartment, and who in the shock of the moment we might have supposed to be Candyman. By the latter the film is not suggesting, of course, that Anne-Marie is herself monstrous. Rather, both she and Candyman offer a challenge to the comfortable certainties of Helen's investigation and of her broader worldview. They both give voice to an African-American experience of which Helen is entirely ignorant. What Candyman's reflection in the photograph also confirms is that Helen has unwittingly summoned up a monster not just by playfully calling his name five times but by the presumptions of her enquiries in Cabrini-Green, presumptions we may ourselves have gone along with.

Fig. 5.11

Helen invokes not just a monster from tales around the campfire, or even the 'unselfconscious reflection of the fears of urban society' as Trevor variously describes urban legends in his lecture, but a whole raft of experience which is kept at arms length at Cabrini-Green. In *Candyman* that experience intrudes where it is not expected; it refuses to fit into the comfortable academic certainties beloved of Purcell, and aspired to by Helen. As Candyman stands in the Lincoln Village apartment, against a backdrop of bookcases and carefully displayed artefacts, it is clear that he cannot be contained in photographs, or collected, or classified. In these moments – Anne-Marie's testimony, Candyman's visceral appearance at Helen's, to which we might add the funeral and the death of Dr Burke (Stanley DeSantis) – which challenge the order and decorum of the academic world, and of the broader white middle class for which it stands, a comforting veneer, like the plaster which has been applied to the naked cinderblock of Lincoln Village, is ripped away to reveal the uncomfortable truth underneath: that there is an African-American underclass whose experience of late twentieth-century life is totally different from the white middle-class hegemony.

In the closing stages of the film, Helen climbs through Ruthie Jean's mirror once again. This time, the portal has grown so large that she can step through it, and the space beyond has grown beyond any naturalistic representation to the extent that Candyman's domain fills the whole width of the building, several stories high. The walls and the space are still full of rubbish and rubble but in addition to the graffiti, the walls are decorated with paintings representing the torture and murder of Candyman. The space also resembles a church, with an aisle bordered by columns formed by the steel frame of the building and paint sprayed across the windows giving the impression of stained glass. In this awful Wonderland Helen finds Candyman sleeping on an altar, and first attacks him but is then partially seduced by him, on the promise of the safe return of Anne-Marie's child.

Two major dynamics emerge in the later stages of the film. The first is the way Helen and the audience are moved away from the possibility of a return to 'normality'. Bernadette is murdered, Helen immured in a mental institution where she and we come suddenly to the chilling realisation that she has been under sedation for a month. When she escapes, her husband is revealed in his true colours as she gets home to find him and Stacey repainting the condominium in baby pink.

Candyman has a hand, or rather a hook, in much of this, committing the crimes for which Helen is incriminated. At first his motive seems to be to restore his reputation with his 'congregation', but gradually the prospect of a romantic relationship between the him and Helen begins to emerge – the second of the emphases which become central to the latter part of the film. Candyman demands 'one exquisite kiss' as he floats above the trolley on which she is restrained in the mental institution, and later, as he carries her toward the altar he promises: 'The pain, I can assure you, will be exquisite. As for our deaths there is nothing to fear. Our names will be written on a thousand walls, our crimes told, and retold, by our faithful believers. We shall die together in front of their very eyes, and give them something to be haunted by. Come with me and be immortal.' His attacks have the effect not of re-establishing his own reputation (except in Helen's and the audience's eyes) but rather establishing Helen's credentials as a monster – and suitable partner.

Candyman manages to make the prospect of ghoulish immortality quite attractive, not least because he has ensured that Helen has no possibility of returning to her previous life – as his disembodied voice reminds her, 'all you have left is my desire for you'. But when Helen succumbs to his embrace upon the altar, swarms of bees crawl and fly out of his mouth and rib cage and she faints. On waking alone, she finds her likeness illuminated on one of the murals depicting the murder of Candyman: it seems not just that Candyman wants her to join him in monstrous immortality but that she is some kind of reincarnation of his earlier love.

In certain respects the film has prepared us for these scenes. Helen's encounters with Candyman often replay the motif of her gently highlighted eyes – in the car park scene, when Candyman begins to talk after she has attacked him, when she wakes on the altar – which was introduced as she listened to the story of his torture. When Helen finds her face on the walls of Candyman's lair, the eyes again feature strongly, the camera zooming to reinforce this through framing.[5] And when, before the attack/ embrace, she found the paintings of the assault on Candyman, the movement of her torch beam on his painted face achieves a similar effect, reminding us of the graphic match from her face in the restaurant to the eyes of the graffiti mural.[6] This treatment, then, alerts us to a sympathy between Helen and Candyman, but the film now begins to suggest that Helen is destined to replay the post-bellum story by forming a new couple (and even a new family, with the abducted baby Anthony replacing the nascent child).

Fig. 5.12

Fig. 5.13

It is logical that there should be a sexual component in the film's return of the repressed as the original injustice perpetrated on Candyman was punishment for miscegenation. (Recognising this enables us to get a better analytical purchase even on the version of the story told by the university students, one in which a black monster murders a young white woman who has strayed from the socially approved forms of sexuality. In this context the Candyman legend has been turned into a cautionary tale about sexual behaviour more generally, but one which trades on a notion of an African-American 'other', racial stereotypes about black sexuality and the taboo of sexual relations between black men and white women.) Indeed, there is a sexual element to Candyman's appearances throughout the film: his strength and size, his handsomeness and charisma, the quality of his tailoring, not to mention the phallic properties of his hook: ripping his victims, punching into bathrooms, lifting Helen's skirt in the seduction scene. The idea that Helen is the earlier woman reincarnated implies that similar social structures apply between the mutually exclusive twentieth-century social worlds explored in the film and the restrictive social structures that the upwardly mobile Candyman attempted to move between in the years after the Civil War. Their relationship is another bridge between segregated social worlds.

Damagingly, however, Candyman's motives become increasing unclear during the second half of the film. By a sleight of hand, the film has changed his stated reasons for appearing from being about the need to re-establish his credibility to a pre-destined romance. He had seemed intent on killing Helen in the apartment until Bernadette turned up. Almost imperceptibly, his mantra moves from 'Believe in me' to 'Be my victim' to 'Come with me, and be immortal' to 'It was always you'.

This becomes critical in the final scenes at Cabrini-Green where the gaps in logic become more difficult to accept – certainly, these passages do not seem to be able to sustain the same level of scrutiny as the earlier parts of the film. What exactly is Candyman trying to do with baby Anthony, and why does he break his bargain with Helen? What is the difference between the death he seems to be planning for the three of them and the 'death' that Helen inflicts on him in the bonfire, or her death in the bonfire? What can 'dying together' mean if he is already dead? Why does he have to lure her out to the bonfire when he already appears to have won her consent the moment before the bees appear? One of the film's most remarkable achievements is the way its heroine steps outside 'normality' entirely and becomes a monster herself, but it is regrettable that the film is not able to offer us a monstrous couple at its end – Helen replaces Candyman rather than tempers his more despicable acts through their union. If my account of this part of the film is a little threadbare, it reflects a conviction on my part that this area of the film is not so densely achieved and the ending not fully coherent.[7]

We have, however, been successfully prepared for the final scene in the bathroom. If there is no monstrous couple, the last sequence of the film gives us Helen-as-monster, and the destruction of a different couple, in the setting of the Lincoln Village apartment. The ending of the film reveals another pattern of damaging behaviour receiving its comeuppance – this time Trevor's. The earlier scenes charting his duplicity led to the moment when Helen discovers the lovers repainting the apartment: as well as being a sequence which eloquently demonstrates Helen's dismay at the betrayal, and the breaking of her ties with a compromised reality – 'Trevor, you were all I had left' – it is also the occasion when Helen begins to try out her new monstrous persona, inspired by the frightened reaction of her husband and Stacey. A line she speaks on that occasion – 'What's the matter Trevor? Scared of something?' – is uttered again in the final scene as she appears behind Trevor, after he has lamented her name into the mirror five times, and ecstatically hacks him to death with Candyman's hook, leaving Stacey as prime suspect. The credits roll over a slow track toward a new mural, depicting Helen's death, behind the altar at Cabrini-Green. Helen has gone native.

Conclusion

Candyman might be described as the *Imitation of Life* of the horror genre. In both movies architecture is central to the dramatisation of racial and economic segregation and the underlying relationships that such distinctions seek to deny. In this film, however, we do not just observe the blonde, career-building heroine's failure to recognise African-American experience: Helen is pitched into it in the most vivid way imaginable and, because it is a genuinely terrifying, carefully crafted, horror film, so are we.[8] In the tradition of the genre she, and we, experience a return of the repressed/oppressed, but also in the best, and most radical, traditions of that genre we come to realise that the monster is not without qualities, and that her own world is compromised. In the battle between normality and the monster, the monster has – the monsters have – more of our sympathy.

NOTES

chapter one

1 For further discussion of the commutation test, its usefulness in relation to casting and performance, and its origins in structural linguistics, see Thompson (1978).

2 *The Blank Wall* was initially published in an abbreviated form in *The Ladies' Home Journal*, and this is how it is referred to in the credits of *The Reckless Moment*.

3 I have followed Holding's spelling of Bee, which is also how Lucia spells her daughter's name in writing to her husband in *The Reckless Moment*. Judging by the material that Lutz Bacher quotes in *Max Ophuls in the Hollywood Studios* (1996), the production documents may refer to 'Bea'.

4 For a fuller account, see Robin Wood's article in *CineAction* (2002) which, provoked by the appearance of *The Deep End*, returns to *The Reckless Moment* and explores this sequence in particular.

5 For the record, the close-up was shot during retakes (Bacher 1996: 307).

6 The fact that all the city scenes involving Darby, Nagle or Donnelly take place in the same setting is eloquent beyond any necessity of financial economy. The parallel between Donnelly and Lucia is only enhanced by the fact that we saw her walking through these urban spaces in a markedly similar way in the first major sequence of the film – that this is also the telephone box that Darby used to telephone Bee is not without irony. The fact that all the scenes of the Los Angeles underworld are played out in this same space enhances the film's play with its two locations, the genres which they evoke for the audience, and the sociological/psychological relationship between them.

7 The film's ending also accentuates the parallel between its leads, when both Lucia and Donnelly are ready to sacrifice everything for the other. In terms of Donnelly's constraint, we might note the further irony that the telephone call was not just designed to tell Lucia Nagle's demands but was actually made at the insistence of Nagle.

8 In the novel we actually meet Nagle before Donnelly, but when Donnelly refers to his partner for the first time Lucia suspects him of playing 'the oldest trick in the world' before realising that he is talking about Nagle (2003: 61).

9 In the context of *The Reckless Moment* these areas, including the idea that Donnelly acts as a return of the repressed, are discussed by Andrew Britton (1976) and Michael Walker (1982b). In *The Blank Wall* Lucia does not offer to go to the police – in fact, she is much more active in trying to evade the police than Donnelly who has slipped into a fatalistic mood after killing Nagle.

10 In the novel Sybil is a character rather like Annie (Juanita Moore) in *Imitation of Life* (Douglas Sirk, 1959), in that Sybil's abilities and labours support the successful façade of Lucia's household, but Lucia knows nothing about her. When she and we learn a little more about Sybil, it transpires that she has held a life-long desire to travel the world, and her husband was jailed in dubious circumstances after fighting a ticket salesman who refused to sell him steamship

tickets on racial grounds (2003: 143).

11 When I visited Kent, Andrew Klevan pointed out that smoking would provide another fruitful point of comparison between the two films.

chapter two

1 Brecht's *verfremdungseffekt* 'is itself a translation of the Russian critic Viktor Shklovskij's phrase "Priem Ostrannenija", or "device for making strange"' (Willet 1974: 99).

2 The script suggests that Quick Mike's eyes are 'inflamed with whiskey' when he attacks Delilah.

3 That the town itself is called Big Whiskey corresponds the extent to which it becomes a battle-ground for different men and competing definitions of masculinity. The absence of settled women – and families – gives us a hollow picture of 'civilisation', bearing few of the positive values conventionally associated with it.

chapter three

1 *Lured* is also known as *Personal Column*, the name changed part way through its run in the United States, to the detriment of the takings according to Sirk (Halliday 1997: 84, 153).

2 The exceptions are the shot which match cuts from the close-up, shot 2, the only cut to break the alternating cross-cutting between office and bar, and shot 6 which is the same set up as shot 4, and shot 12 which is the same as 10.

3 In saying to Wilde, later in our scene, 'Let's take a look at the pretty little girls in their dancing shoes', Fleming even speaks the same language as Pickering, if sardonically.

4 Sanders is one of the film's stars, so it is unlikely that he is going to be a minor figure. Perhaps this also makes it unlikely that he is going to be the murderer, but he had more of a reputation for playing roguish, and often rather ruthless, character parts than for romantic leads (*Rebecca* (Alfred Hitchcock, 1939), *Summer Storm* (Douglas Sirk, 1944)), and it would be difficult to think of an introduction that more effectively established a character as 'an unmitigated cad'.

5 There are also elements like the comic motif around Barrett's crossword which move the film in this direction.

6 The terms I am employing here come from the critical framework set out by Michael Walker (1982a).

7 The three writers credited on *Pièges* are also credited on *Lured* – 'from a story by...' – while the screenplay credit is reserved for Leo Rosten.

8 A historian of the effect of the Motion Production Picture Code could make a profitable comparison of certain sequences in each film, as a way of establishing what was acceptable on the French screen in 1939 and what on the American in 1947. The scene in the heroine's bedroom with Maxime/Maxwell is a case in point, as is the fact that in *Pièges* Robert Fleury initially asks Adrienne to be his mistress and they only become engaged after her violent response.

9 It seems to me that there is one special sequence in the original. That is the equivalent to the scene with van Druten, where Adrienne Charpentier encounters a designer called Pears. Differences in the way the scene is organised and played contribute to a very different tone: there are

no dummies or pug dogs in the audience for the fashion show, just empty seats; Adrienne has actually heard of Pears, which immediately gives greater credibility to the deluded designer; he has (better) reason to consider Adrienne an industrial spy, as he sees her communicating with her police tail from the window. The sequence does not end with Pears being tumbled into the dustbins by the equivalent of Barrett, instead he locks himself and Adrienne into a room containing all the clothes he has designed and starts a conflagration: our last view of the sequence is Adrianne apparently succumbing to smoke inhalation. Above all, it has one of those extraordinarily poignant performances by Eric von Stroheim in his portrayal of Pears.

chapter four

1 It seems a deliberate decision to frame this shot within the frame of the photograph: earlier in the sequence, when Marco had been standing nearer the wall on which it hangs, we had seen the whole photograph, some of the wall, and the nearby standard lamp.
2 This description owes something to Steve Neale's discussion of the 'relay' of looks, as well as to Mulvey's original phrasing (1980: 57).
3 Given the emphasis on partial or restricted viewpoint, one of the questions which the film provokes through its complicated structure of flashbacks and inserted narratives, and in its focus on characters who are unconscious yet to whom feelings are attributed, is whether the flashbacks and recounted narratives in the film can be trusted as objective accounts, or whether they are partial, shaped by the tellers in ways which belie the conventions of flashback narration? On close reflection, it can be argue that the flashbacks and inserted narratives are as reliable as the main body of the narration. Even Marco's recollection of the evening when he and Lydia heard Caetano Veloso sing, which the film suggests may be a dream and which does not receive the imprimatur of a title, clearly gives us perspectives broader than those of the character to whom the flashback is (at least partially) tied. The other flashbacks identified as belonging to particular characters share the same qualities of balance in the construction of point of view, and the same potential to challenge our preconceptions, that characterise the rest of the film.
4 Both of these examples appear in chapter three of *Ways of Seeing* (1972), where John Berger uses them to discuss the nude as a tradition of painting designed to gratify a male spectator.
5 This shot follows an earlier one in which the camera was on other side of the partition and the effect of the reflections exactly the reverse, where Benigno also does most, but not all on this occasion, of the talking. It does not have quite such an immediately interpretable effect, but it does appear in the context of a number of other elements – the highly symmetrical framing and reverse-field cutting throughout the conversation, the similarity through contrast of the red (Marco) and blue (Benigno) tops that the men wear, the broader narrative parallels discussed earlier in the chapter – which collectively suggest a relationship between the two. The psycho-analytic reading – see below – might also take these compositions as evoking a more general failure by Benigno to distinguish between himself and others.
6 *Vertigo* (Alfred Hitchcock, 1958), too, is about what living by a limited perspective can lead to, but the destructive consequences are there even more nakedly revealed.

chapter five

1   It is certainly an invention of the film. Clive Barker's short story *The Forbidden*, on which *Candyman* is based, has an interest in architecture, and makes some comparisons between the quadrangles of the Spector Street Estate (the story is set in Liverpool) and the carpeted corridors of the University. But although there is some emphasis on the way in which the architects (who live in Georgian townhouses in another part of the city) and the planners have left the estate to its own devices, the sense of a vital connection between two worlds, which is such a strength of the film, is not developed.

2   The long-shot which shows Jake leading Helen past the bonfire, on the occasion of her second visit, appears to have been shot on the other side of Chicago from Cabrini-Green and included by means of 'creative geography', such is the desire to show bonfire, wasteland and skyline simultaneously.

3   Each of these images are constructed using point-source lighting to create prominent 'eye-lights' – and this is picked up in the painting, where highlights to the eyes are part of the composition.

4   A photograph of Helen in front of a Mayan pyramid is prominent next to the unanswered telephone when she leaves a message with her one call. From this moment on she is increasingly part of the phenomena her earlier self would have sought to capture and document.

5   This also happens with the new mural of Helen in the last shot of the film, providing its closing image. It is worth recalling, too, that at its beginning, the film had dissolved from a view of the Chicago skyline to a close-up of Helen's face, her eyes prominent, just after we heard Candyman's voice intone the words 'I came for you'.

6   A handful of frames of the graffiti painting and the flash of Helen's camera are often cut into subsequent sequences creating a percussive effect, particularly when Candyman communicates with Helen.

7   While writing up these observations about *Candyman*, I encountered two other accounts of the film, one published in *CineAction* (Kydd 1995) and one in *Camera Obscura* (Briefel & Ngai 1996). They discuss some of the same elements that have been important to this chapter, but their arguments have different emphases and work toward rather different conclusions.

8   Like *Imitation of Life*, *Candyman* also closes with an unexpected show of respect at a funeral. At Helen's funeral Trevor, Purcell, Stacey and Archie Walsh are surprised to see a procession of mourners from Cabrini-Green making their way across the cemetery to pay tribute. It is Archie – a bit-part played by the director – who notices the approach of Jake, Anne-Marie and the others. Archie also makes an appearance in the restaurant scene, playing an unspeaking member of the academic dinner party. These appearances by the architect of *Candyman* acknowledge Bernard Rose's own limited perspective in relation to the world of the real Cabrini-Green, but claim slightly greater farsightedness than Trevor or Purcell.

BIBLIOGRAPHY

Bacher, L. (1996) *Max Ophuls in the Hollywood Studios*. New Brunswick: Rutgers University Press.

Barr, C. (1999) *English Hitchcock*. Moffat: Cameron & Hollis.

Berger, J. (1972) *Ways of Seeing*. Harmondsworth, London: BBC and Penguin.

Brecht, B. (1979) *The Threepenny Opera* [translated and edited by Ralph Manheim and John Willett]. London: Methuen.

Briefel, A. and S. Ngai (1996) '"How much did you pay for this place?": Fear, Entitlement, and Urban Space in Bernard Rose's *Candyman*', *Camera Obscura*, 37, 70–91.

Britton, A. (1976) 'The Family in *The Reckless Moment*', *Framework*, 4, 21–4.

Cavell, S. (1979) *The World Viewed: Reflections on the Ontology of Film* (enlarged edition). Cambridge, MA and London: Harvard University Press.

Cawelti, J. (1970) *The Six-Gun Mystique*. Ohio: Bowling Green University Popular Press.

_____ (1995 [1979]) '*Chinatown* and Generic Transformation in Recent American Films', in B. Grant (ed.) *Film Genre Reader II*. Austin: Texas University Press, 227–45.

_____ (1999) *The Six-Gun Mystique Sequel*. Ohio: Bowling Green University Popular Press.

Elsaesser, T. (1972) 'Tales of Sound and Fury: Observations on the Family Melodrama', *Monogram*, 4, 2–15.

Gallafent, E. (1994) *Clint Eastwood: Filmmaker and Star*. New York: Continuum.

Gibbs, J. (2002) *Mise-en-scène: Film Style and Interpretation*. London: Wallflower Press.

Halliday, J. (1997) *Sirk on Sirk* (second edition). London: Faber.

Holding, E. S. (2003 [1947]) *The Blank Wall*. London: Persephone.

Kydd, E. (1995) 'Guess Who Else is Coming to Dinner: Racial Sexual Hysteria in *Candyman*', *Cine-Action*, 36, 63–72.

Matthews, P. (2001) '*The Deep End*', *Sight and Sound*, 11, 11, 43–4.

Mulvey, L. (1975) 'Visual Pleasure and Narrative Cinema', *Screen*, 16, 3, 6–18.

Neale, S. (1980) *Genre*. London: British Film Institute.

Perkins, V. F. (1981) 'Moments of Choice', *The Movie*, 58, 1141–5.

_____ (1990) 'Film Authorship: The Premature Burial', *CineAction!*, 21/22, 57–64.

Pumphrey, M. (1996) 'Why do cowboys wear their hats in the bath?: Style politics for the older man', in I. Cameron and D. Pye (eds) *The Movie Book of the Western*. London: Studio Vista, 50–62.

Pye, D. (2000) 'Movies and Point of View', *Movie*, 36, 2–34.

Thomas, D. (2000) *Beyond Genre*. Moffat: Cameron & Hollis.

Thompson, J. O. (1978) 'Screen Acting and the Commutation Test', *Screen*, 19, 2, 55–69.

Thomson, D. (2002) *The New Biographical Dictionary of Film*. London: Little, Brown.

Walker, M. (1982a) 'Melodrama and the American Cinema', *Movie*, 29/30, 2–38.

_____ (1982b) 'Ophuls in Hollywood', *Movie*, 29/30, 39–60.

Willet, J. (ed.) (1974) *Brecht on Theatre*. London: Methuen.

Wood, R. (1976) *Personal Views*. London: Gordon Fraser.

_____ (1986) *Hollywood from Vietnam to Reagan*. New York: Columbia University Press.

_____ (2002) 'Plunging off *The Deep End* into *The Reckless Moment*', *CineAction*, 59, 14–19.

1.2 THE POP SONG IN FILM
Ian Garwood

ACKNOWLEDGEMENTS

I would like to thank the *Close-Up* series editors, John Gibbs and Douglas Pye, for their extremely useful comments on the various drafts of this study, and their tremendous patience in helping me through the editing process. At an even earlier stage, Richard Dyer offered me great intellectual guidance and personal support, for which I will always be immensely grateful. My sincere appreciation goes to Andrew Klevan and Heather Laing, who were instrumental in helping me think through my initial ideas. The encouraging and incisive comments of Victor Perkins and Simon Frith helped to improve this study greatly. I would also like to thank my colleagues at the University of Glasgow for their support, as well as the students on the various film music courses I have taught in my time here. Finally, I would like to offer very heartfelt thanks to my parents, who have provided me with support in every way imaginable long before this project began.

INTRODUCTION

This is a study of the pop song *in* film narrative, rather than an account of the pop song *and* narrative film. The distinction indicates my interest in understanding the transformations pop songs undergo when they are asked to accompany the events of a fiction film: at these moments the song is no longer something that stands alone; its meanings can only be fully apprehended by understanding its placement within a particular narrative cocoon. When pop songs are used in narrative cinema, they become an integral part of a particular fictional world, whilst simultaneously retaining their status as pop music. It is the interaction between the pop song and the narrative situation to which it contributes that this study will explore.

The interactions between pop song and narrative situation result from a series of choices made by filmmakers. In the first place, a decision has to be made about the selection of a particular song to accompany specific narrative events. What is it about *this* song that makes it appropriate to *this* dramatic context? There are also often choices to be made to do with the *form* the song will take within the fictional world of the film: will an on-screen source be established for it, or will it take its place in the position traditionally reserved for the specially composed film score, which has no discernible on-screen source? Decisions are made about the *choreography* between visual action and song: for instance, will visual elements be made to correspond with particular rhythmic or musical aspects of the song, and/or will the correspondence between music and image be understood more according to their shared 'themes'? Choices are also made concerning the relationship between the song and other elements of the soundtrack. Will other sounds be audible as the song is heard, or will it dominate the film's soundscape at that moment entirely? What other kinds of (musical) sounds are used in the film, in relation to which the use of a pop song at a particular moment will be placed?

These choices affect the manner in which the viewer is encouraged to understand the narrative status of a song in relation to the fictional world it inhabits. The vast majority of the songs contained in this study come to their films with a history already behind them: unlike the specially-composed score, these songs have enjoyed an existence in their own right before being selected for use in a particular film. The pre-existing quality of these songs does not, however, lead to a simple importation of meanings into the films in which they are used. The choices made by filmmakers as to the relative weight given to both the song's purely musical and culturally resonant qualities in relation to a particular dramatic situation are decisive in shaping the viewer's understanding of the role the music plays.

To demonstrate the importance of these acts of selection, chapters one, two and three will each consider two uses of pop music that are comparable in terms of raw material (whether that be comparable types of music or similar narrative contexts), but differentiated through the specific interactions contrived between pop song and the dramatic situation. Chapter one compares the use of the same song (Portishead's 'Glory

Box') in two films, *Stealing Beauty* (Bernardo Bertolucci, 1996) and *Chacun cherche son chat* (*When the Cat's Away*, Cédric Klapisch, 1996), to illustrate how exactly the same musical material can generate different meanings according to its particular positioning within a filmed fictional world.

In these opening examples, the pop song figures as a *narrational device*. That is to say, it helps to present the film's story to the viewer and to offer a particular perspective on that story, in the same manner as other elements of narration such as camerawork, the organisation of mise-en-scène, editing or the specially composed film score. Chapter two will consider the pop song in the fiction film in a different guise: as a *narrative element*. The pop songs discussed in this chapter are rendered through on-screen performances, as the result of the visible and audible activity of characters within the drama, rather than existing as a disembodied presence on the soundtrack. This is not the only way the pop song can appear as a narrative element. Pop songs often appear as part of the 'visible' world of the film by being played through stereos, jukeboxes, in club scenes, or simply being 'in the air' as background noise in street scenes. Such instances will be discussed in chapter four, through the detailed analysis of *Baby, It's You* (John Sayles, 1983).

The case studies in chapter two consist of two star-vehicle musicals from the mid-1950s, *Young at Heart* (Gordon Douglas, 1954) and *Pal Joey* (George Sidney, 1957), where the central (but not only) musical performances are enacted on-screen by Frank Sinatra, the biggest pop star, along with Elvis Presley, that the era had to offer. In certain ways, the genre these films inhabit, the musical, marks them apart from the other films discussed in this study. The musical offers a specialist space in which pop songs can be performed, and which usually guarantees that attention will be dedicated to the detail of the song being delivered. There is no such guarantee that the song will be the main focus of attention in the non-musical. In addition the type of attachments made between the song used as narrational device and the song performed by character on-screen, as narrative element, are different: the 'distance' between song and film character in the first instance gives the potential for the music to act as commentary on the character's situation (as a musical type of voiceover), whereas the song performed by an on-screen character works more directly (as a musical form of first-person speech).

However, in other respects, an understanding of the number in the musical as an instance of the *pop song's* involvement in narrative cinema is important to what I wish to say about the use of pop music in other contexts. Firstly, the song sequence in the musical provides a limit case, in terms of the extent to which the pop song is fully embodied by a particular character or characters. I discuss a number of sequences throughout this study where filmmakers arrange the relationship between pop song and non-singing character in a way which suggests that the character aspires to act in a manner fitting to the music on the soundtrack, even when it is not indicated that the song has a literal on-screen source. The extent to which the desire on the part of the character to 'embody' the song is allowed to be achieved, or is seen to fail, is a crucial way in which the interaction between song and character activity can be made meaningful.

Secondly, the Frank Sinatra musicals help to map out the cultural territory occupied by the type of pop song that is focused upon throughout this study: that is to say, a kind of overtly commercial popular music which differentiates itself from other types of music in terms of commonly held perceptions about its cultural currency. This specificity will be described more closely in chapter one, but for now it is enough to say that both *Young at Heart* and *Pal Joey* point to the centrality of notions of *pop stardom* to the delivery and understanding of the pop song. When filmmakers make use of a particular pop song, the persona of the star who sings it becomes a possible element to be referred to and made meaningful to the dramatic situation. The Frank Sinatra musicals provide a setting where the inter-relationship between the pop song and the pop star, and the implications this has for understanding the pop song's place in a particular narrative context, is tackled head on.

Finally, chapter two corresponds to the overall aims of the study in its attention to the relationship between the pop song and film character. The song sequences in these musicals negotiate between representing Sinatra as a star, performing in a style for which he is already renowned, and tailoring the performances to the particular dramatic requirements of the film. In keeping with my interest in exploring the consequences of filmmakers making different choices with regard to the same source material (here the material is Sinatra himself), I have chosen two films which represent two different sides of the Sinatra persona, and which handle the 'fit' between star persona and fictional character in different ways.

Chapter three returns to the use of pop songs with no discernible on-screen source, as a kind of commentary on the characters for whose movements they provide the soundtrack. Like chapter two, this section engages with the cultural specificity of the pop song, but this time in terms of its consumption by *fans*, rather than its production through the agency of stars. I suggest, following work on pop music by Simon Frith, that the pop song represents a particularly 'possessable' cultural form. The affiliations struck between the pop music listener, the pop song and the pop star(s) associated with it have been viewed as exhibiting a unique intensity. In this chapter, I relate this understanding of the pop song's cultural value generally to its functioning as dramatic film music in sequences from *Midnight Cowboy* (John Schlesinger, 1969) and *Saturday Night Fever* (John Badham, 1977). I argue that the assumption that the pop song can take a role in constructing identities in everyday life is another area filmmakers can play upon when using songs to help construct the identities of their films' characters.

Chapters two and three, then, are interested in understanding both different formal aspects of the use of the pop song in narrative films (as narrative element or narrational device) and the specific cultural qualities commonly associated with the particular type of pop music under discussion in this study (pop stardom and pop fandom respectively). Chapter four offers an extended analysis of a film where the formal and cultural qualities discussed in the previous two chapters are brought together. *Baby, It's You* makes use of the pop song as narrative element *and* narrational device. It also identifies the cultural specificity of the pop song as lying in its emphasis on notions of both stardom *and* fandom. In the film, Sheik (Vincent Spano) is a huge fan of Frank Sinatra who tries to forge a pop career of his own. *Baby, It's You* constructs a fictional world in which common assumptions about pop music culture are central, whilst also holding those assumptions up for scrutiny, as they are worked through in a particular narrative context.

As such, *Baby, It's You* brings to the fore the double nature of the pop song in film: as a culturally meaningful object in its own right on the one hand, and as an integral part of the film's fictional world on the other. My interest throughout is in exploring how filmmakers enable specific songs to tell a story about themselves at the same time as these songs are made to help tell the story of a particular film.

Chapter one begins by clarifying key terms and concepts. Thereafter, the study relies on close readings of sequences and films to make its arguments, and as such, the reader will ideally have viewed the film before reading the analysis. I have attempted to use language that is precise and evocative, without resorting to the jargon of film studies or musicology.

However, on occasion I do use two terms that require brief explanation: when I refer to 'non-diegetic music', I am discussing music that does not have any visible or plausible on-screen source. This is the type of film music traditionally associated with the composed orchestral score, but which can also be provided by the pop song when it is used as a narrational device; 'diegetic music', on the other hand, is music which *does* emanate from an on-screen source. In practice, some of the most interesting examples of the use of pop music in film are those when the status of a song crosses over between these two categories.

1. Pop music as film music

Defining the pop song

Pop music has always had a role to play in cinema, even before sound film became the industry standard in the late 1920s. In the earliest film showings, a live pianist and singer would play accompaniment to song slides illustrating the popular hits of the day, to cover the time it took to change film reels (see Altman 2001). Live music also accompanied the screenings of silent films, with melodies as likely to be culled from popular songs as they were from the more 'respectable' classical repertoire recommended in the cue sheets sent to theatres by distributors (Reay 2004: 10). The musical, one of Hollywood's most buoyant genres between the coming of sound in the late 1920s and the mid-1950s, showcased performers and songs whose star status and popularity were established through radio, musical theatre and record sales, as well as through the movie screen. It is also the case that a number of non-musical films have used pop music on their soundtracks in imaginative ways, from the earliest days of sound cinema (*The Public Enemy* (William Wellman, 1931) is just one early example).

The particular focus of this study is the *pop song* in narrative film, and, as a first step, it is necessary for me to explain what I take the term to cover.

Pop music as a particular mode of performance

The pop song in narrative film provides a special instance of the popular film music score more generally, a form whose distinctiveness from the classical score lies, according to Jeff Smith,

> in its greater sense of rhythmic and melodic freedom and its emphasis on unique timbres ... things that cannot be captured in traditional Western notation, but rather are identifiable by a certain 'feel' to the music, a feel that is only actualised in the process of performance. Unlike classical music, the individual character of a pop piece is not inherent in its form, but rather in the materiality of its sound. (1998: 10)

This distinction is not absolute: for instance, the 'individual character' of a classical music performance can be registered through its 'unique timbre', but Smith argues that due to the 'comparatively rigorous performance standards of classical music ... [the range of interpretive possibilities] is much narrower than that of popular music' (1998: 9). One element of pop music where this difference is particularly apparent is in the singer's voice: one of the ways pop singers differentiate themselves from each other is through the idiosyncrasies of their vocal delivery, rather than their attainment of a classical standard.

Pop music as a particular kind of sound

The materiality of sound to which Smith refers is created by instrumentation that is also different to the conventional classical combinations, whether the big-band arrangements bolstering Frank Sinatra's swing jazz style in *Pal Joey*, the sparse ensemble of bass, drums and sampled effects that accompanies Beth Gibbons' brittle singing of 'Glory Box' discussed below, or the urgent combination of strings, clipped guitar and funk rhythms that accompanies Bobby Womack's soulful rendition of 'Across 110th Street', heard at the beginning of *Jackie Brown* (Quentin Tarantino, 1997), discussed in the conclusion.

Not all pop music includes the voice as part of its sonic material, but this study does focus on such instances. The concentration on the song's use in film is due, in part, to the especially important role the lyrics can play as a kind of commentary on a narrative situation, or, when the song is performed by an on-screen character, as a particularly heightened form of self-expression.

The pop song as a particular commercial cultural form

The connotations surrounding particular songs will be discussed at relevant points, but it is useful here to make some broad claims about the pop song as a cultural form. The pop songs discussed in this study belong to a musical canon that has been constructed within certain commercial parameters. The pop music industry as it exists today is generally viewed as taking shape in the mid-1920s, with the development of electrical recording techniques and the establishing of radio networks such as NBC and CBS. These developments allowed for the effective mass distribution of popular music, and the packaging of it as a particular type of commodity form.

One aspect of this commercial process is the common association of the individual song with a particular star or group. The song is routinely understood as helping to articulate the star persona of the singer or group who performs it, as well as existing as a discrete entity in its own right. Simon Frith identifies the importance of the star to the production and reception of the pop song in his book *Sound Effects*:

> The music business doesn't only turn music into commodities, as records, it also turns musicians into commodities, as stars ... Record companies (like film studios) seek to reverse the 'rational' relationship between stardom and music (or films) – if acts become stars because people like their records, the commercial object is to get people to buy their records because they are stars. (1983: 134)

Commenting specifically on rock music, Frith continues:

> 'Stardom' describes a relationship between performer and audience ... rock records, however privately used, take their resonance from public leisure, from the public ways in which stars are made. (1983: 135)

It is part of the cultural currency of this type of pop music that the individual song is wrapped up in the revealing of the musical persona of its performer. The resonance of the pop star persona, therefore, provides a powerful resource to be made use of by film-makers when they involve a particular performer's songs in their fictional scenarios.

Frith's description of stardom as a 'relationship between performer and *audience*' (my italics) points to the second feature associated with the cultural functioning of the type of pop music discussed in this study: namely, the relationship between pop stars, songs and the construction of the individual and group identities of pop music fans. It has been commonly accepted that pop fans use music imaginatively in the construction of their own identities, in a more intense manner than is associated with most other cultural forms. In chapter four, I shall discuss the role of the pop song in the formation of identity, as it is conventionally understood, and suggest equivalences between this wider cultural process and the specific use of the pop song in providing identities for film characters.

The first two features discussed above refer to pop music generally as a type of sound and mode of performance that is distinguishable from classical music (which has traditionally formed the basis for the specially composed orchestral score). The pop song, that is to say pop music with words, exists as a special example of this musical form. The final feature, the significance of particular modes of stardom and fandom, differentiates the pop song from other forms of popular music. This precludes from my study such instances of popular music in film as the 'pop score' (that is, the specially composed in-strumental score which makes use of pop music styles and idioms rather than classical ones). It also excludes a consideration of types of popular music which are lyric-less or do not revolve around notions of pop stardom and fandom in the manner characteristic of the pop song (for example, the folk music which pervades the soundtrack of, in par-ticular, the Hollywood western).

The importance of voice and notions of stardom and fandom to the operation of the pop song in narrative cinema are what mark it out as distinctive from other types of film music. This is not to say, however, that these are the only elements that are important. Lyrics may be made meaningful to the particular narrative event which they accompany; viewers may be encouraged to appreciate the star persona of the singer behind the song as part of their understanding of the song's function in relation to a particular scene. However, the emphasis on these particular qualities of the music is only the result of decisions made by the filmmaker. The pop song provides rich source material, in terms of both its 'musical' and 'cultural' qualities. Filmmakers choose to exploit the expressive potential of certain of these qualities through the manner in which the song is made to interact with the other material that constitutes the film's fictional world.

Two uses of Portishead's 'Glory Box'

In order to demonstrate the rich potential of using a pop song as dramatic film music, I will examine the use of the same song in two different films. The purpose of this analysis is to demonstrate how the filmmakers make a different set of choices with regard to their source material, the song, due to the different dramatic effects each filmmaker is pursuing. In its transformation from pop song to film music, the song retains a certain sense of its own cultural and musical specificity, whilst also taking its place within the unique context of the film's fictional world.

Portishead achieved international commercial and critical success with their debut album 'Dummy' (1994) and one of its most well-known songs, 'Glory Box', was used in Bernardo Bertolucci's international art movie, *Stealing Beauty* and Cédric Klapisch's French drama, *Chacun cherche son chat* (*When the Cat's Away*), both released in 1996. The version of 'Glory Box' featured on 'Dummy' fades in gently with a simple, leisurely descending bass figure (b flat up to e flat, then notes down the scale played twice on its way back to b flat), a snare drum sounding out in the gaps between the pairs of bass notes, with a more complicated 'roll' at the end of the riff. A swirling strings melody is also repeated, continuing when singer Beth Gibbons begins the first verse, her voice somewhat brittle as she intones the lyrics with cool precision:

I'm so tired ... of playing
Playing with this bow and arrow
Gonna give my heart away
Leave it to the other girls to play
For I've been a temp-ter-ess too long

Gibbons' detached vocals give way to the throaty 'yes' which follows the verse and heralds the entrance of the chorus. Whilst the same bassline, drum pattern and strings continue unchanged (as they do throughout the entire song), a churning, distorted guitar riff lurches to the fore, and Gibbons' voice discovers new-found body and flow:

Give me a reason to love you
Give me a reason to be ... a woman

On both occasions, there is a melodic turn on 'reason', 'be' is stretched at high pitch, and 'a woman' is delivered dreamily in the breath that follows. The guitar riff runs out and Gibbons sings 'I just wanna be a woman' in a more conversational tone, as if making sure the listener understands the point she had made so passionately in the preceding two lines. In short, the chorus is as revealing of the grain of Gibbons' voice as the verse is determined to bestow a feeling of iciness upon it.

This description of the song up until the end of the first chorus is intended to identify the musical elements available to be made use of by each sequence: the spare drum pattern and simple bass riff, each allowing the other room to be heard, offering a sense of musical space; the icy vocals of the verse, detailing a desire to throw off the shackles which the maintenance of this coolness imposes; and the shedding of inhibitions of the chorus as Gibbons pleads for a reason to abandon her distanced poise, whilst the lurching guitar ranges over the measured space of the other instrumentation.

Stealing Beauty uses 'Glory Box' to accompany a scene in which a teenage girl exhibits a yearning with parallels to that voiced in the song. Lucy (Liv Tyler) is an American teenager spending her vacation in an Italian village. Seeking out Niccolo (Roberto Zibetti), the local lad she had enjoyed a childhood romance with some years earlier, she patrols the foyer of his family's villa, before spying on him making love to another woman in a grove outside.

The opening passage of the song offers the sense of waiting for something else to be released. If the standard practice of fading out a pop song represents a gradual climbing down from the intensity which had preceded it, the gentle fade-in of 'Glory Box' suggests a building towards something more intense. Gibbons is demonstrably holding her emotions back in the first verse and the words she sings anticipate an untethering from this restraint. Furthermore the spaciousness of the musical backing seems to be leaving room for something else to emerge to fill out the sound. This impression of anticipating something more intense finds a correspondence in the sequence, choreographed to Lucy's gangly wandering about and wide-eyed gazing. Lucy is shown first cycling down the avenue leading to the villa, densely tangled trees arching over her, then walking down the fresco-decorated reception hall, the earthy paintings she gazes upon featuring carnival scenes, men and women dancing and finally two bulls staring out of the picture (and looming to the front of the frame with a zoom). The setting is lush, in terms of both the natural landscape and the vibrant frescoes, the sights she registers heavy with eroticism (through the frescoes) and history (through the maturity of the natural setting and the age of the buildings) that is at odds with her own sexual inexperience and youth. At the same time, Lucy demonstrates a fascination with these sights and a sense of expectation: she is, after all, searching for the man who had provided her with her first romantic experience.

The song, then, represents on the soundtrack both Lucy's lack of experience and her anticipation. However, during the chorus, when music and vocal gain more body, the force of the transition is lost as Lucy drowns out the music by asking a maid where Niccolo is. The sequence wards off any sense of climactic release being associated with

Fig. 1.1

Lucy at this moment. Instead, after she has walked through the villa's garden towards a dense grove during the second verse (sung in the same terse style as the first and with a similarly yearning lyric) – 'From this time unchained/we're all looking at a different picture/through this new frame of mind/a thousand flowers could bloom/move over and give us some room' – she discovers and watches Niccolo having sex with a woman against a tree. The camera begins to dolly around the couple as the grinding guitar kicks in, the view obscured by foliage, before a cut to Lucy looking away and up. Here the repetition of the guitar riff continues over a brief, but expansive, dolly around part of the crumbling villa wall, dominated by a baroque statue. Whilst the first chorus is cut off in its prime by Lucy's questioning, here its increased passion is allowed a correlative in the imagery, which intensifies a spectacle of uninhibited eroticism (as she watches Niccolo having sex) and ancient environment (represented by the villa's architecture and state of repair) with which Lucy is at odds.

Fig. 1.2

By overlaying the first chorus with Lucy's everyday conversation, and by diverting attention away from her in its choreography of the second, the sequence withholds from Lucy the leap into passion enacted by the song: Lucy remains conspicuously the innocent onlooker. This is in fact more appropriate to the spirit of the song than it may at first appear, in that, despite its more engaged delivery, the lyric of the chorus still finds the singer pleading for something to happen, rather than celebrating it happening.

In *When the Cat's Away*, by contrast, 'Glory Box' is used at the film's climax and actually becomes the soundtrack for just such a celebration, providing the spectacle of a woman revelling in the feeling of experiencing something new. Chloé (Garance Clavel),

Fig. 1.3

the woman in question, has struggled throughout the film to find contentment in her home city of Paris, her unease exacerbated by the disappearance of her cat. Forced to team up with the tight-knit network of old ladies who live in her block of flats, all of whom display unshakeable confidence in their cat-finding abilities, Chloé gradually comes into contact with the outside world more generally, with mixed results. By the end of the film,

however, her cat has returned and she has unexpectedly begun to form a relationship with her artist neighbour Bel Canto (Joel Brisse), who, ironically, she has only got to know by helping him move out. 'Glory Box' emerges on the non-diegetic soundtrack as she stands on the street outside the local café, pictured from shoulders up, smiling broadly whilst watching Bel Canto's removal van disappear into the distance. She giggles to herself and then turns away. The cut after her turning coincides exactly with the beginning of the first verse, the camera tracking with her in a

Fig. 1.4

shot from waist up as she runs joyfully along the pavement, still laughing. On the first lurching guitar riff that immediately precedes the chorus, the camera also 'lurches' down as it blurs past a parked car, then lifts itself up again, to follow Chloé's movement once more, but this time with only her head and shoulders in view (the result of a jump cut). When the chorus is finished, the film cuts to the credits, the song fading out as they end.

This sequence is more specific in its articulation of the meanings the song can be taken to convey than the *Stealing Beauty* sequence. Firstly, the song is far more precisely placed in relation to a particular character. If the conventional orchestral score, appealing as it does to assumptions about music's special access to, and expression of, emotional states, is routinely used to convey what is on a character's mind, it may be that pop music, with its more immediate association with the body and physical movement, is often made to give the impression that it is actually playing in a character's head. Here, Chloé turns and runs as if on command, in response to the emergence of Beth Gibbons' voice. The combination of the diving camera, the jump cut and Chloé's carefree stumbling with the introduction of the lurching guitar riff provides a reciprocity between sound and image to indicate that both are in fact exhibiting the same degree of 'giddiness'.

Furthermore, 'Glory Box' emerges as the sound 'playing in Chloé's head' by fading in behind, then swiftly superseding, the off-camera, diegetic singing of the old women in the café. Their song, 'Ça, c'est Paris', is in the French cabaret tradition (originally popularised by the legendary music hall singer Mistinguett) and it is the emphatically repeated chant of its title that is heard as 'Glory Box' makes its presence felt. The version of the song heard in the film begins off-screen as we watch Bel Canto waving goodbye to Chloé and climbing into his van (with close shots of Chloé interspersed). Only then does the film move inside the café to focus upon the leading singers (including the old lady behind whose cooker the titular cat had in fact been stuck), before returning to a shot of the van finally departing and then the mid-close shot of Chloé which signals the arrival of 'Glory Box'.

The lyrics to 'Ça, c'est Paris', as translated in the subtitles, run as follows:

Paris, Queen of the world
Paris is a blond
Her nose in the air, mockingly
Her eyes always smiling
Everyone who knows her leaves in the thrall of her caresses
But they always come back
Paris, here's to our love!
That's Paris!

The 'Glory Box' sequence leaves 'Ça, c'est Paris' behind in five ways. Firstly, it replaces the demonstration of music being used communally with a song undergoing a personal attachment to one character. Secondly, the use of the woman as a metaphor for the city in 'Ça, c'est Paris' is replaced by the display of a real woman experiencing freedom in the real city for the first time. Thirdly, the assertion that Paris remains inescapable is overlaid with images of Bel Canto in fact 'escaping', and followed by the demonstration of a personal sense of freedom within the city that is represented by Chloé's giddy run. Fourthly, 'Glory Box' offers a contrastingly spacious sound to the raucous sing-song it replaces, as well as an international one. Except for 'So Tired of Being Alone' by Al Green, which accompanies Chloé's assistance of Bel Canto packing, 'Glory Box' is the only English-language song in the film. As a pair, both accompany moments which show Chloé escaping the oppressive feelings of loneliness that have stifled her throughout. Finally, the lyrics of 'Glory Box' contrast with 'Ça, c'est Paris' in their insistence on the personal ('give *me* a reason to love you' as opposed to 'here's to *our* love'), and the desire to change a situation ('I'm so tired of playing...'), rather than the celebration of the status quo ('her eyes *always* smiling ... they *always* come back' [my italics]).

The transition from one song to the other, then, enacts a movement away from the communal to the private, from the parochial to the international, from woman as metaphor to woman as real, from vocal descriptions of entrapment by the city (no matter how benign) to images of the self-sufficient pleasures provided by feeling comfortable in one's own skin, and from the celebration of an unchanging situation to the depiction of a key moment of change. The film demonstrates 'Glory Box' to be an appropriate soundtrack for this movement by virtue of its audible difference to what has been heard before it.

Stealing Beauty casts 'Glory Box' in tandem with a young woman's unfulfilled yearning, while *When the Cat's Away* has it accompanying a woman demonstrating that her shackles have been cast off. *Stealing Beauty* may be more faithful to the reasonable interpretation of the song's lyric as one of unfulfilled desire, but *When the Cat's Away* is more specific about its potential resonances as a pop song and more responsive to its sense of musical space, even if it proposes the lyrics as a strident clarion call for action rather than as a desperate plea.

Areas of choice: obtrusiveness, cultural resonance and quality of distance

We can derive from these analyses a number of key concepts for considering the choices filmmakers can exercise in terms of the relationship a song will have to its narrative context. Three issues seem central: (i) the pop song's quality of obtrusiveness; (ii) the cultural connotations associated with a particular song or type of pop music, before its use in the film in question; and, in all but the special case of the on-screen performance in the musical, (iii) a quality of potential 'distance' from narrative events. This comes as a result of both the song having a life of its own, rather than being designed specifically for a moment in the film, as is customary with the specially composed film score, and as a consequence of the song's physical separation from a particular on-screen body.

Obtrusiveness

Much criticism of the use of the pop song in narrative cinema has revolved around the perception that it is excessively obtrusive, when compared to the more traditional orchestral score. This obtrusiveness has been seen to derive from: (i) the supposed lack of flexibility of the song form, which, due to its existence as a pre-determined structure in its own right, has been perceived to be less malleable than the specially-composed score, which is often constructed of deliberately short phrases, designed to weave in and out of the soundtrack with the maximum dexterity and minimum of fuss; (ii) the presence of words in the pop song, which have been seen to offer a potential source of distraction for the viewer, leading them away from an engagement with the dramatic content of the narrative; and (iii) an obtrusiveness in terms of the cultural connotations a well-known song may 'import' in to a particular film (this will be dealt with further below).[1]

It is the contention of this study that these elements of obtrusiveness, far from being blocks to the expressive potential of the pop song as dramatic film music, lay the ground for such a potential. In the uses of 'Glory Box' already cited and in several of the examples that follow, the specific form of the pop song is integral to the manner in which the filmmaker co-opts it for the requirements of a particular scene. It becomes a matter of choice on the filmmaker's part to choreograph the other elements of the film's fictional world in relationship with this structure.

It is not inevitable that the song's integrity as a pre-existing structure will determine its placement within a particular scene. The filmmaker is at liberty to select which part of the song is to be used for dramatic effect, and to weave the song in and out of the soundtrack (for instance to allow dialogue to remain intelligible) in a manner characteristic of the conventional specially-composed score. Furthermore, the extent to which the different structural units of a song are allowed full expression in a film can be decisive in guiding the viewer's understanding of the relationship between the music and its dramatic context. For instance, in the example from *Stealing Beauty* the sense of unfulfillment associated with Lucy's character is represented, in part, by the reduction of the song's obtrusiveness at a key structural point of the song (that is, the first chorus). *When the Cat's Away* highlights the unusual fade-in intro of 'Glory Box' by making it sound out in between the gaps of the final chorus of 'Ça, c'est Paris' and attaching it to a close-up of Chloé. In so doing, the sequence draws attention to an element of the song so that it becomes associated with aspects of the protagonist's subjectivity (the rising quality of the song's introduction comes to represent the rising feeling of freedom experienced by Chloé at this point).

The 'obtrusiveness' of the singer's voice can also be a source of rich expressive potential, rather than distraction, when the pop song is transformed into film music. Both *Stealing Beauty* and *When the Cat's Away* encourage the viewer to understand the lyrics as a commentary on Lucy's and Chloé's situations. In the case of *When the Cat's Away* the lyrics take on an extra significance through the contrast made between the sentiments expressed in 'Ça, c'est Paris' and those of 'Glory Box'.

Cultural resonance

The extent to which the pre-existing histories of the pop song, the artist singing the song, and/or the song as representative of a specific genre of pop music is taken into account is another area of choice for the filmmaker when a pop song is chosen to accompany a particular dramatic situation in a film.

It is undoubtedly the case that viewers will bring different levels of knowledge of a particular song with them when confronted with the use of an 'imported' pop song in a particular film: this is not something under the control of the filmmaker. However, the filmmaker *can* decide which existing connotations will be made meaningful to the dramatic situation at hand. For example, in the comparison between the two uses of 'Glory Box', I identified a distinct difference in the manner in which the song is made to refer to itself as a particular kind of pop sound in each case. Whereas the acknowledgement of the song as a specific kind of pop music is *not* especially determining to its narrative effect in the case of *Stealing Beauty*, *When the Cat's Away* is very careful to differentiate it from other types of pop music in the film.

In *When the Cat's Away*, the immediate contrast between the old women singing the Mistinguett staple 'Ça, c'est Paris' and the non-diegetic rendition of 'Glory Box' is made significant at a number of levels, as has already been noted. The awareness of Mistinguett and Portishead as different but related types of artists can add an extra level in the understanding of this contrast. Both have been placed in a tradition of female cabaret performance: Mistinguett directly, through her career in French music hall in the early twentieth century; and Portishead more obliquely, through Beth Gibbons' adoption of a 'torch singer' performing style, in terms of the music itself and the iconography associated with it.[2] As such, both Mistinguett and Gibbons represent a specific kind of female performer that is then associated with particular female characters within the dramatic context of the film.

Understood in this way, the old women in the café gain a sense of group identity by singing together a song popularised by Mistinguett, a female voice from their youth. In a related manner, Chloé's identity is posed as a more individual one by the decision to accompany *her* final actions non-diegetically by Gibbons, a female voice from her youth, which, unlike the old women, she is currently experiencing. Mistinguett, therefore, figures as a present absence in this scene. An awareness of the song's association with her can help the viewer to understand 'Ça, c'est Paris' and 'Glory Box' as comparable material in certain respects, if 'Glory Box' is accepted as referring to the female cabaret tradition represented by Mistinguett. However, the scene works to emphasise the differences between the two songs, rather than their similarities, by involving them in the representation of contrasting narrative situations. The scene's use of both songs is appropriate in its response to the cultural connotations surrounding each piece of music. Both Mistinguett and Beth Gibbons embody a particular type of youthful female musical identity and the scene does make reference to an understanding of them as such. However, these cultural identities are then integrated into the dramatic situation in different ways: the Mistinguett song becomes the occasion for a communal and nostalgic remembrance of youth, whereas the Portishead song accompanies a moment of intimate and immediate experience on the part of the film's young protagonist.

According to Jeff Smith, the meanings generated by a pop song when it is used as film music are 'often dependent upon the meaning of pop music in the larger spheres of society and culture' (1998: 155). Whilst agreeing that the pop song represents an excessively familiar element of the film soundtrack, I do not believe that the pre-existing connotations of a pop song are as all-determining to the meanings it generates in a particular film as Smith and other writers have suggested. A song may carry any number of potential connotations into the film with it, but, as the example of *When the Cat's Away* suggests, it is up to the filmmaker to make certain of these connotations relevant to an understanding of the narrative situation at hand.

Distance

When the pop song is used instead of the specially-composed score as a narrational device, it brings with it a capacity to maintain a sense of 'distance' between itself and the narrative action it accompanies. The specially-composed score appears in a film with the sense that it has been brought into being precisely for the particular moment it accompanies. The obtrusiveness and cultural resonance of the pop song offers an alternative sense that the song is not necessarily reliant on this particular moment in the film for its very existence. The filmmaker has to make what might be called an effort of attachment for the song to be understood as meaningful in relation to particular aspects of the film's fictional world.

One of the most significant ways a filmmaker can modulate the narrative significance of a particular song is to close the gap between song and other elements of the fictional world to a greater or lesser extent and this relationship will be discussed further in subsequent chapters.

2. The pop song as narrative element

The special case of the star-vehicle musical

This chapter has two main aims. Firstly, it provides case studies of the use of the pop song as a narrative element in its most fully embodied guise: the on-screen performances of the pop song within the special context of the musical offer examples of a complete attachment between character and song, against which subsequent examples may be judged. The second aim of this chapter is to expand upon the notion of the pop song as 'culturally resonant'. In particular, this section discusses the importance of *stardom* to the kind of pop music featured in this study.

The pop song in the musical is generally heard within the context of the number, a structural unit which is crucial to the musical's specificity as a genre. Within the space of the number, an expectation exists that other narrative elements (for example, the characters, objects and settings) and the film's narrational devices (such as camerawork, the organisation of mise-en-scène, editing, lighting and so on) will be deployed in considered relationship to qualities of the song itself.

The song sequence of the musical offers a privileged space, in which the focus usually remains on the details of the featured performer's rendition of the song. This means that the manipulation of a distance between the song and other narrative elements is uncommon as a decisive factor in such sequences.

The concentration on the particulars of the performer's on-screen rendition of the song is even more likely when that musical is conceived as a star vehicle for an established pop musician, as has often been the case. As Steven Cohan explains in relation to the musical in the Classical Hollywood era, these stars were likely to have cultivated their public personas in a number of arenas *outside* of the movie musical itself:

> One may usually think of Hollywood performers being discovered at an early age and then groomed by a studio into major stardom, as was the case with Judy Garland at MGM, but most stars of movie musicals (Fred Astaire at RKO, Eleanor Powell and Gene Kelly at MGM, Alice Faye and Carmen Miranda at Fox, Bing Crosby and Betty Hutton at Paramount, Dick Powell and Doris Day at Warners), first found renown in another entertainment industry, if not radio, then Broadway, records, or one of the big bands. (2002: 7)

This chapter focuses on two star-vehicle musicals for Frank Sinatra, whose status as a pop star was cultivated initially through records, live performances, radio and the promotional machinery of the music industry, and whose film appearances were always only one component amongst many through which his musical persona was articulated.

In the musicals under discussion, Gordon Douglas's *Young at Heart* from 1954 and George Sidney's *Pal Joey* of 1957, the most important decisions made by the filmmakers are those to do with the second area of choice discussed in chapter one: the pop song's cultural resonance. There are three significant components to this resonance. Firstly, the song itself may already be well known before its use in the film, and this may be taken in to account in the way it is integrated in to the film's fictional world. In the case of *Young at Heart*, only one of the songs was composed specifically for the film itself, and I suggest that there is a marked difference between the way Sinatra performs this and the rest of his songs in the film. *Pal Joey* is a screen adaptation of a 1940 Rodgers and Hart Broadway musical, and as such its songs had already enjoyed wide circulation, through the performances (on stage and record) of a number of stars. A number of the songs were composed for the original show and therefore deliberately narrativised, but the film also features Rodgers and Hart songs culled from their other musicals (as was the custom of Hollywood adaptations of Broadway musicals). Two of these, 'The Lady is a Tramp' and 'My Funny Valentine', had already enjoyed a particular association with Sinatra. For those viewers aware of it, this prior association becomes an informing feature (but crucially not the only one) of their understanding of the songs' performances in the film.

This points to the second aspect of the song's potential cultural resonance in the star-vehicle musical: its propensity to be used to establish a relationship between the pop star's performance in the film and his or her musical persona more generally. This can be achieved by providing a space for the singer to perform songs on-screen for which he or she is already known, but the relationship can also be established more indirectly. The song sequence allows aspects of the performer's musical persona to be translated into a cinematically specific context. On a general level, this may involve a particular kind of 'fit' between the star's pre-existing persona and the kind of character he or she is asked to play. Within the space of the song sequence itself, the articulation of a star persona is achieved through both the performance of the singer (the way the song is sung, and the manner in which the performer moves through this performance) and the style in which this performance is framed cinematically. In my analyses of both *Young at Heart* and *Pal Joey*, I pay particular attention to how film space is organised in relation to the musical performances, arguing that, in each case, Sinatra's character is allowed a privileged kind of space in which to perform that is not at the disposal of the other characters.

The third, related, aspect of the pop song's cultural resonance is its potential to disclose assumptions about popular music culture generally. As well as providing a space in which the unique qualities of a star persona can be demonstrated, the song sequence can also reveal underlying assumptions about pop music, which, for example, make stars so important to the manner in which the commercial pop song is produced and consumed.

By their very nature, as pop star vehicles, *Young at Heart* and *Pal Joey* are testament to the importance of stardom for this type of popular music. In addition, each film casts Sinatra in the role of a *fictional* professional musician. This decision allows the films to make explicit arguments about the centrality of stardom to commercial pop music. In

Young at Heart, this argument is made by contrasting the Sinatra character's charismatic individual musical performances to the more 'folk-oriented' communal performances of the other characters. In *Pal Joey*, Sinatra plays a character whose musical performances and worldview are in sync with the performing style and lifestyle associated with the Sinatra star persona during the 1950s: that of the 'playboy'. Within the song sequences of the film, the specialness of the pop star playboy asserts itself through a freedom of movement and vocal delivery which is denied to the other characters.

Cohan notes the tendency for performers to address the camera directly, as if facing a live audience, in the song sequence, and concludes:

> As a musical moves back and forth between the diegetic realism of story and extra-diegetic awareness of the star's performance in numbers, the oscillation between indirect and direct address heightens the audience's sense of not observing the star play a character so much as witnessing her or his own authenticity, charisma and talent without the mediation of fictional narrative or cinematic technology. (2002: 13)

This chapter attempts to understand how a star persona is embodied through a specific fictional characterisation. In the song sequences under discussion, Sinatra the star and the fictional characters the star embodies are present and significant at one and the same time. The particular choices made by the filmmakers in relating selected aspects of the star persona to the fictional character are what give each film its distinctiveness.

Young at Heart: making music popular

A star entrance

Frank Sinatra's entrance in *Young at Heart* is boldly iconographic. A door is opened to disclose a suited figure with his back to the camera. As he turns around, a close-up of Sinatra's face shows his hat tipped back in his trademark style, as depicted on his album covers throughout the 1950s. A further cut to accommodate his movement through the door reveals a tie lowered to half-mast and a collar whose wings flop loosely around the neck, in the manner shared by the carefree hipster on the cover of 'Swing Easy', the moody balladeer of 'In The Wee Small Hours' and the avuncular figure looking over a courting couple on 'Songs For Swinging Lovers'. Released in 1954, the same year as the first of these albums,

Fig. 2.1

the nature of Sinatra's first appearance in *Young At Heart* demonstrates how familiar his new public image had already become.

Sinatra's presence is felt before his on-screen entrance, however, with the airing of his rendition of 'Young at Heart' over the film's opening credits. His first number one hit for eight years, the song was one element, along with his Academy Award-winning role in *From Here to Eternity* (Fred Zinnemann, 1953) and his debut Capitol LP 'Songs For Young Lovers', in his celebrated return to popular acclaim, described by *The Penguin Encyclopaedia of Popular Music* as 'the most famous comeback in history' (Clarke 1998: 1194). He had reinvented both his singing style and screen persona, revealing an artistry which stridently announced its own integrity and intensity, as opposed to the softer romanticism and sweetness which characterised his musical and acting performances in the 1940s.

Young at Heart casts Sinatra as Barney Sloan, a morose but talented composer whose defences are broken down by the decidedly more cheery Laurie Tuttle (Doris Day). Throughout the narrative, Barney's music is held in consistently high regard, yet his incorporation into Laurie's world of suburban domesticity, registered in the final scene of the film, requires not just a thawing out of his character, but also a change in his musical style. *Young at Heart* undoubtedly exploits Sinatra's reputation as a high-quality singer outside his role in the film, and allows his newly 'matured' voice an uncluttered musical platform (his numbers are all performed at an on-screen piano, and his voice stays firmly on top of any non-diegetic backing that does emerge). However, the narrative does not simply serve as a fictionalised showcase for the virtues that have allowed the real-life singer to get back to the top. Indeed, the closing scene of the film features Sinatra performing in a manner which can be heard as running counter to the reinvented vocal style that had marked his comeback.

The role of music in the Tuttles' household

Music is important to the lives of all the main characters in *Young at Heart*, and before Barney makes his entrance the film demonstrates how music circulates within the Tuttles' contented household. As Sinatra's rendition of the title song finishes and the opening credits end, the camera moves from the street outside into the Tuttles' sitting room, where Laurie's father, Gregory (Robert Keith), continues to play the song's melody on his flute. Gregory reads from a music sheet as he plays, as do his daughters in their later performance of 'Until My Lover Comes To Me'. Even when Laurie launches into a spontaneous version of the hit 'Ready, Willing and Able' on the beach, she reads the lyrics off a song sheet. In the opening sequence, a close-up of the father's doctoral diploma in music, framed on the wall, further testifies to his learned credentials.

Yet the association of the Tuttles with music in its written form is not offered as a sign of the family's stuffiness. As the father continues playing the flute, he ambles away from his music stand over to Aunt Jessie (Ethel Barrymore), who is watching a boxing match on television. The raucous sound of the crowd clashes with his melodious playing, but Gregory does not retreat (as it turns out, he is waiting to see the outcome of the fight – he duly pockets a quarter from Aunt Jessie when 'his' man wins, without dropping a note). Later, after leading a recital by his daughters, the father complains: 'the orchestra, no matter how small, should have only one voice', to which his daughters mockingly interject, 'the conductor's', showing they have obviously heard this maxim many times before. When Laurie sings 'Ready, Willing and Able', she is both reading from a sheet and singing along to the record as it plays on their portable gramophone. The Tuttles' attitude towards music is not precious; their evident formal musical training is used as a means by which they can enjoy music as a shared, sociable experience.

Jane Feuer identifies the 'singalong' as one of the song formats used by the musical in its attempts to present itself as a folk rather than mass art (1982: 16). Laurie leads her family in a campfire rendition of 'Hold Me In Your Arms', a romantic ballad with lyrics directed to a single lover, but which Laurie addresses to the whole group. It is clear that the song does play a part in her courtship rituals with her genial companion Alex Burke (Gig Young), as she snuggles closer to him as the song progresses. However, a sustained shot of the whole family sitting around the fire at the beginning of the song, together with cuts to the reactions of her two envious sisters (who are both besotted by Burke), stresses the wider environment in which her singing is received. The family's democratic vision of how popular song should be performed means that even the most intimate of musical moments is rendered

Fig. 2.2

within a discourse of sociability. Furthermore, this sharing of musical experience is not necessarily an entirely comforting one: Laurie's sisters show their jealousy both here and during Laurie's later duet of 'There's A Rising Moon For Every Falling Star' with Alex around the family piano.

Thus, before Barney Sloan makes his entrance (over half an hour into the film), a way of performing and listening to music has been mapped out which has formality without dryness and sociability that is not completely idealised. The mode of musical appreciation with which Barney's initial performances contrast is not criticised by the film, even though his character is played by the singer who, at that time, was supposed to embody the virtues that made music popular in the 'real world'.

Barney Sloan's 'anti-social' musical performances

Barney's entrance follows the rendition of 'Hold Me In Your Arms'. Brought in by Alex to help compose the musical score he is working on, he comments sarcastically on his friend's neat notation, and soon disregards the sheet music in front of him as he effortlessly embellishes and expands Alex's basic melody. Laurie's first encounter with Barney is a reversal of her initial meeting with Alex. Laurie mistakes Alex for a vet as she happens upon him helping out with the delivery of puppies on the next door front lawn. Her first impression of him is felt through the easy social charm he displays, rather than through his musical abilities (he is actually on his way to see her father about his musical project). In contrast, Laurie's introduction to Barney is through his music, as his piano playing filters through to the kitchen into which she has just walked. Laurie is immediately impressed by Barney's improvisational flair, and this moment constitutes a new type of listening in the film: for the first time music is appreciated outside a context of explicit social interaction.

However, once face to face with Barney in the living room, Laurie is appalled by his off-hand attitude to his own talents. When he absently plays one of his own unfinished compositions, which eventually becomes 'You My Love', the ballad played in the film's closing scene, she urges him to complete it, arguing that it is a crime to leave a song 'without face or feet'. Yet at this point Barney sees no value in articulating his intense musical vision in a form which would make it more accessible to others.

The film, then, features an explicit argument about the pop song as a structured experience, in terms both of the form it takes and the manner in which it is consumed. The specificity of the song as a cultural form, discussed in chapter one, becomes the subject of debate by the film's characters. It also becomes an informing feature of the structuring of the song sequences themselves. In the numbers led by the Tuttles, the song offers a vehicle for group participation. This participation is made possible due to the characters' shared awareness of the conventional form the song will take. The progress of Barney's solo numbers, by contrast, is more idiosyncratic. In these sequences, the performances are made more intimate by being choreographed around Barney's private emotions, even when the numbers are being played in public settings. These performances are played out in a series of stages, moving towards a more and more narrow mode of address on the part of the singer.

The musical provides a space for a song to be played out in its entirety as the central focus of the scene. As such, filmmakers are less likely to exercise choice in their use of a pop song by modulating its obtrusiveness in terms of volume, by choosing to use only one part of the song, or by combining a particular structural unit with the narrative situation in a specific way. However, *Young at Heart* demonstrates that issues of song form can still be made significant to the understanding of the dramatic situation in the musical. In this instance, the invitingly open form of the numbers associated with the Tuttles is contrasted to the comparatively closed form imposed on the songs by Barney's solo performances.

The narrow focus of Barney's musical performances is demonstrated in his rendition of 'Someone To Watch Over Me'. Playing to a disinterested clientele in a bar, the sequence is split into three stages, each with a distinct mode of address. He begins the song against a hubbub of background noise, in the foreground of a shot which shows the diners with their backs turned away from him. A shot looking along the people chatting at the bar emphasises their inattentiveness, as does the cut to Laurie, her sister Amy (Elisabeth Fraser) and Alex, with Laurie asking 'why don't they keep quiet?' A return to the original shot of Barney at the piano shows him looking around distractedly, as background chatter continues to dominate the soundtrack.

At this stage Barney is singing just for himself, playing on regardless of his unappreciative audience. However, as he sings, 'I'm a little lamb who's lost in the woods', in the first close-up of the sequence, he looks to his right, clearly directing his singing at Laurie,

Fig. 2.3

with whom he has fallen in love. A two-shot of Laurie and Alex shows her trying to pay attention to the song, whilst Alex works on his own score. Laurie is not yet transfixed by the performance, however, and she is distracted by a couple arguing behind her, the camera panning across to them as their words flood onto the soundtrack.

There then follows an exchange of glances between Amy and Alex before the camera returns to Barney. As he sings 'but to her heart I'll carry the key', again in close-up, his gaze reverts to Laurie, who is now looking on more attentively. The final two close-ups of Barney and Laurie acknowledge the fact that his heart-felt singing has enraptured her as the sound of the diners fades out for the final few lines of the song. The final shot of the sequence views Laurie in a close-up, no longer part of her group, with non-diegetic strings lending the song an emotional final flourish.

'Someone To Watch Over Me' is performed in such a way as to bypass any address to its primary audience – the patrons of the bar. Barney directs his

Fig. 2.4

song inwardly at first, but then gradually out toward Laurie, until the mise-en-scène and soundtrack is completely dominated by their two faces and the song which connects them. At the beginning of the film, Laurie had told her sister Amy that she demanded one thing from marriage: 'lots of laughs'. The charming Alex, to whom she becomes engaged, would seem to fulfil this criterion admirably. However, her reaction to the pleading of 'Someone To Watch Over Me' (in both the style of vocal delivery and the lyrical content) demonstrates a deeper attraction to Barney's vulnerability, at the same time as it offers the possibility for a musical performance to create intimacy. In contrast, Laurie's singing of 'Hold Me In Your Arms', despite its specific message of love to Alex, is offered to everyone sitting around the campfire, so that all may gain comfort (or, as it turns out, feel envy) from its emotional resonance.

The film continues to interiorise and personalise space and sound during Barney's remaining nightclub performances. 'Just One Of Those Things' features him alone after the bar has closed, seeking solace in a song to ward off the pain after Laurie has announced her marriage to Alex. Again a non-diegetic backing fills out the emotional space, and Barney sings with such self-absorption that he fails to notice the presence of Laurie who has been standing behind him.

His rendition of 'One For My Baby (And One More For the Road)' occurs at a point in the narrative where he and Laurie are most divorced from the stable domestic life offered by the Tuttle household. By this time, Laurie has jilted Alex at the altar and married Barney. Relocated to another city, the couple are trying to make ends meet through his song-writing and nightclub engagements. He has just challenged Laurie to pawn a bracelet given to her by Alex, in order to show she no longer feels anything for him. Storming out of the flat, he goes to fulfil a date at a bar, playing 'One For My Baby' to yet another uninterested audience. Midway through the song Laurie enters and pulls up her sleeve to show Barney that she has sacrificed her bracelet as a signal of her love for him.

The sequence is filmed in such a way that the song becomes a soundtrack to the resolution of their domestic dispute. From the second verse onwards, background noise is obliterated, non-diegetic instruments come to the fore and the camera focuses on the exchanges between Barney and Laurie. As in 'Someone To Watch Over Me', 'One For My Baby' is shown to channel its address to an audience of one, but this time Laurie accepts the intense focus of this address without hesitation.

Yet even Barney knows the act of sacrifice for which the song provides a soundtrack is one that he should have never asked Laurie to make. In the following sequence, as the couple return to Laurie's family for Christmas, he returns the bracelet to her, having rescued it from the pawnshop. *Young at Heart* identifies Barney's intensity of feeling (evidenced by the interior focus of his singing) and his artistic integrity (his refusal to give his songs recognisable 'face and feet') as faults which inhibit him from a full-hearted engagement with the sociable world represented by the Tuttles. Only when given a second chance after a near fatal (and deliberate) car crash does he apply his particular musical talent in a manner appropriate to the idea of what music means to the Tuttle family.

Barney's transformation

The final sequence begins with the same crane-shot through a window which had

opened the film. This time a lush string arrangement gives way to Barney's full-bodied piano accompaniment to his self-composed 'You My Love', the song he has been encouraged to finish by Laurie throughout the film. As he expresses his new-found love of life to Laurie, singing from the song sheets he had previously mocked, the camera cuts between close shots of the two. Midway through, Barney tells Laurie 'It's got a face and feet now, how d'ya like it?'. When she responds favourably he invites her to 'come on in and join the family' and they duet in a two-shot.

Fig. 2.5

By referring to his creation in human terms, Barney acknowledges his song as an entity

separate from himself, with the ability to communicate more widely even as it serves as a means
of personal expression. Although it is performed
with only Laurie and Barney in shot, as it ends the
whole family gathers around the piano to congratu-
late him on the song's success, and by extension, on
his adoption of an outgoing mode of performance to
which they can all relate.

Fig. 2.6

'You My Love' differs from the earlier numbers
Barney performs not just because it is framed more
sociably, but also due to it being a different type of
song. Here, the cultural resonance of Sinatra as a performer outside of the film ceases to
inform the development of his character within the fictional world of the film.

Of all the songs performed by Sinatra in *Young at Heart*, 'You My Love' is the only
one to have been written especially for the film. Even the title track was a hit before
Sinatra was cast in the role, the movie naming itself after the song rather than vice versa.
'Someone To Watch Over Me' had been recorded by the singer ten years previously with
the Tommy Dorsey Band and 'Just One Of Those Things' was chosen as the opening
track on his second Capitol album, 'Swing Easy', released in the same year as *Young at
Heart* (not surprisingly Sinatra's phrasing in both versions is very similar, even down to
the 'improvised' quality of the last verse's opening line, 'so goodbye, goodbye, bye, bye,
baby and now and then'). 'One For My Baby', the Johnny Mercer/Harold Arlen 'saloon
song' detailing a man's broken-hearted conversation with his barman, had already been
interpreted by Sinatra in 1947, and was to become the stand-out track on his 1958
album 'Only the Lonely', often cited as his greatest work.

The version of 'One For My Baby' sung in *Young at Heart* demonstrates the interpretive, storytelling quality that Sinatra was being praised for at the time. One example
of this is the way he deals with the song's rhymes. The first lines ('It's quarter to three/
There's no-one in the place except you and me') are lost amongst the chatter of the bar's
clientele, but Barney's voice takes prominence on the soundtrack from then on. The following four bars introduce the intentions of the singer: to have a few drinks and pour his
heart out, as far as his male pride will allow, to the bartender: 'So set 'em up Joe, I got
a little story you ought-a know.' The phrases, 'set 'em up Joe' and 'you ought-a know',
are covered by the same notes (although the final note on 'know' is longer than that on
'Joe'), but Barney sings the first with brisk authority and the second more tenderly. This
sets the mood of a song whose protagonist wants to get down to business ('set 'em up'),
but whose melancholy may get the better of him (he never gets around to delivering the
details of his 'little story'). This pattern of briskness followed by melancholy is repeated
in the internal rhyme of the next line, 'We're drinking my friend to the end of a brief episode' – 'friend' is sung with most emphasis during the line, the singer convincing himself
of his close ties to his bartending confessor, whilst 'to the end' is more wistful, as if the
very mention of the word 'end' is bringing on new pangs of sorrow.

After the chorus line ('So make it one for my baby and one more for the road'), Barney sings, 'I got the routine, put another nickel in the machine'. By pausing slightly before singing 'I' and then elongating its sound, Barney has to tumble out the phrase 'got the routine' in the manner of 'set 'em up' in order to keep in time. This gives the words a suitably off-hand quality (the singer has done this before), but once again the corresponding rhyme 'in the machine' is sung more softly: even the commonplace act of dropping a coin into the jukebox has become poignant. The next line's opening declaration, 'I'm feeling so bad', sees 'so bad' being almost thrown away, whilst the passage that follows, 'won't you make the music easy and sad', finds 'music' being lovingly caressed and 'sad' sung with far more regret than 'bad' had been. Once again this reinforces the struggle of the singer to articulate his sorrow specifically (shrugging it off with the general observation that he feels 'bad'), whilst at the same time making that sorrow clear (the music does his talking for him).

However, this contrasting of briskly delivered phrases and more melancholy rhymes is not slavishly followed throughout the song. The next line features an internal rhyme between 'lot' and 'got' ('I could tell you a lot, but you got to be true to your code'), but here the first part of the line is sung far more dramatically than the second: the singer seems ready to pour out his heart, but then is held back by his own sense of how a man should display his emotions (punching out 'you've got to be' far more conversationally). The subsequent phrase, 'You'd never know it but buddy I'm a kind of poet', finds both 'know it' and 'poet' sung in a comparatively brusque manner, rather than contrastingly, the importance of the line being to underplay the singer's poetic credentials at the same time he announces them (with the clumsy metre and slanginess of the words 'buddy, I'm a kind of poet'). From this point on, however, Barney's vocals do become more evenly melancholy and conventionally lyrical, so that even the hectoring line 'you simply gotta listen to me' is sung as dreamily as its preceding rhyme ('and when I'm gloomy'). Whilst the singer manages not to give anything away of the specifics of his situation (thereby remaining true to his code), he does betray his emotions through the manner in which he delivers his words, before realising that he must stop his confession before he is overwhelmed by emotion entirely ('But this torch that I found must be drowned/for it soon might explode'). This struggle between the singer's attempts to shrug off his situation and need to voice it lyrically is most clearly felt in the way he apologises to the bartender for 'bending your ear', a phrase that may suggest nagging, but which is delivered with a distinctly non-onomatopoeic gentle melodic twist.

This description of Sinatra's delivery of the song's rhymes is intended to highlight how his phrasing is tied up with acting out the developing themes of the song rather than simply delivering the notes on the page. John Rockwell, in his analysis of Sinatra's 1958 recording of 'One For My Baby', identifies it as his finest moment because 'it most completely calls upon his skills as both singer and actor' (1995: 73), and it is this sensitivity of vocal interpretation that has been taken as one of the hallmarks of Sinatra's singing during the Capitol years (1953–61). However, in *Young at Heart*, Barney's excessive immersion in the narratives of the songs he performs is part of what delays the happiness he eventually finds at the end of the film.

'You My Love' does not display the nuanced storytelling characteristics of 'One For My Baby'. In fact, the number does not fit at all with the two main strands that constituted Sinatra's songbook of the time: it is neither a 'saloon song' like 'One For My Baby' nor a swing number, such as the ones featured in *Pal Joey*. Written especially for the film by Mack Gordon and Jimmy van Heusen, the lyrics are appropriate to the narrative context, with Barney thanking Laurie, through song, for walking into his lonely world and bringing him peace of mind. However, the style of the singing does jar with how Barney has been seen to perform earlier in the film, the careful phrasing of the earlier numbers abandoned for a more uniform 'open' vocal delivery which sees Barney emphasising every vowel sound to a consistently full-bodied piano accompaniment. The effect is as 'innocently balladic' as that attributed to Sinatra's 1947 version of 'One For My Baby' by John Rockwell (1995: 71). The final scene of *Young at Heart* does indeed reveal a 'younger' Sinatra, eschewing the more worldly-wise musical delivery that had become the defining feature of his comeback.

Young at Heart is a musical remake of *Four Daughters* (Michael Curtiz, 1938). In the original, the Sloan character (John Garfield in his first role) commits suicide. Once it had been decided that this would not be the case in *Young at Heart*, and that Barney would find contentment with the Tuttle family, it was reasonable that the character should adopt a less immersed musical style at the end. Within the terms of a fictional world seeking a source of narrative closure, Barney's completion of a song that Laurie had been pleading him to finish throughout the film, and his adoption of a performing style that signals his new-found comfort in the family home, does provide a suitable closure. However, if *Young at Heart* closes events in a congruous manner, the narrative is itself enclosed by a voice which may cast doubt on the ending's appropriateness. The film in fact closes with the voice of Sinatra, outside of his role in the film, reprising the title song. Like many of his singles throughout the 1950s (for example, 'Love and Marriage' and 'High Hopes'), 'Young At Heart' is more straightforwardly spry than the material he recorded for his albums. However, his new 'mature' singing style is still evident: in the playfulness of phrasing as he sings the title first swooningly and then more matter-of-factly, as if the idea should now be sinking in; in the fuller grain discernible in his voice on the 'you' of 'if you should survive to 105' (the more weathered quality of his vocals valued as a positive side-effect of the vocal haemorrhage he sustained in the early 1950s); and in the restraint he displays by keeping the singing low-key until the affirming crescendo of 'alive'. Whilst the film provides a place for the showcasing of these musical qualities, it also contrives a narrative which ultimately denies their articulation by the character Sinatra plays.

I have stated that songs in the musical do not usually feature the quality of distance between music and narrative situation which can be crucial to the storytelling role of the pop song in the non-musical. However, *Young at Heart* does conclude with a song which is marked by a sense of distance, Sinatra's weathered singing of the title number contrasting with the performing style adopted by his character towards the end of the film. The song sequence of the musical offers a secured space where the viewer may be *particularly* encouraged to relate fictional events to the performance history of the star(s) involved. As such the cultural resonance of the performer outside the film becomes a crucial factor in the understanding of the performance within it. However, within this environment, issues of obtrusiveness and distance, the two other areas of choice discussed in chapter one can also be of importance. In *Young at Heart* the obtrusiveness of the pop song is made meaningful by the contrast presented between the open form of the Tuttles' musical performances, and the closed form of Barney's numbers. The distance suggested between Sinatra's non-diegetic performance of 'Young at Heart' at the end of the film and the on-screen number that has preceded it casts doubt on the appropriateness of aspects of the narrative's conclusion.

In these concluding events, Barney determines to complete the composition of 'You My Love', thereby acting upon Laurie's entreaties that he should discipline his unquestionable musical talent. *Young at Heart* presents the results of Barney's acquiescence to her encouragement at the same time that it demonstrates his new-found ease within the Tuttle household: the song is presented as a sign that he has eventually found a place in their suburban home. Unlike certain melodramas of this period (such as *All That Heaven Allows* (Douglas Sirk, 1955) and *Rebel Without a Cause* (Nicholas Ray, 1955), the landscape in which the household is set remains uncriticised. Barney's transformation at the end of the film is rendered as a willing surrender to the nurturing warmth of the family rather than, as he had earlier feared, the capitulation to a restrictive domestic regime. That Barney needs to be brought in from the 'outside' at all indicates that this world holds carefully-set limits and rules, but these are never articulated in aggressive terms. Barney's initial antagonistic stance towards the family is viewed as a self-imposed exile, the cessation of which can only be to his benefit.

The disciplining of music is also integral to the film version of Rodgers and Hart's *Pal Joey*, conceived as a star-vehicle for Sinatra. However, whereas in *Young at Heart* this involves a sudden change in the singer's performing style, *Pal Joey* allows a particular strand of Sinatra's musical personality to dominate throughout. At the conclusion of *Young at Heart*, Sinatra's unique qualities as a pop star after his 'comeback' do not find expression through his fictional character. Instead, the final sequence presents his character performing the song as a type of 'folk music', whose most important function is its communal, social use. Within the film's fictional world, this involves the rejection of the view that pop musicians represent unique kinds of stars, *separated* from their audience by virtue of their charismatic talent. As such the ending of the film rejects an assumption which underpins the production and consumption of commercial pop music, and which motivates, amongst other things, the manufacturing of star-vehicle musicals such as itself. The problems of making such a move narratively, in the context of a pop star film vehicle, are indicated by the isolated nature of Sinatra's musical performance in this final scene, which is quite unlike any that he had enacted previously, and which also contrasts to the non-diegetic rendition of the title song which succeeds it.

Pal Joey: the disciplines of the 1950s playboy

Access all areas? The disciplining of musical performance

Pal Joey is much more consistent in its celebration of commercial pop music as a cultural form which relies on the performances of charismatic stars. Throughout the film, the character Sinatra plays embodies star qualities commonly associated with him at the time of the film's release in 1957. These qualities are of a different order to the ones of intensity and integrity made use of (and, at the film's conclusion, momentarily subdued) in the fictional world of Young at Heart. Instead, Pal Joey plays on Sinatra's status as the era's most renowned pop star 'playboy'. The star presence of Sinatra, as an embodiment of the 1950s' playboy, is allowed to exert an exceptionally dominating influence over the manner in which the song sequences are played out. Pop song, pop star persona and fictional character are set in a relationship whereby all three elements reinforce each other to an extent not matched by any of the other examples in this study. In Pal Joey, the title character is allowed the fictional authority to present an ideal version of himself through song in a manner to which the other characters discussed in this study can only aspire – and fail. As a direct comparison, this failure is witnessed most poignantly in Sheik in Baby, It's You, which scrutinises his unsuccessful attempts to construct his identity through pop music, and an image of Sinatra in particular.

The unique mutually reinforcing quality of the relationship between song, Sinatra as star, and fictional character in Pal Joey is not just registered by its comparison to other instances of the relationship between pop song and fictional character in other films. Within the fictional world of Pal Joey itself, Joey's musical performances are allowed an authority that exceeds those of other characters who break into song (that is to say Joey's benefactor Vera (Rita Hayworth) and the chorus girl Linda (Kim Novak)). In fact, the male-centred playboy discourse embodied in Sinatra's fictional role resonates across the film so thoroughly that even when the female characters sing, they are still often playing to Joey's tune. The song sequence in the musical is often presented as a utopian moment, in which problems and inequalities present in the rest of the narrative find ideal solutions.[1] Pal Joey's version of a musical utopia, however, is one which continues to privilege the male character's perspective. The film is so heavily involved in the cultural resonances associated with its star that it distorts the conventional utopian possibilities of the musical genre.

Pal Joey displays an unusually combative tone in its musical segments, with songs being predominantly sung at, rather than to or with, other characters. It features only one duet, and even this is played out in unequal terms. In the original stage production, nightclub heel Joey seduces the innocent Linda through his rendition of the romantic ballad 'I Could Write A Book'. She responds to his (false) entreaties of love by taking over the number, expressing her feelings within exactly the same musical structure used by Joey. The same song in the film, however, finds Joey dictating how it is to be performed. He drags Linda onto a nightclub stage unexpectedly, leads her in all the dance steps, and tells her when to sing (she is given two lines). When Linda nevertheless shows that she has enjoyed the performance, Joey deflates her romantic musing by snapping 'How's it feel to work with a star?'

All three of the main characters (Joey, Linda and Vera) are given the opportunity to sing at one another during the course of the film. However, Joey's performances display a form of mastery withheld from those of Linda and Vera, a mastery secured by the film's commitment to the ideals embodied in the 1950s' playboy.

The publicity surrounding the release of the Kinsey Reports on male and female sexual behaviour (in 1948 and 1953 respectively) indicated an increasing openness in public debates about sexuality. Throughout the 1950s new magazines like *Confidential* and in particular *Playboy* circulated stories and images which sought to define how this new awareness should be articulated. The playboy embodied a particular type of 'ideal' masculinity and, during the decade, Sinatra was the entertainer most associated publicly with this mode of masculinity, as Karen McNally notes:

> The figure of the playboy is one of the lasting masculine images of the 1950s. Its associations of sexual predatoriness and invulnerable confidence were set up as a stark contrast to the world of steady propriety within which the suburban husband was said to exist. Frank Sinatra seemingly fit the mould of this symbol of the age to a tee, his life and art combining in an image of the affluent urban swinger which stretched across the breadth of his popular cultural depictions of the American male. (2002)[2]

In this description, McNally points to the key qualities of the 1950s playboy: sexually predatory, immensely self-confident, affluent and associated with the sophistication of city life rather than the domesticity of the suburbs.

Crucially, as will be discussed at further length presently, the swing jazz style which was central to Sinatra's comeback in 1953 was seen as the musical equivalent of the playboy lifestyle. In *Pal Joey* Sinatra's character demonstrates a freedom of movement *and* musical expression in keeping with the discourse of the 1950s playboy. This freedom, however, was only secured by regulating those elements which might threaten it, and in its orchestration of its musical numbers the film demonstrates the unequal distribution of power which allows the playboy his liberty.

Pal Joey as star vehicle

The original production of *Pal Joey* introduced an unprecedented tone of cynicism and frankness about sexual behaviour to the Broadway musical when it premiered in 1940. As Gerald Mast notes: 'There had never been a musical like *Pal Joey*; bitter, cynical, seamy, sordid, with no romantic resolution, no change of heart, no happy ending – no ending at all' (1987: 181). Its two main characters, Joey and the philandering millionairess Vera, remain steadfast in their determination to act solely according to their own self-interest. The show ends with Joey out of work and broke, after being thrown out by

Vera when a blackmailer threatens to reveal their affair to her husband. Earlier, Linda, the innocent chorus girl whose desire for Joey would exert a transforming influence in a more conventional musical, had been disabused of any romantic notions by his callous seduction and subsequent discarding of her.

Contemporary reviews of the film version of *Pal Joey*, whether favourable or disparaging, generally recognised two differences from the original production: a watering down of the stage show's uncompromising bleakness; and the shaping of the source material to provide a star vehicle for Frank Sinatra. Evidence of the film's comparatively lighter tone was provided by what *Variety* termed the 'happy ending stuff' of the finale, in which Joey leaves town with Linda amidst intimations (but no declaration on his part) of marriage.[3] In addition, Vera has changed from an adulterous wife to a lonely widow, and she selflessly clears the way to true love by telling Linda where to find Joey as he prepares to sneak away.

Yet the language used to describe Sinatra's performance suggests that the dilution of the original's bleakly unromantic vision was felt to be compensated for by his charismatic star turn. The *Hollywood Citizen-News* called it 'almost a one-man show' (Shaw 1970: 230). *Variety* described Sinatra as 'forceful' and 'potent', ideal as 'the irreverent, freewheeling, glib Joey'.[4] Rose Pelswick of the *Journal-American* echoed these sentiments, commenting: 'He brings vividly alive the glib, egotistical, raffish opportunism of John O'Hara's well-known story, and invests the part with such tremendous charm that he simply wraps up the picture' (quoted in Shaw 1970: 230). Whilst Pelswick uses negative adjectives to describe the nature of the source material, she also acknowledges how Sinatra's particular brand of 'charm' renders these qualities attractive. The uniformity of language used to describe Sinatra's role and performance suggests that the film of *Pal Joey* placed itself within a well-defined discourse. By common consent, 'there had never been a musical like *Pal Joey*' when it arrived on Broadway, but by the time it appeared on film there had grown a framework of accepted male sexual behaviour within which Joey's rakish actions could be accepted by, and even 'charm', a mainstream audience.

The cultural resonance of Sinatra as a performer is reflected throughout the film in terms of the character Sinatra plays, and in the way the fictional performance is framed. This offers a contrast to *Young at Heart* which ultimately constructs a rift between Sinatra's star persona and the development of the character within the film. In the song sequences of *Pal Joey*, Sinatra's playboy persona is embodied in Joey in two ways: through the particular manner in which the songs are performed vocally; and through the physical movement of the character as he sings. My analysis of these sequences will take each element – voice and movement – in turn, before considering the relative lack of vocal or physical freedom allowed to the other characters in their song sequences. What is also crucial, however, as already indicated, is that numbers not written for the musical have been inserted into the film. Particular attention is thus given to the ways in which these work on and with their previous associations as Sinatra numbers.

The playboy's singing style: 'The Lady Is A Tramp'

A number of Sinatra's albums in the 1950s elaborated the swing ballad style inaugurated in his first Capitol albums. 'Songs for Swingin' Lovers' (1956), 'A Swingin' Affair' (1957) and 'Come Fly With Me' (1958) featured ebullient, big-band arrangements with Sinatra stretching his lyrical phrasing more audaciously than ever. This vocal audacity is evidenced in his playful rendition of 'The Lady Is A Tramp' in *Pal Joey*, which had become a staple of Sinatra's live set in the year leading up to the film's release.

In the film, Joey directs this song at Vera (Rita Hayworth), as an impertinent dismissal of the social gap between them. One of the ways in which he demonstrates his mastery over her, and eventually captivates her attention, is to surprise her with unexpected variations in his vocalising. Commanded to grant her a private audience, Joey begins the song seated at a piano. He renders the first verse with low-key precision, stretching a vowel sound at the same point in every line and clipping the words at their end:

> She gets too hun**gry** for dinner at eight
> She likes the thea**tre**, never comes late
> She'd never both**er** with people she'd hate
> That's why the lad**y** is a tramp
> (elongated sounds bold and underlined)

The first three lines of the second verse reverse this strategy, with each beginning with every syllable precisely spelled out and ending with the elongated singing of 'earls', 'pearls' and 'girls':

> Doesn't like crap games with barons and earls
> Won't go to Harlem in ermine and pearls
> Won't dish the dirt with the rest of the girls

The repeated refrain of 'that's why the lady is a tramp' is sung as before, the film cutting both times to Vera in order to note her discomfort.

During the release of the song, Joey pushes the piano away and begins striding in a predatory way around Vera as he sings. When he returns to the lyrics of the first two verses, he changes the words slightly and takes liberties with the melody, allowing it to see-saw up and down, instead of contrasting elongated sounds with staccato phrasing as before. 'She gets too hungry for dinner at eight' becomes 'She gets far too hungry for dinner at eight', and 'She likes the theatre, never comes late' is changed to 'she adores (sung with parodic affectation) the theatre and she doesn't arrive late'. The witty bravado of his performance begins to seduce Vera, so that by the time he substitutes a self-satisfied shrug for the expected repetition of 'OK' in the second release, she is held in his thrall, pictured seated in the bottom edge of the frame with Joey towering above her, arms held open.

On his Capitol albums, Sinatra often demonstrates his mastery over the song he is singing by twisting its melody, changing its structure, or unexpectedly shortening or stretching a vocal line. Yet as Steven Petkov notes:

Classical musicians use such terms as glissando, tempo rubato and mordent to describe many of these practices; they can all be found in Sinatra's singing. But the listener must pay attention because Sinatra makes it seem casual and effortless and never calls attention to the techniques being employed. All he does sounds natural and inevitable, as if it were being composed on the spot. (1995: 82)

The offsetting of uninhibited displays of skilled vocalising with a seemingly off-hand naturalness was fundamental to Sinatra's 'swinging' singing style of the 1950s. In an analysis of his performance of 'I've Got You Under My Skin' (from 'Songs For Swingin' Lovers'), Stephen Holden identifies what this balance between vocal dexterity and naturalness articulates:

In the song's climax, Sinatra admits that for the moment he's a smitten fool, and this exhilarating expression of a perfect balance between intoxication and wry knowingness may be the apex of all his 'swinging' music ... Sinatra's artfully casual readings of Porter embody ... [an] enviable ideal of grown-up fun. (1995: 68)

Sinatra's singing style and the mode of male sexual behaviour (its 'ideal of grown-up fun') that *Playboy* sought to popularise in the 1950s share common properties. As Richard Dyer has noted, the magazine's philosophy was based on a 'drive reduction model' of sexuality, positing the sex drive as 'a basic biological mandate' seeking 'expression' or 'release' (1987: 31). Thus the magazine's unprecedented openness in sexual matters was justified as something healthy, paying heed to natural desires that ought not to be repressed.

On the other hand, the playboy differentiated himself from the other major male non-conformist stereotype of the time, the 'beatnik', by the worldly sophistication with which this free expression was exercised. Whereas beat writers sought to detach themselves completely from mainstream American culture, engaged in a desperate search for an alternative, *Playboy* offered a 'square counterpart' who operated within a widely recognised milieu, yet demonstrated a greater freedom than the common man by casting a sceptic's eye over society's limiting institutions and conventions, most predominantly marriage (Reynolds & Press 1995: 10).

It is this seemingly paradoxical imperative to allow oneself to be overwhelmed by desire, yet also to remain self-aware and to act within certain boundaries that finds its musical counterpart in Sinatra's combination of 'intoxication' and 'wry knowingness'. It is in this manner that his 'swinging' music can be identified as part of the homology that constructs the playboy lifestyle. As Joey's performance of 'The Lady Is A Tramp' shows, the freedom of movement (musically and culturally) associated with the pop star playboy had to be reasserted aggressively, dictating in the process the relative lack of mobility afforded those who constituted the 'norm' against which he defined himself. Neither Linda nor Vera is allowed the casual mastery over a lyric displayed by Joey. Vera's emotional rendition of 'Bewitched, Bothered and Bewildered', for example, is immediately undercut by the first seconds of the following scene.

Vera is moved to song after spending a night with Joey. She wanders around her apartment the following morning in a state of heightened sensuality, dreamily testifying to her reawakened passions through her movement and singing. The action then cuts from her bathroom to Joey's, where he is absent-mindedly humming the tune to 'The Lady Is A Tramp' whilst shaving in front of the mirror. The reprise of this melody at this moment is not only a reminder that Vera was originally seduced by the power of Joey's rendition of the song. It also contrasts the heart-felt mode of her musical interpretation (she sings what cannot be adequately expressed in speech) with the attitude Joey displays in relation to vocal performance. Here, in a moment of privacy, Joey's performance of music is light-hearted and flippant. On other occasions, Joey uses his musical voice to demand attention (his spontaneous rendition of 'I Didn't Know What Time It Was' convinces the nightclub owner to hire him) or exert control (his hijacking of the duet 'I Could Write A Book' and performance of 'The Lady Is A Tramp'). In none of these instances does Joey perform the song to articulate emotions that cannot be spoken, as Vera does throughout 'Bewitched, Bothered and Bewildered'.

Moving with a playboy's freedom

It is only towards the end of the film, during 'I Can Do Without Dames', that Joey's mastery over the songs he sings begins to slip, as if it is there to represent his emotions tumbling out, in the same way that 'Bewitched, Bothered and Bewildered' works in relation to Vera. This demonstrates the extent to which Joey's freedom of expression is being threatened at this moment, by both Vera's patronage (she has just withdrawn her financial backing for the club) and Linda's devotion (his underlying feelings for her caused the confrontation between him and Vera which led to her decision to pull out of the club). All his other performances are delivered with the cultivated 'sexual insouciance' which John Rockwell identifies as one of the main interpretive strands of Sinatra's singing (1984: 142). This confidence of musical expression is complemented in the film by an equally forceful display of physical movement, and it is to this aspect of the performance that I will now turn. In particular, the film refers to an irreverent style of live performance, involving the transgression of conventional boundaries between stage and audience that was commonly associated with Sinatra and like-minded entertainers at the time. Within the film's fictional world, this style of performance is only allowed in relation to Joey, thereby adding a physical dimension to the relative freedom that is also asserted vocally.

The Clan, a loose collective of freewheeling entertainers led by Sinatra, was renowned for an irreverence towards the boundaries of the stage during the 1950s, as Arnold Shaw notes:

The en masse appearance of The Clan at an important club engagement of one of its members and the staging of an improvised, unbuttoned show, proved the peak point of night-clubbing for many customers, an offence to some, and a matter for adverse comment by others. (1970: 236)

Reports detailing The Clan's hijacking of other entertainers' shows proliferated during the late 1950s. Such a display of high-spirited non-conformism finds expression in *Pal Joey* in Joey's very first number, when he jumps onto the stage uninvited, cracks a few gags and then launches into a version of 'I Didn't Know What Time It Was' which leaves the audience transfixed.

Later, at the high society ball hosted by Vera, he enacts the opposite process, cultivating a presumptuous intimacy with her from the stage as he sings, rather than simply providing a soundtrack to which the guests can dance. During 'There's A Small Hotel' he directs the last line of each verse specifically at Vera, and, playing as the lines do on variations of spending the night together, prompts a shocked reaction from her. He continues to ignore the boundaries of class which map out the space of the ballroom (the high society partygoers on the dance-floor and the hired help on stage) when he forces Vera to perform 'Zip', a number which sees her unwillingly acting out a striptease routine in front of her guests.

The stages of seduction: 'The Lady Is A Tramp'

Joey's ability to move freely in space reaches its peak with his rendition of 'The Lady Is A Tramp'. He begins the number from a position of vulnerability. He has had to beg Vera to turn up at the nightclub, and her reaction to his performance will determine whether he keeps his job. However, Joey transforms this potential trial into an irresistible act of seduction, which thrills through its potent disregard for the conventions of performance, not just vocally but also spatially. Despite its seemingly hostile title, the lyrics of 'The Lady Is A Tramp' are intended as a back-handed compliment to the woman it addresses: she is looked down upon by uptight, polite society only because she refuses to bide by its stiff codes of behaviour. Joey's performance acts as an exercise in forcing Vera to see the joke.

As Joey begins to play at a piano on stage, the camera dollies around the back of the table at which Vera is seated, so that she is placed at the very right edge of the frame whilst Joey occupies the left, viewed sideways on. The seduction begins, then, with both singer and his audience stationary in their conventional positions, one on stage, the other watching on from the floor. The song proceeds with an exchange of medium close-ups between Joey and Vera, he singing the first two verses with ar-

Fig. 2.7

Fig. 2.8

Fig. 2.9

Fig. 2.10

Fig. 2.11

rogant casualness, she registering somewhat more emotion as she realises what he is singing to her. These shots mark an early reversal of the positions they held before Joey began to sing. Vera had arrived at the club to see how Joey would react to the challenge of performing for her, but already the challenge has been reframed, with Joey asking her to react to his performance. Once this transformation has been set underway, Joey rises from his piano (during the first release of the song) and moves towards the band with a swagger. This movement brings Vera back into the right-hand side of the frame, so that they are both in shot again, but now he stands above her, picked out by the stage light above him, band swinging to his command. The exchange of medium close-ups continues with Joey in his new position, growing ever more uninhibited with his gestures, mimicking the brass punches which punctuate the song by snapping his head back and shrugging dramatically. Vera is viewed from the same position as before, but now her features begin to break into a smile as her resistance breaks down.

Joey breaches the division between stage and floor completely when he dances around Vera's table before disappearing from frame back onto the stage. Vera follows his movements, registering delight at his self-assured prowling, before joining Joey on stage to dance, the band striking up an encore in celebration of a seduction fully achieved. The conventional demarcations which mark the nightclub as a place of musical entertainment have been so utterly transformed by Joey's aggressive mobility that even the band leave their posts with their instruments to follow the two lovers as they exit into the night.

Linda's 'naïve' musical performance: 'My Funny Valentine'

'The Lady Is A Tramp' is one of the songs in the film not to have been part of the original Broadway musical. The decision to include it in the film version of *Pal Joey* was no doubt influenced by the fact that the song had become a staple of Sinatra's live act in the year preceding the release of the film. For viewers with an awareness of this, Joey's performance of the song becomes even more seductive: Vera's challenge is combated by a song which has already been recognised as a show-stopper in the act of the performer taking on Joey's role in the film. However, it is important to the wider claims of this study to note that the fictional character's performance is *also* charismatic. Further, the power of the performance is not just the result of Sinatra's singing and movement, but also the consequence of the manner in which the performance is presented through the film's various narrational devices. The *extent* to which the cultural resonance of the song is made important to the drama unfolding in the film's fictional world is a matter of choice on the part of the filmmaker.

A similar point can be made in relation to another song imported into the film: 'My Funny Valentine'. It is highly likely that many viewers at the time of the film's release would have recognised the song as the opening track on Sinatra's 'comeback' album 'Songs for Young Lovers' and as a constant fixture on the set-list of his concerts subsequently (of course, viewers watching the film in *any* historical period may also know this). With this in mind, it may seem odd that Sinatra does not perform the song in the film. Instead, it is sung by Linda. However, as the scene is played out, an awareness of the song's prior association with Sinatra allows an extra layer of understanding on the part of the informed viewer as to the appropriateness of having Linda perform the song in the film. For within the fictional world itself, Joey 'controls' the way Linda's song is presented. The knowledge that this song is intimately connected to the performing career of Sinatra outside of the film adds to the sense that Linda is playing along to someone else's tune. However, it does not provide the whole basis for understanding the scene.

Linda performs 'My Funny Valentine' ostensibly as a love song directed towards Joey, but her performance is characterised by an artlessness that prevents her from exerting control over how her song is received. This lack of control is signalled in the first place by the fact that she is performing the song as part of the show Joey is putting together in his nightclub. The space in which she is allowed to move and the style in which she sings all fall under his supervision. Attention is also diverted away from Linda's use of the song as an expression of love, by the scene being played out in such a way as to emphasise its relevance to the struggle being engaged between Joey and Vera. Whilst Linda tries to display her feelings for Joey within the limited space allowed to her, the camera blocks this effort of self-expression by turning its gaze onto the other two main characters.

When the camera is focused upon Linda, she is either viewed through an ornate love-heart or in an extreme close-up of her face, of a type not to be found elsewhere in the film. Encased within a prop which over-determines her role as a tender-hearted romantic, and dressed in a pure white gown which theatricalises her virginal innocence, the artificial staging of this number ensures that the potential for Linda to express what she 'really' feels through song is severely curtailed. In fact her positioning on stage blocks her attempts to address Joey directly through her song. The curtain closes on her the second she stops singing, to emphasise even more the restrictions placed upon her mode of performance by its setting.

Fig. 2.12

Similarly the two close-ups of her face in this sequence indicate naïvety in the way she addresses the emotions which are contained in her singing. As Joey demonstrates in his performance of 'The Lady Is A Tramp', the film views the control of the gaze as essential for the successful targeting of a song towards a particular person: he counters Vera's initial gaze onto him with an irresistibly aggressive gaze back at her. When Joey sings, the close-ups always allow enough room to make the direction of his gaze clear. The extreme close-ups of Linda, in contrast, transmit the intensity of emotion behind her singing, but do not reveal where this intensity is being directed. The feeling is simply 'there' for Joey to see; it is not projected towards him in the forceful manner displayed in his own performances.

Significantly in this context, the moment at which Joey experiences a crisis that leads to the closing of his club is articulated as an inability to focus his gaze. Vera has threatened to withdraw her funding unless Joey fires Linda. Not able to confront her directly, he asks Linda to perform her striptease routine, hoping she will refuse and walk out on him. When she actually goes through with the number, Joey cannot bring himself to watch. An abrupt zoom into his startled eyes precedes his instruction for the performance to stop, an action which effectively ends his dream of running his own club.

The timidity of Linda's address during 'My Funny Valentine' is emphasised when her performance is relegated to the background upon Vera's arrival onto the scene. Her entrance prompts a dramatic zoom from the stage to her position on the balcony, as if she were physically wresting control of the camera's gaze from Linda. When she begins speaking to Joey (the song now barely audible), the conversation is filmed in medium shot/reverse-shots. The 'naked' emotions of Linda's singing give way to the measured threats exchanged in Joey and Vera's conversation. Joey is not immune to the appeal of Linda's performance, as his subsequent actions bear out. However, Linda cannot keep his attention focused upon her, allowing her relationship with him to become a prop in the power games conducted by Joey and Vera.

Young at Heart offered an example of song form still being made important to the understanding of narrative events, even in the musical genre where the integrity of that form is usually guaranteed. Song form is also a useful point of comparison in *Pal Joey*. The difference between Joey's mastery over his environment and Linda's comparative lack of control is demonstrated, in part, by the sense of expansiveness and contraction associated with their respective performances of 'The Lady Is A Tramp' and 'My Funny Valentine'. The performance of 'The Lady Is A Tramp' exceeds the bounds of the stage on which it is begun and receives a musical reprise as the band provide an instrumental version of the melody to accompany Joey and Vera's dancing. The sense that the vitality of the number is causing the song sequence to burst at its seams is emphasised by the music continuing non-diegetically as the scene transfers to the couple on Vera's boat. By contrast, Linda's performance of 'My Funny Valentine' is utterly constrained, the performance lasting only as long as the original musical script, dictated by Joey, allows. Furthermore, in the middle of the sequence, attention is drawn away from the details of the performance itself, putting the song in the kind of distanced commentary role normally reserved for the non-diegetic pop song in the non-musical.

Vera's musical 'strips': 'Zip' and 'Bewitched, Bothered and Bewildered'

The power struggle between Joey and Vera, alluded to in the 'My Funny Valentine' sequence, begins at Vera's charity ball where, as already demonstrated, Joey challenges her by blatantly ignoring conventions of musical performance and their difference in class. His most obvious attempt to orchestrate events in this scene occurs when he forces Vera into a potentially humiliating position, leaving her no choice but to re-enact her past life as a stripper in front of the high society audience.

'Zip', the number which follows, was sung in the original Broadway production by Melba, a female reporter who had come to interview Joey at his club. Her bookish appearance and obvious intellect convince the enlightened singer that she must be a lesbian. Melba launches into the parodic strip routine of 'Zip' unexpectedly, to convince him that she is heterosexual as well as smart. Clearly then, in keeping with the film's general tendency to allow Joey to orchestrate events, the motivation for the number's appearance has been reversed from the stage version. Whereas Melba exposes Joey's misogyny through the song, in the film Joey uses it to exert his control — he wants to find out if Vera, despite her uptight appearance, can still display what she learned as a stripper.

Yet Vera responds to this challenge with a verve and wit that echoes the bravado of Joey's musical performances. In common with the strategies of 'The Lady Is A Tramp' sequence, this scene gathers the non-performer onto the edge of the frame in order to show how he is seduced by the song's delivery. Despite her unwillingness to reveal her past life to her audience, once the performance is underway Vera moves with a knowing insouciance which resembles that of the playboy, and displays the combative tone characteristic of Joey's performing style. Her freedom of movement here is still contained within the particular vision of female sexuality proposed by the *Playboy* philosophy, however, and not only because it is Joey who initiates her performance.

Vera first appears with her hair brushed back at the sides and curled tightly on top. Her low-cut ballgown reveals broad shoulders and a tight corset ensures that the curves of her body are sharply defined. When called upon to perform her routine, she uses the tightness with which her body is defined to transform the clichéd erotic gyrations of the strip into aggressive, angular movements. It is in this way that Vera, with a great deal of humour, resists Joey's attempts to embarrass her by forcing her in to a 'proper' strip routine. As she sings 'Sigmund Freud has often stated, dreams and drives are all related', for example, her wiggles while she pretends to pull down her gown are so overstated that they describe a sharp zig-zag rather than a shimmering 'S'. Whereas

Fig. 2.13

a stripper might climax her performance with a brazen, open-armed wiggle of what has been revealed, Vera ends the song with a series of symmetrical shrugs of each shoulder, keeping all her movement on an even plane.

If her performance does demonstrate a gestural control reminiscent of Joey, it does not result in the complete reversal of the balance of power between the two that is the effect of Joey's rendition of 'The Lady is a Tramp'. The only way she can signal her resistance to Joey's attempts to take control is by acting as though he is not there. She addresses her performance primarily to the audience in front of her, offering only the occasional withering glance towards Joey. She sometimes delivers her parodic striptease moves as violent swipes in his direction (a back kick, bum wiggles and flicks of her gown), but always avoiding eye contact. She acts in these moments as if she were distractedly swatting away a fly, pretending that the orchestrator of this unwanted performance does not exist, a pretence that Joey is delighted to expose in his subsequent rendition of 'The Lady Is A Tramp'.

Vera's sexuality is performed through a discourse more specific to the *Playboy* philosophy in her rendition of 'Bewitched, Bothered and Bewildered', sung after she has spent her first night with Joey. This is presented as a complement to 'Zip', allowing comparisons to be made between the display of Vera's body before and after the encounter with her lover. Both numbers feature a displaced 'strip' routine, in this case the revealing of Vera's body as she prepares to take a shower. Yet whereas her movement in 'Zip' displays a knowing subversion of the routine's erotic strategies, with her body deliberately hardened, 'Bewitched, Bothered and Bewildered' finds her suddenly soft and supple, conforming to the 1950s ideal of how a woman felt sexual pleasure.

Richard Dyer demonstrates how oceanic imagery dominated descriptions of the female orgasm in popular culture and Freudian psychoanalysis during the 1950s. Despite the suggestion in the Kinsey Report that the vaginal orgasm was a biological impossibility,[5] it continued to be celebrated as an experience which flooded the whole body with sensual ecstasy: 'Where the visible/visual analogue for the male experience derives from the penis, for the female it is everywhere. The visual analogue of the vaginal orgasm is the female body itself' (Dyer 1987: 55).

Pal Joey is remarkable for the way it so over-determines Vera's transition from the deliberately 'hardened' physicality displayed in 'Zip' to the soft and blurred 'feminine' sexuality portrayed in 'Bewitched, Bothered and Bewildered'. The contrast between Vera's appearance before and after her night with Joey is evident as soon as she awakes the next morning. Viewed in medium close-up from above, her hair has been let down and her arms stretch wide to either side. Whilst she sings 'I'm in love, but don't I show it, like a babe in arms' she rolls down her bed towards the camera, her whole body laid across the frame, before gathering herself up into a sitting position, arms trailing behind her. Later in the song, the camera cranes above her as she reclines on her chaise-longue, once again offering the viewer the spectacle of her whole body loosely stretched. By this time her naturally broad shoulders have been covered (and blurred) by the bushy fur lining of her dressing gown.

When the camera shows Vera's whole body in 'Zip' it reveals how strictly she marshals the standard poses of the strip through her tautly controlled performance. She wittily prevents each gesture functioning as part of a seamless erotic whole (culminating in the spectacle of the woman in her 'natural' state), by making each movement appear discrete and mechanical. During 'Bewitched, Bothered and Bewildered', in contrast, she shows how her sexual encounter with Joey has caused her body to blur with sen-sual pleasure, her movements no longer clipped and discrete, but rather languorous and diffuse. At the end of the sequence, she enters the shower sing-ing, 'the way to my heart is unzipped again', after which she throws her arms open and pushes her breasts forward, albeit behind the shower's frosted glass. Even though the sequence is only a 'strip' for the viewer (whereas 'Zip' is diegetically marked as such), Vera's newly sexualised body conforms far more closely to the conventional poses of a public strip routine than before.

Fig. 2.14

The song itself has been cut considerably from its original incarnation on Broadway. In the stage show, Vera awakes from her wild night with Joey singing:

> After one whole quart of brandy,
> Like a daisy I awake.
> With no Bromo Seltzer handy
> I don't even shake.

The implication is that sex with Joey has been the ideal hangover cure, one type of in-toxication counteracting the effects of another. In contrast, the film's version runs:

> He's a fool and don't I know it,
> But a fool can have his charm.
> I'm in love, but don't I show it,
> Like a babe in arms.

The imagery here is immediately associated with the enveloping warmth provided by love ('like a babe in arms'). Both versions then continue in a similar vein, celebrating a reawakening of passion with the standard imagery of romantic song (she has turned into 'a simpering, whimpering child again', 'has lost [her] heart, but what of it'). However, in the film, as Vera moves from bedroom to bathroom, she begins humming the melody rather than singing the lyrics, thereby disguising the twist which the Broadway version takes. In the original, the clichéd romantic imagery of the first line of each verse begins to be followed by ever more explicit descriptions of the physical sensation which has moved Vera to song. It is worth quoting some of these lines to demonstrate how they articulate a sexual response far removed from the oceanic model popularised in the 1950s:

> I'll sing to him, each spring to him,
> And worship the trousers that cling to him.

> When he talks he is seeking, words to get off his chest.
> Horizontally speaking, he's at his very best.

> Vexed again, perplexed again.
> Thank God I can be oversexed again.

and finally:

> I'm dumb again, numb again,
> A rich, ready, ripe little plum again.

Whilst both versions maintain a faith in male penetration as the ultimate source of female sexual pleasure (the vaginal orgasm), the stage show is far more specific about the biological origins of this pleasure. In the film Joey provides Vera with an experience that prevents her from thinking of her body in terms of individual parts, thus robbing her of the awareness she had previously demonstrated in her performance of 'Zip'. Joey's 'unzipping' of her defences transforms her body instead into the ideal of diffused female sexuality which was integral to the male-produced playboy discourse.

The 'perfect' fit between pop star and film character

A fundamental difference between the original stage version of *Pal Joey* and the film version discussed here lies in the fact that by the time the film was made Joey's freewheeling behaviour could be viewed through the prism of a newly articulated male lifestyle – that of the playboy. If, as Gerald Mast claims, Joey and Vera were 'two of a kind' in the original production, they have lost that parity in the film (1987: 181). Instead both Linda and Vera are framed within the power mechanisms which ensure Joey's ability to roam freely.

Pal Joey is illuminating because it shows how these structures of power have to be kept aggressively in place, even within the space of the song, which has often been the occasion within the musical for utopian flights from social realities. In the original series of letters by John O'Hara, upon which the musical was based, Joey is cut down to size by an obvious limitation of the epistolary form (O'Hara 1952). He continually boasts about his singing talent to his pen-pal Ted, but as the reader cannot hear him in action and he never seems to get anywhere, we are not inclined to believe him. By giving a voice to Joey, the Broadway musical allowed the character a chance to prove his claims (the role in fact made a star of Gene Kelly). By making that voice Sinatra's in the film version, Joey gains access to both a performing style that was predicated in part on a display of mastery through song, and to the performer who most prominently acted out the fantasy of male freedom offered by the playboy. With Joey's character so safely guarded by its performer, the narrative 'threats' posed by Linda and Vera to his boundless mobility carry little weight. They are never allowed to speak entirely in their own voices or move with their own freedom, Joey's orchestration of events being achieved through a charismatically controlling use of voice, space and the direction of the gaze.

Conclusion

The different ways in which the musical persona of Frank Sinatra is accommodated in *Young at Heart* and *Pal Joey* demonstrate that the choices filmmakers make are just as decisive to the understanding of the performance of a pop star within a particular fictional scenario, as they are when a 'disembodied' song is used to accompany a specific narrative situation. There are two processes at work that result in the differences between the relationship of pop song, star and fictional characterisation in each film. Firstly, each film makes use of two different aspects of the Sinatra persona, both of which were equally prevalent during the mid-1950s. The character of Barney Sloan in *Young at Heart* refers to Sinatra's status as an exceptionally sensitive interpreter of popular song. The character of Joey Evans in *Pal Joey* embodies the qualities of musical virtuosity and free-wheeling sexual swagger which exemplified Sinatra's 'swinging' singing style and the mode of performance and playboy lifestyle associated with it.

Secondly, these qualities are then represented through characters who inhabit their fictional worlds in crucially different ways. *Young at Heart* simultaneously provides a showcase for, and offers a critique of, the qualities of intimacy and intensity displayed through the musical performances of the character Sinatra plays. *Pal Joey*, by contrast, embraces the task of embodying Sinatra's playboy persona in a fictional setting so enthusiastically that the persona's presence is made to be felt even in those song sequences in which Joey is not the main performer. As well as referring to popular music culture outside of its own fictional bounds, through the casting of Sinatra, each film also offers the viewer its own unique perspective on that pop music culture within its fictional world. The song sequences provide the most appropriate setting in which this unique perspective can be established and developed.

3. The pop song as narrational device

In this chapter, I return to a discussion of the pop song as a narrational device to consider how filmmakers have made creative use of the pop song's propensity to be understood as existing in a particularly intense relationship with its fans.

The sequences from John Schlesinger's *Midnight Cowboy* from 1969 and John Badham's *Saturday Night Fever* of 1977, discussed presently, are both marked by a series of 'incomplete' attachments, including those between non-diegetic pop song and film character. The relationship between song and character, and the attachment of both to other features of the fictional world, allows the viewer to understand, in a way that the characters themselves do not, the extent to which each character fails to project his desired self-image onto the world around him. The pop song is able to communicate this failure of self-expression so powerfully because of the status pop has achieved as a cultural form with a privileged role in the construction of identity.

The pop song and possession

The commercial pop song, as defined in this study, takes its place within a popular music culture that encourages its audience to 'possess' the music in a special way. As Simon Frith notes:

> Popular music is something possessed … In 'possessing' music, we make it part of our own identity and build it into a sense of ourselves … the intensity of this relationship between taste and self-definition seems peculiar to popular music – it is 'possessable' in ways that other cultural forms (except, perhaps, sports teams) are not. (1987: 143–4)

The conscious mapping out of identity through an affiliation with a particular song, musical style or artist has played an integral part in people's everyday use of pop music and in accounts of that use, whether it be rock'n'roll's role in the cultural production of the teenager or sub-cultural theory's emphasis on music's potential to be used as a tool of resistance against hegemonic forces.

Cultural conventions guide the consumption of all types of music. The classical concert, for example, provides a particular kind of setting for its listeners to register their identification with and appreciation of classical music. However, this setting constructs a relationship between audience and performer which is marked by a certain outward passivity on the part of the listener. Put another way, the activity of the classical music fan in this case is meant to lie in their listening attentively, rather than being encouraged to adopt a more overtly participatory response.

The rituals of pop music consumption, by contrast, are marked by more ostentatious displays of affiliation. Unlike the audience of a classical concert, attendees of a pop concert are typically encouraged to join in with the music through activities such as singing along, clapping in time with the music, or dancing. Different genres of pop music encourage such participation to a greater or lesser degree, and each genre's rituals of participation take different forms. However, it is one of the distinctive features of pop music overall that such participation forms at least part of the music-listening experience. To use Simon Frith's phrase, the consumption of pop music is a particularly 'bodily matter' (1996: 274).

As well as encouraging a physical response in the listener, the consumption of pop music is also a 'bodily matter' in terms of physical appearance. One way this is registered is through the importance of particular dress codes to different types of pop music. The history of pop music is also a history of changing fashions, as pop fans have asserted their affiliation to particular genres of music by the clothes they wear, whether that be the oversized zoot suits sported by fans of Latin/Mexican swing jazz in 1940s America, the 'Rasta' style typical in the late 1970s UK reggae scene, or the 'baggy' look associated with rave culture in the late 1980s. In *Midnight Cowboy*, *Saturday Night Fever* and *Baby It's You*, all three of the male protagonists are particularly interested in their appearance. In the latter two cases, the way the characters dress is explicitly connected to a particular type of pop music (disco in the case of Tony (John Travolta) in *Saturday Night Fever*, the 1950s playboy in the case of Sheik (Vincent Spano) in *Baby It's You*). Without being as explicitly stated, Joe's (Jon Voight) cowboy outfit in *Midnight Cowboy* is also associated with the country-folk of 'Everybody's Talkin'', the song that provides him with a theme tune throughout the film.

The 'possession' of pop music on the part of the fan, then, is often demonstrated through the body. However, this possession is a psychological as well as a physical matter. Music in general has been considered to be an art form that is particularly adept at accessing the emotions of its listeners. Indeed, the idea that music resonates emotionally with the viewer in a way that other aspects of a film, such as dialogue, cannot, has provided a common justification for the necessity of the composed score. This view is represented by Claudia Gorbman:

> Music enters to satisfy a need to compensate for, fill in, the emotional depth not verbally representable. Bernard Herrmann [film composer]: 'The real reason for music is that a piece of film, by its nature, lacks a certain ability to convey emotional overtones. Many times in many films, dialogue may not give a clue to the feelings of a character...' All music, say [cultural theorists] Eisler and Adorno, 'belongs primarily to the sphere of subjective inwardness'. (1987: 67)

In the case of the commercial pop song, the fan can be seen to identify emotionally with three aspects of the song: its 'purely musical' qualities, which may prompt an emotional as well as physical response (in fact, the physical activity can be viewed as a particular expression of the emotional reaction); the lyrics, which fans can relate imaginatively to their own identities; and the star through whose performance the song is embodied. This type of identification gives an emotional justification for the physical display of affiliation to a particular piece of pop music. The pop fan demonstrates identification with a pop song by 'exterior' means because it also connects with them 'inside'.

When filmmakers include pop music in their fictional worlds, they exercise choice in deciding which of the cultural assumptions associated with it in terms of its consumption (as well as other aspects of its cultural resonance) are to be made relevant in the particular narrative context. The sequences from *Midnight Cowboy* and *Saturday Night Fever* display a number of similarities: they both feature their characters walking along the streets of New York, accompanied by a non-diegetic pop song; both characters display an interest in presenting themselves ostentatiously to the world around them. In *Midnight Cowboy*, Joe is a male prostitute hustling for business. In *Saturday Night Fever*, Tony is simply walking to work, but he does so in a manner which suggests a desire to differentiate himself from the crowd, something that is illustrated later through his performances on the disco dance floor.

The sequence from *Midnight Cowboy* makes use of 'Everybody's Talkin'' in a way which privileges the psychological or interior affiliations between pop song and film character. By contrast, in the opening sequence of *Saturday Night Fever*, more emphasis is placed on understanding the character's identification with the song ('Stayin' Alive') through physical or exterior means. In neither case, however, do the filmmakers present an unproblematic fit between song and the character's identity.

Many of the songs discussed in the rest of this study act as ideal identities against which the viewer can judge the characters' actual situations. As suggested at the end of the previous chapter, Joey's performances in *Pal Joey* offer an example of song and character being coordinated to produce just such an ideal identity. In neither the sequence from *Midnight Cowboy* nor *Saturday Night Fever* are character and song allowed to cohere to produce this type of ideal representation. Instead, in *Midnight Cowboy*, a certain attachment is made between the song and aspects of Joe's state of mind, but the viewer is discouraged from understanding the music simply as a representation of the character's subjectivity. In *Saturday Night Fever*, moments of 'ideal' coordination between character and song are made to co-exist with moments where these attachments falter. Both of these examples prepare the ground for the extended analysis of *Baby It's You* in chapter four. This film interrogates, throughout the entire course of its narrative, the differences between the ideal identities seemingly offered by the pop song and the actual existence of the characters whose lives the songs accompany.

The 'psychological' attachment between song and character: 'Everybody's Talkin'' in *Midnight Cowboy*

Harry Nilsson's country-tinged ballad 'Everybody's Talkin'' accompanies the hustler Joe Buck at various points in *Midnight Cowboy*. In the sequence in which he walks around New York for the first time, apparently on the look out for rich women to pick up, the song is affiliated, to a certain extent, with Joe's subjective experience of finding himself in a new environment. However, the relationship between song and character and the other elements of the fictional world remain deliberately detached. Despite moving to New York to find his fortune, Joe's identity is constructed through an attachment between song and character that only serves to highlight the indifference to Joe displayed by the world around him. Furthermore, the song is used to propose an ideal identity with which to combat the city's indifference that Joe fails to claim as his own.

The invitation to understand the attachment between song and character as psychological rather than physical is made, in part, by the lack of formal interaction between the music and image. In this sequence, there are no rhythmic matches between song and image. Shot transitions occur in the middle of lines or cut across melodic phrases, whilst Joe's movement does not correlate to the pace of the music.

The song first appears in tandem with a deliberately disorderly image and in the company of soundtrack elements which reduce the impact of its introduction (in terms of showcasing its musical qualities). In the first shot of the sequence, the camera zooms up from street level to Joe looking out from the window of his high-rise apartment. The speed of the zoom is so quick that it blurs his body until it is unrecognisable, and then halts suddenly, still a distance away from its intended target. This violent camera movement is the cue for the song to begin, but the arpeggiated guitar intro is disrupted by the sound of a car-horn beeping. The song's partial alignment with the perspective of Joe, discussed below, exists in a fictional world where other narrational devices are used to demonstrate a self-conscious lack of interest in Joe's activities. For instance, later in the scene shots pull from shop windows onto brief glimpses of Joe passing by (a pan from someone opening a safe; a zoom from a jewel in a display case), as if desperately trying to maintain an interest in charting his progress through the streets, even though there are so many distractions to lure that attention away.

Both song and character, through their country styling (whether that be the country folk-style of the music or the cowboy outfit worn by Joe), exhibit qualities that jar with the city environment. Both are also made to struggle to align themselves with other aspects of the fictional world (as evidenced by the lack of formal interaction between song and image and the preponderance of framings that prevent Joe from being the centre of attention). In this way, the song can be seen to parallel the character's feelings at this particular moment: both are struggling to fit in.

However, the song also provides a more distanced commentary on Joe by proposing, through its lyrics, an 'ideal' solution to his situation which is not taken up by the character. In so doing, it offers an example of the pop song's ability both to represent a character's subjectivity and to indicate that character's limited understanding of his or her situation.

The lyrics to 'Everybody's Talkin'' are narrated by a character who is lost in reverie:

Everybody's talkin' at me
I don't hear a word they're saying
Only the echoes of my mind

People stopping staring
I can't see their faces
Only the shadows of their eyes

I'm going where the sun keeps shining
Through the pouring rain
Going where the weather suits my clothes
Banking off of the North East wind
Sailing on a summer breeze
And skipping over the ocean like a stone

Everybody's talkin' at me
I don't hear a word they're saying
Only the echoes of my mind
And I won't let you leave my love behind
I won't let you leave my love behind

The character in the song seeks protection from the real world by immersing himself in his own imagination. In the film as a whole, suggestions are made that Joe, too, lives in a kind of fantasy world. He is actually first heard, rather than seen, singing a song representing his anticipation of moving from his country home to New York, over a shot of a blank screen at a drive-in theatre. This immediately associates him with the world of fantasy represented by the movies. He is then shown grooming himself and striking poses in front of his bedroom mirror, intercut with shots of him addressing the camera directly to respond aggressively to his co-workers in the kitchen which he is evidently leaving behind. The direct address to camera and the disruptive nature of the intercutting imply quite clearly that these confrontational exchanges are taking place in his imagination (whether as memories or complete fabrications). The suggestion is made at the very start of the film that Joe's expectations of how he will cope in New York are based on a fantasy image of himself.

Joe's fantasy unravels after he arrives in New York and is forced to come to terms with the harsh realities of city life. However, at the point in the narrative considered in detail below, Joe has no understanding of the gap between his image of himself in the world and the reality of his situation. The scene could have been represented from Joe's point of view, to demonstrate how *he* imagined his arrival on the streets of New York to have been received. Had this been done, the sentiments of the song would have been aligned more straightforwardly with Joe's subjectivity: the characters in both song and film seek protection from the outside world by immersing themselves in their own imagination. However, this is not the way the sequence is actually constructed. Instead, the scene shows Joe attempting and failing to impose himself on the 'real world'.

The sequence makes an issue of, rather than wards off, the city's obliviousness to his presence. Shots marked as being from Joe's point of view do not just receive indifference from the women under his gaze. They also lead to a relay of shots that efface the presence of his look entirely. The second shot of the sequence films Joe from a distance, in the middle of a crowd, marked out by his distinctive hat, walking towards the camera. A closer shot singles him out further, chewing gum, swaggering his shoulders, and looking about. A glance to his right is followed by a cut to a woman shot ostensibly from his point of view: she is walking in the same direction (from right to left) as Joe, and the track from her side that traces her movement could be seen as a representation of Joe's gaze following her. However the tracking shot is considerably quicker than Joe's walking. Furthermore, this image is rapidly succeeded by a similar tracking shot of another woman walking in the opposite direction, from left to right, and then by a slower track from right to left that depicts a woman turning away from the camera and heading towards a shop window at the back of the frame (see overleaf). Joe's initial look becomes disorientated in shots that display a tangle of movement from right to left, left to right, right to left again, and then front to back.

Fig. 3.1

Fig. 3.2

A return to a tracking shot of Joe, now walking from left to right, on the left-hand side of the road, is followed by a similarly-paced tracking shot in the same direction of a group of women greeting each other. However, it is shot from the opposite side of the street, cars cutting across in the front of the frame, making it impossible to consider as a literal point-of-view shot.

Point-of-view shots are always only representations and approximations of what a character is meant to be seeing. Yet in this sequence, Joe's looks are mismatched in a deliberately sustained way. At one point he comes to a stop and looks ahead, as

Fig. 3.3

if someone has caught his eye. The next shot tracks behind a woman with a handbag draped over her shoulder, before cutting to a very brief head and shoulders' backward tracking shot of Joe striding after her. The return to the camera trailing behind the woman reinforces the impression that the image represents Joe's pursuit of her. However, the next shot cuts away from the chase completely and consists merely of a bus blurring quickly past the camera in extreme close-up. When we return to Joe, he is now at the shoulder of a different woman altogether. It is not just the case that Joe fails to catch

Fig. 3.4

Fig. 3.5

up with any of the women he pursues. His gaze is robbed of any authority, so that we cannot even be sure if the chase is taking place at all.

The relationship of the song to all of this is two-fold: firstly, an attachment is made between elements of the music and aspects of Joe's situation. Both strike a note of incongruity in the city setting, and neither song nor character is given support by the film's other narrational devices. The song also bears some relation to the character's subjective state of mind, in that its lyrics describe a character who lives in an 'interior' world, like Joe.

However, the song depicts a character who *knows* this to be the case, and who succeeds in protecting himself by immersing himself in his imagination. Joe, by contrast, is depicted trying and failing to impose the fantasy he has of himself on the outside world. In this way, 'Everybody's Talkin'' offers a vivid illustration of a pop song being used to propose an ideal identity which the character associated with the song cannot actually match. The repeated use of 'Everybody's Talkin'' throughout the film provides the opportunity to understand how Joe's situation relates to the ideal solution proposed by the song at any given moment.

The 'physical' attachment between song and character: 'Stayin' Alive' in *SaturdayNight Fever*

The opening credit sequence of *Saturday Night Fever* offers an example of the pop song enjoying a much more visible, 'physical' attachment to a particular character than is the case in the example discussed from *Midnight Cowboy*. As Tony walks through the streets of Brooklyn to the strains of the Bee Gees' 'Stayin' Alive', a coordination between character movement and pop song is achieved that resembles that more normally associated with the fully embodied performances that can take place in the musical (as was evidenced most strongly in the song sequences involving the title character in *Pal Joey*). In addition, a sense of the fictional world as a whole being shaped around the musical performance is provided by the manner in which various narrational devices (chiefly editing and shot composition) seem governed by particular rhythmic qualities of the song.

Apart from 'You My Love' in *Young at Heart*, 'Stayin' Alive' is the only song featured in this study that was composed specifically for its film. Although Tony does not literally sing the song as he walks through Brooklyn, and no on-screen source is provided to imply that Tony is actually listening to it, this scene *does*, in parts, resemble the song-and-dance sequence of the musical in its close choreography between song, performer and other aspects of the fictional world (*Saturday Night Fever* is, indeed, often described as a musical). As such, there are moments when Tony's character is understood as being embodied *fully* through the song and the way he performs in relation to it. At these points the distance between song and character is reduced to an absolute minimum, with the result that the viewer is encouraged to understand the identity of Tony as being revealed through the ideal identity of the song. However, the instances of maximum synchronicity between character, song and other narrational devices are also the moments in which Tony is depicted as occupying an abstract, fantastic environment rather than the actual streets of Brooklyn. This is a problem for a character who wishes to mark himself out as special within *this* particular social milieu, a desire most vividly expressed through his performances on the dance floor of the local disco, a venue which acts as a microcosm for the Brooklyn community as a whole.

'Stayin' Alive' plays non-diegetically over a title sequence in which the film's hero Tony struts down the streets of Brooklyn, pausing to chat up women, grab a bite of pizza and pop into a clothes' shop, the song fading out when he reaches the DIY store where he works. All the shots of Tony 'just' walking are cut to the beat of the song: two bars of 'Stayin' Alive's well-known opening riff accompany Tony's entrance, registered by a close-up of his shoe as he raises it to compare it to one in a shop window. At the end of the shot, he resumes his walk, the gliding motion of his foot coinciding with an upturn in the melody of the song which leads to the introduction of the swooping strings that rise at the beginning of the next image. This melodic escalation and addition of strings suggests an increase in musical intensity, and this is registered in the mise-en-scène by having the camera pushed back by Tony's pounding gait. This retreating of camera establishes Tony's irresistible ability to forge through space, to define his own channel of movement. The alignment of this power with the rhythm of the song is intensified by having each footfall stamp onto the pavement in time with the accented snare drums. This shot appears twice more, on both occasions at the beginning of the section that signals an ascent to the song's chorus ('and now it's all right, it's OK'), the driving back of the camera equated to the doubling of the song's efforts as it drives towards its refrain.

As the singing of the first verse begins, there is a cut to a backward tracking shot that pans up from Tony's feet to his upper torso, his shoulders swaying in time to the music. The image places Tony at its centre, the railway bridge to his right and the buildings to his left meeting at a point behind his head and stretching out in a pronounced perspective to the opposite edges of the frame. Additionally his movement is singled out as being particularly attuned to the rhythm of the song, with people cutting across the frame behind him or walking the opposite way, but with no one moving toward the camera in his direction. The camera accommodates Tony's rhythmic swagger by tracking backward at his pace, the shot covering the verse until it reaches the bridge that ascends to its chorus (where it is superseded by the close-up of his feet). The second verse is filmed in the same manner, a backward tracking view of Tony, now eating pizza, followed by the close shot of his feet.

Three other shots, which occupy two each of the first six bars of the second chorus, are cut to the beat of the song, all of them presenting Tony's body as being lost in musical rhythm. The first two are mirror images of each other, taken from angles that suggest they are filmed with the camera pointing upwards from a position around Tony's feet. The first shot has Tony's body (from waist up) canted to the right, blue sky behind him, the railway bridge creeping into the top-left corner of the frame. The second pictures him tilted to the left, the buildings cutting across the right corner of the frame. The next shot returns to the perspectival image with Tony's head at its centre that occurred at the start of the first verse.

Fig. 3.6

Fig. 3.7

Fig. 3.8

The odd angles of the first two shots result in an abstraction of the objects which surround Tony. The bridge and buildings in these shots appear to float at the top of the screen, as a kind of frame for Tony's performance (rather than appearing more straightforwardly as part of the busy backdrop in front of which Tony walks as is the case in other parts of the sequence). The sense of these objects as frames for Tony's moving body in these shots is intensified by the manner in which they are made to 'rhyme' with each other (the bridge cutting across the left corner of one shot, the buildings cutting across the right corner of the other). The symmetry of the following shot is also highly stylised, turning a bustling, cluttered street into a corridor that Tony's movement perfectly bisects. The close-ups of his feet, meanwhile, are so tightly choreographed to the pulse of the song, that the pavement gains the character of a percussive instrument, his shoes rapping out the beat. Every shot in which Tony appears to be most attuned to the rhythm of the song is marked by the suggestion that in doing so he transcends the real space of the busy streets around him.

These moments of transcendence are not maintained throughout the entire sequence. Whenever Tony becomes engaged with the life of the streets, either through contact with fellow pedestrians or by diverting his path into the neighbouring shops, the rhythmic presentation of his walking falters. The first shot that does not accompany a regular number of bars of music is also the one in which Tony's thrusting swagger is interrupted for the first time. The end of the opening verse and most of the chorus runs over a long shot of Tony walking along the street, pausing as a woman going the other way catches his eye, chasing back after her, before thinking better of it and picking up his stride once more.

It is not just the narrative detail (failing to pick up a woman) that delivers a blow to the confidence with which Tony has hitherto strutted along. The whole composition of the frame denotes a weakening of attachment between the music and his body and of the effect this combination has in 'musicalising' the image (by which I mean the or-ganisation of all the elements in a shot to provide a frame for Tony's rhythmic movement). Tony's figure is no longer central to the frame. The perspective of the previous upper-torso backward tracking shot has been lost, shop fronts stretching off to the right without the balance of the railway bridge on the left. With the names of the supporting cast obscuring Tony's body at the beginning of the shot, the most striking line of motion in the frame is supplied by a train which cuts across the back at the top of the screen from left to right, diverting attention away

Fig. 3.9

from Tony's trajectory of movement towards the camera. A closer view of the train cutting across from left to right, with diegetic sound spreading over the song, is in fact the image that succeeds this shot, cutting in off the beat as the Bee Gees harmonise on an elongated '…alive'. Additionally the increased distance between camera and body allows passers-by to cut in front of him or become visible walking in the same direction, thereby compromising the unique attention given to his particular strutting in the previous shots. The visible stutter in Tony's stride is surrounded by a mise-en-scène that has already placed in the balance his efforts to impose his presence on his environment.

Tony's thrusting forward, emphasised by the backward tracking of the camera, is the key to the differentiation of his movement. The camera movement contained in the first shots of the film, before the music starts, shifts *across* the frame: an aerial pan sweeps from left to right across Brooklyn Bridge; a train exits the right-hand side of the screen, and then is viewed from the back, pulling away from the left of the frame. Tony's first paces also take place on a horizontal axis, but his act of turning the corner, accompanied by swooping strings as the music hits its stride, is the moment his movement is singled out as unique. However, the narrative landmarks of this sequence all divert him from his forward trajectory, whether he is buying a pizza (chronicled in a shot/reverse-shot that cuts across the street rather than along it), darting into the clothes store to order his shirt, or chasing after another woman (the backward tracking shot abandoned in favour of a forward tracking point-of-view shot that ends up filming the street from the opposite direction and excludes Tony from the frame entirely).

The moments in which Tony is most closely attached to the music physically are also the moments where he is depicted as being most removed from the real-life hustle-

and-bustle of the Brooklyn streets through which he walks. One section of 'Stayin' Alive', obscured by dialogue in this sequence, begins with the lyric 'life goin' nowhere'. The repetition of exactly the same upper-torso tracking shot at the end of the second chorus as was used at the beginning of the first verse, suggests that Tony's self-confident swagger is not actually getting him anywhere. The rhythmic qualities of the song provide a base upon which Tony is shown to construct a sense of his physical identity. However, at the same time the attachment robs him of a culturally-specific identity (he loses his connection with a particular social environment). In its very first moments, then, *Saturday Night Fever* suggests that Tony's physical investment in music, later embodied in scenes where he dances to diegetic music (that is to say music which appears as a narrative element, rather than in a narrational role), will not be enough on its own to provide him with a secure sense of identity within his community.

Conclusion

Both the sequences discussed in this chapter make reference to assumptions about the pop song's role in the process of forming identities. However, each of them does so with a productive sense of cynicism. The characters do not simply take on the identities proposed by the songs. Instead a distance is left between the song's qualities (whether musical or lyrical) and the character's activities. The establishing of this distance allows the viewer to understand each character through the *constructed relationship between* character and song, rather than accepting the song simply as a reflection of the character. Even when the distance between character and song is reduced to a minimum, as it is at times in the *Saturday Night Fever* sequence, other aspects of the scene serve to contextualise such moments and question their 'ideal' nature (that is, is being 'lost in music' really an effective way for Tony to construct a sense of his own identity if it is seen to remove him from the very social environment in which he wishes to shine?).

The next, final chapter features an extended analysis of *Baby It's You*. The film provides an appropriate conclusion to this study, as it engages with all the aspects of the pop song's use in narrative film discussed so far.

4. Pop music culture and screen identities

Baby, It's You: two-part structure

John Sayles' *Baby, It's You* from 1983 focuses upon the relationship through high school and beyond of two teenagers, both of whom seek a sense of self through excessive role-playing: middle-class Jill (Rosanna Arquette) as an aspiring actress; and the working-class Italian-American Sheik (Vincent Spano) as a would-be singer in the style of his hero Frank Sinatra. In its use of pop songs from the period (the film is set in 1966 and 1967) and through the anachronistic non-diegetic presence of Bruce Springsteen songs from the 1970s, the film casts its music as an element in Jill and Sheik's role-playing and as a commentary upon them, as both individuals and as a couple. At the same time, the film also undermines the music's status as a source of ideal identities by the nature of the narrative action it is asked to accompany.

Baby, It's You, unusually for a 'teen romance', splits its action between high school and college, rather than choosing between the two. Paramount, the film's backers, were sceptical about this two-part structure, as writer-director Sayles explains:

> My distanced opinion on it is that they had seen *Valley Girl* and *Porkys* and *Fast Times at Ridgemont High* and felt, 'Jeez, we could have a big hit high school comedy' and *Baby, It's You* just was never going to turn into a high school comedy. So they said to me, 'Look, the high school section is really great, and we really want to cut down on the college parts, because it's kind of long and it's kind of a downer. (Smith 1998: 92)

A re-edit by Jerry Greenberg was rejected by Sayles, who threatened to take his name off the credits should the film come out in that form. Eventually, Paramount backed down and Sayles retained the right to the final cut.

The extension of the narrative into Jill's first year at college and Sheik's attempts to make it as a singer in Miami is crucial to the film's use of pop music as a source of possible identities and to its reflections upon the nature of this provision. The two parts reflect on each other more generally, being paralleled in terms of location, narrative progression, rhyming characters and in repeated references by Jill in the second half to events that had occurred in the first. The care with which these parallels are set up is indicated in the first four scenes of each section, which echo each other exactly in terms of location:

Section One	Section Two
School	University
Drama hall	Drama class
Jill at home with parents	Parents reading letter from Jill
School canteen	University canteen

The two parts also close with parallel sequences – of Sheik driving frantically and with the school/college prom. Both also include one sequence away from each section's two main sites of action, Jill and Sheik's hometown of Trenton, New Jersey, and Jill's university. In the first section, Sheik persuades Jill to skip school and drive out to Astbury Park, and, in the second, Jill visits Sheik in Miami. These two sequences in turn reflect upon each other in their dramatic structure. In the first, Jill and Sheik drive out to the pier and walk along the beach before dancing to Frank Sinatra, playing on a diner jukebox. They then kiss goodbye passionately by Sheik's car. The Miami sequence also opens with Jill driving towards and walking along a beach, this time with an old school-friend. The diner episode is echoed by Jill's arrival at the bar where Sheik is making a living lip-synching to Frank Sinatra: he has become the jukebox. Finally, their passionate car-side kiss is paralleled in the unsatisfying sexual encounter undertaken by the couple in Sheik's apartment, and their cold goodbye at the airport.

If the Miami sequence recalls the Astbury Park episode, but replays it with characters who have conspicuously drifted apart from one another, the various pieces of music that accompany the scenes are just as telling in their different dramatic roles. In the first, Ben E. King's 'Stand By Me' strikes up powerfully on the soundtrack as Sheik and Jill hit the road, whilst in the diner Sheik tells Jill what buttons to press on the jukebox to select Sinatra's 'Strangers in the Night'. I will attend to the specific alliance of music and narrative action and the sonic profiling of the songs later, but it is enough to note now that there is at least an indication that 'Stand By Me' expresses what the characters feel at that moment and that 'Strangers in the Night' helps Sheik to deliver a performance of feeling in front of Jill. 'Stand By Me' takes its place in, and seems in its lyric to aptly comment upon, a familiar display of transcendent coupledom: as long as Sheik and Jill remain true to each other, they can overcome the social divides that threaten to tear them apart. Sheik manufactures a moment of intimacy on his terms in the diner by encouraging Jill to put on the Sinatra track.

By contrast, the Miami sequence is typical of the film's concluding section in its refusal to allow music a role in the representation of characters' emotional states. This episode signals Sheik's reappearance into the narrative after his absence from the opening of the second part. His miming to Sinatra (and, later, 1960s crooner Jack Jones) is both a humbling display of his lack of progress in becoming a successful performer in his own right and a vocal reminder of how much the presentation of his character in the first section had relied on the musical voices of others. In the opening section, Sheik reveals his obsession with Sinatra, but it is accompanied non-diegetically and anachronistically by Bruce Springsteen songs from the 1970s. The suggestion that Sheik's performance is enabled, rather than simply accompanied, by the Springsteen songs, is discussed below, but his miming to Sinatra here puts such a suggestion in an entirely transparent form: the tape of Sinatra singing is literally what allows the performance to take place. This episode brings the contrivance of Sheik's performance onto a concrete diegetic level.

In Jill's case, the first section of the film shows her incorporating the music she listens to into her efforts of self-display, whether dancing in front of the mirror to 'Stop!

In the Name of Love', or singing 'Chapel of Love' with her friends in the car as they tease her about her relationship with Sheik. As we will see, the film, even in its opening section, reflects upon, rather than merely represents, this spectacle of Jill performing to pop. However, in the second part, Jill is pointedly disinterested in the music that plays in the background. She crouches disconsolately in the corner of the college disco as a 1960s beat band thrash out a soundtrack for the raucous crowd. 'Venus in Furs', Velvet Underground's paean to sado-masochism, plays in a student's room as Jill regales her fellow dorm residents with yet another story about Sheik. Finally, the 'unapplied' nature of the music in relation to Jill is asserted to such an extent that Simon and Garfunkel's 'Bookends' album moves quietly from track to track in the background whilst Jill casually asks her new friend Steve if he wants to sleep with her.

Jill is unconcerned about the music she hears in the second half of the film, and the attachments made between her character and a song when it appears non-diegetically in this section also indicate that pop music is no longer as important to the construction of her identity as it had been. The first song of the second section is Procul Harum's 'Whiter Shade of Pale', which plays quietly (non-diegetically) as Jill's mother reads aloud a letter from her daughter describing her first semester. The visual montage of events of the past term that accompanies the letter clearly contradicts much of what she has written: as her mother reads that Jill is taking the 'wonderful opportunity to make friends among people I would never have met in Trenton', we see her walking to her room alone and then sitting on her bed, morosely inspecting a sandwich. Her letter claims that she is concentrating on her acting skills rather than worrying about the size of the parts she gets, yet we see Jill looking deflated as she scans a cast list to see if her name is included.

Significantly, 'Whiter Shade of Pale' does not take part in this mismatching of information: it simply indicates the period to which the action has now moved (1967). The letter montage signals that pop will no longer be associated with Jill in order to express her subjectivity. In so doing, it draws a line under the tendency of the first half of the film to first propose, and then increasingly call into question, homologies between different types of music and different types of character.

Suggesting homologies between music and character

Jill's singing of 'Chapel of Love' in the car with her friends is indicative of the film's perspective on pop music as a source of identity that can only be utilised as such through self-conscious performance. After quizzing Jill about her recent first date with Sheik, her friends serenade her with a chorus from the song (Jill soon joins in), a Number One hit for girl-group The Dixie Cups, of the period in which the film is set. This scene could be regarded as paying testament to a popular notion of how closely teenage girls related to girl-group pop in the early 1960s. Susan Douglas, for example, states:

> The most important thing about this music, the reason it spoke to us so powerfully, was that it gave voice to all of the warring selves inside us struggling, blindly and with

a crushing sense of insecurity, to forge something resembling a coherent identity … In the early 1960s, pop music became the one area of popular culture in which adolescent female voices could be clearly heard. (1994: 77)

In *Baby, It's You*, Jill is indeed associated initially with girl-group songs, but the songs are never made to 'speak' for her in a transparent manner. 'Chapel of Love' follows a conversation which has dwelt on Sheik's incongruity, in terms of both race and class, as a suitor for Jill. The song is sung mockingly, rather than seriously, as if the simplicity of its romantic scenario ('going to the chapel and we're gonna get married') bears no relation to the complexities of Jill and Sheik's socially-problematic relationship. Throughout its course, *Baby, It's You* hints at a homology between the gender, class and race of its characters and particular types of music, only for the strength of those attachments to founder as the musical sequences are enacted.

The film opens conventionally for a teen movie, by introducing two lead characters occupying disparate positions within the rigorously defined social order operating in their high school. The rock'n'roll song 'Woolly Bully' by Sam the Sham and the Pharaohs has been playing over the titles, and continues throughout the opening sequence. The transition from the credits is signalled by the sound of the school bell whereupon the film fades into a shot of an empty school corridor. The bell prompts a speedy exodus from the classrooms to either side of the passageway, and the hall floods with students, the space suddenly awash with noise and movement in all directions. Out of the melée, the camera settles upon Jill and her three friends, tracking back to accommodate their movement. Clutching her books to her chest, Jill heads the group and leads the conversation, their chat finally resting on the forthcoming meeting of the sorority, of which Jill has been elected president. On the ringing of another school bell, Jill enters the classroom to the left, exiting the frame, as the corridor empties of bodies and noise as quickly as it had been filled.

Jill's movement is choreographed between the diegetic sound of the two school bells that frame her passage from one classroom to another. In this manner, despite the presence of a non-diegetic song on the soundtrack, she is located in 'school time'. Sheik is also introduced in this sequence but in contrast to Jill, moves in 'song time'. The ringing of the first bell heralds the subduing of 'Woolly Bully' on the soundtrack in favour of the sounds of the school and, in particular, Jill's chatter. Sheik's first appearance prompts both an interruption in Jill's conversation, a disruption of the smooth backward tracking shot that had chronicled her movement, and the re-emergence of the song to prominence on the soundtrack.

Underneath the dialogue, the song is about to reach its sax solo. Jill's description of a film she has just seen is interrupted when a boy greets her as he walks past. This acknowledgement of her existence causes great speculation amongst the girls, although Jill laughs off any suggestion of romance. Turned to her friend, rather than looking forward, she bumps into Sheik, who has emerged in the middle of the corridor, front of frame, with his back to the camera. At this point, the tracking shot is abandoned in favour of a glide into a mid-close shot of Sheik as he turns around coolly to appraise Jill. Up to this moment, the sax solo had aped the chugging rhythm of the song's verses, but in tandem with the glide in on Sheik the sax dips down the scale and then sallies upwards. A correlation is thereby suggested between the disruption of the regular pattern of the solo and the suspension of the smooth tracking shot, as well as a parallel between the movement upwards of the melody and the shot's gliding towards Sheik's face.

Fig. 4.1

There is a brief close shot of Jill as she looks at Sheik and begins to turn away, before a return to the tracking shot that dominates the sequence, Sheik remaining stationary in the background. The second bell clears the hall, leaving Sheik alone. At this point his movement is made to fall in time with the music. The impression is given that the singer's concluding cry, 'watch it now, here he comes!', triggers Sheik's movement, as he begins to stride towards the camera, his steps choreographed to chime with the emphatically slammed down guitar chords and snare beats that form the song's climax. In this manner, Sheik becomes associated with the wild bull of the lyrics. Sheik's brief entrance isolates him from the flow of students walking between classes, his movement associated instead with elements of a song (the sax solo and climax) that has no source in the diegesis and is otherwise subdued when attached to the activities of other characters in the scene.

Fig. 4.2

The opening sequence places Jill in a position of comfort in relation to her surroundings, whilst Sheik is isolated from them, not party to the movement from one room to the next marshalled by the school bells, and instead singled out through association with elements of 'Woolly Bully'. The next two musical sequences continue to secure Jill within the

Fig. 4.3

diegesis whilst identifying Sheik with a non-diegetic song whose narrational role is to mark his difference. The two scenes are also played out in such a way as to make the music on the soundtrack gender specific. Jill plays the intro to 'You Don't Have To Say You Love Me' by Dusty Springfield on her bedroom Dansette, a scene which is immediately followed by Sheik walking into the school canteen to the non-diegetic strains of Bruce Springsteen's 'It's Hard To Be A Saint In The City'. The first sequence is conveyed in one static shot and renders naturalistically the tinny sound coming from Jill's record player, whereas in the second the comparatively glistening production values of Springsteen's song are displayed to their best advantage without any competing diegetic sounds. Fur-

thermore, the sequence cuts around Sheik's strutting body to emphasise equivalences between Sheik and the streetwise character Springsteen sings about.

It has been common to equate cultural expressions of femininity with passivity and those of masculinity with activity. These two sequences throw those distinctions into sharp relief, Jill reclined on her bed, toying distractedly with her teddy bear, Sheik making his presence felt as he swaggers around the dinner hall. 'You Don't Have To Say You Love Me' shares with the film's title song, 'Baby, It's You', a lyric that

Fig. 4.4

describes a woman's self-sacrificing devotion to her partner. 'It's Hard To Be A Saint In The City', on the other hand, details a man ranging through the city streets, taking from them whatever he desires. The fact that one song is identifiably 'pop' and the other 'rock' also demonstrates an awareness of a familiar alliance between the feminine and pop and the masculine and rock. The manner in which the numbers are sonically presented inflects yet another assumption that stems from this division: the appeal of 'You Don't Have To Say You Love Me' lies in its ephemerality (it offers Jill comfort at that moment in her bedroom, but is also limited to that space); 'It's Hard To Be A Saint In The City' has a more pervasive and lasting stature, actually 'cheating' time (a 1970s rock song playing in a film set in the 1960s) and ranging over diegetic space and sound.

Problematising homologies between music and character

'You Don't Have To Say You Love Me' and 'It's Hard To Be A Saint In The City' both indulge conventionally-coded displays of feminine and masculine behaviour. However, these sequences also exhibit a strain between the situations which the songs accompany and the actual rendering of them. I have noted that Sheik's miming to Sinatra in the Miami bar in the second section of the film crystallises his lack of an original voice and reliance on his hero to provide him with a sense of identity. The school canteen sequence provides the first full expression of this self-conscious 'trying on' of musical personas, and in the process suggests the possibility that pop songs set the scene for on-screen action rather than simply accompanying it.

Bruce Springsteen's song is, in itself, concerned with performance. A first-person description of a man swaggering through the tough city streets, it makes constant recourse to simile or metaphor: he has 'skin like leather', 'the diamond-hard look of a cobra', bursts 'just like a supernova', walks 'like Brando right into the sun' and dances 'just like a Casanova'. The song describes its protagonist's activity by reference to phenomena outside of himself, just as Sheik's journey through the canteen relies on a deliberate manufacturing of alliances with the song for its impressive effect.

'Woolly Bully' brings itself to a full stop in a conspicuous manner: its emphatic guitar chords combine with the altered drum pattern (forsaking its rolling 4/4 rhythm by dropping the bass drum and hi-hat, leaving the snare to sound out in tandem with the guitar) to signal that the song has reached its climax. The beginning of 'It's Hard To Be A Saint In The City' is as self-consciously an introduction to a song as the 'Woolly Bully' ending is a climax. It features the musicians gearing up before launching into the swaggering attack of the main body of the song. The drummer taps his hi-hat whilst the guitarist tentatively strokes, rather than continuously strums, the opening chords, and the pianist plays a wandering melody which only acquires a coherent, vamping rhythm when the full drums kick in.

Fig. 4.5

This impression of getting musically organised plays over Sheik's own efforts at organisation, as he looks at his reflection in a pane of glass on the canteen door and combs his hair ('slicked sweet' in the manner described in the song later on), his actions choreographed exactly in sync with the first stroke of guitar and the two hi-hats that play underneath it. Satisfied with his appearance, Sheik walks into the canteen and stands by the entrance, surveying the scene. Two cutaways show students glancing over their shoulder or looking up, presumably in his direction. At this point, the song is still in its intro. When Springsteen begins to sing, the camera returns to Sheik in medium close-up. His first action is to turn his head to the right and shift his eyes from side to side. Springsteen, meanwhile, sings 'I had skin like leather and the diamond-hard look of a cobra'. Sheik's studied movement gives the impression that he is displaying his body in terms of the song (he is indeed tanned, and his gaze is steely). Furthermore, it is only at the end of this line that he begins to walk around the room, as the film cuts to a side-tracking shot. The deliberation with which Sheik is made to wait for Springsteen's lyric before moving emphasises the extent to which the song is instrumental in providing his movement with a sense of authority. Later, Sheik stands still during the piano crescendo that separates the first and second verse, and only moves when the singing starts again. The lyric,

Fig. 4.6

Fig. 4.7

'I could walk like Brando right into the sun', plays over a profile shot of Sheik, who turns his head on the mention of Brando and, at the end of the line, tips his finger. Without the presence of an on-screen recipient for Sheik's action, the gesture gives the impression of acknowledging the compliment of being compared to Brando by the song. Immediately after the following line 'dance like a Casanova', there are more cutaways to two girls looking towards him, the reference to the renowned lover in the song again seeming to encourage the display of on-screen action, rather than simply accompany it.

Without the presence of 'It's Hard To Be A Saint In The City' on the soundtrack, Sheik's pacing around the dinner hall would appear undynamic. The chief dramatic incident of the scene, after all, involves him stealing a French fry from someone's plate, an episode which is choreographed to a moment of musical drama in the song (the drums dropping out momentarily to foreground the racing electric-acoustic guitar). The deliberately uncanny synchronisation between Sheik's movement and the song begins to indicate his over-reliance on pop music to provide him with a sense of identity. In this way, the song is not made simply to 'speak for' Sheik throughout the sequence. Rather, his mannered movement suggests that the music is a necessary requirement if he is to be allowed to 'speak' in such a way at all.

The intro of 'You Don't Have To Say You Love Me' immediately precedes the canteen sequence as Jill listens to it in her room. The notion that this may be a natural choice to provide the soundtrack for Jill's passive posing on her bed is undermined, this time by manufacturing ambiguity over the state of mind Jill is in when she plays the song.

In the penultimate scene of *Baby, It's You*, Jill admits that she does not know what she wants. Throughout the film, she remains in a state of conjecture: dreaming about winning the lead part in the school play; fretting over whether she has been accepted to university; and then, once at college, retelling stories about her relationship with Sheik, even though she claims to have disowned him. In its opening sequences, the film performs a series of juxtapositions that cast doubts over what Jill is dreaming about at any one time.

The early sequences of the film indicate the two factors occupying Jill's mind: her audition for the school play and her first encounter with Sheik. After 'Woolly Bully' ends, towards the close of the first scene, Sheik is seen in close-up looking silently through the classroom window at Jill, who does not see him. The scene cuts to Jill's audition, where she immediately intones the line 'I dream about him all the time': the audition speech becomes a reciprocation of the interest Sheik displays in her in the previous shot. The next scene shows Jill returning home and discussing the importance of getting the main part in the play with her parents. She then goes into her room and puts on the Dusty Springfield record, apparently preoccupied with the outcome of the audition (she is meant to be doing her homework).

The question of what Jill is feeling as she lies on her bed listening to 'You Don't Have To Say You Love Me' is problematised by its positioning within a network of scenes that deliberately re-orientate the direction of her daydreams. The film undercuts the viewer's assumption that Jill is thinking about the audition by pairing the scene with Sheik's performance to 'It's Hard To Be A Saint In The City', the intro to 'You Don't Have To Say You Love Me' becoming a subdued preliminary to the bolder sound of the Springsteen song. 'It's Hard To Be A Saint In The City' fades out when Sheik begins to chat up Jill, in their first sustained encounter. The next scene features Jill daydreaming in class, writing something in her exercise book. At this point it would be plausible to assume she may be thinking about Sheik, but the film thwarts this expectation when it reveals that Jill has been drawing a picture of her own name up in lights.

I have argued that the use of 'Whiter Shade of Pale' over the montage of Jill's first weeks at college and the contradictory voiceover reading the letter she has written to her parents, signals the abandonment of any attempt to associate Jill's subjectivity with the music that accompanies her actions. However, the letter montage also compresses into one sequence this initial strategy of juxtaposing various narrative elements to call into question the version of events as they are presented by Jill. Even at the moments when alliances between Sheik and Jill with particular types of music are first being suggested, the film undermines the 'naturalness' of these alliances: in Sheik's case by marking his entrance into the canteen as a performance enabled rather than simply accompanied by the music; and in Jill's by resisting the characterisation of the song as 'giving voice' to her emotional state, by deliberately creating ambiguity about what that emotional state precisely is.

Viewing music from the 'wrong' perspective

A Bruce Springsteen track and girl-group song are subsequently used to undermine further the simple equation of Sheik with male rock and Jill with female pop. 'E Street Shuffle' by Springsteen and 'Baby, It's You' by the Shirelles both feature in sequences that deny the perspective that might be expected: namely, they become attached to the point of view of the 'wrong' character.

'E Street Shuffle' plays non-diegetically when Sheik takes Jill on their first date to Joey D's, an Italian-American bar which he frequents and which is obviously unfamiliar to Jill. Like 'It's Hard To Be A Saint In The City', the song provides a street-level view of the hustle of city life. Whereas in the first sequence, Sheik's attach-ment to the song is made to seem too dependent, here the scene is wrested from his perspective en-tirely, so that the energy of the song and its confi-dent appraisal of the environment it surveys are not registered visually. Instead the chance to see Sheik impose himself in his 'natural' habitat is deliberately confounded in favour of chronicling the far less dy-namic inter-action with the location offered by Jill's bewildered and bored glances around the bar.

Fig. 4.8

'Baby, It's You' also accompanies a sequence whose action would seem to make the choice of song inappropriate. The lyric concerns a woman's undying love for a man despite his indifference towards her:

It's not the way you smile that touched my heart
It's not the way you kiss that tears me apart
But many nights roll by, I sit alone at home and cry
Over you, what can I do?
I can't help myself, 'cos baby, it's you

Yet the scene features Sheik fruitlessly pursuing Jill after they have had an argument. Apart from the discrepancy in giving Sheik a female 'voice', there is another displace-

Fig. 4.9

ment involved. The song describes the woman's love as a passive longing, but Sheik's efforts are charac- terised by active harassment (soon after this scene, he even goes as far as kidnapping Jill). From the initial indication in the opening sequences that Jill and Sheik are to be connected with distinct types of music, the film reaches a point here where Sheik is accompanied by 'Jill's' music. The certainty with which the song can be related to character action is further problematised by the disparity between Sheik's behaviour and that narrated in the song. Both Sheik and the singer are convinced their lover is made for them, but each display exactly opposite methods of demonstrating their devotion (one longing passively, the other actively harassing). These acts of placing the pop song in 'inappropriate' relation- ships with the film's characters further call in to question pop music's ability to provide the characters with a secure sense of identity.

Pop music and cars

The concentration on the role of music in characters' performances within the film and its undermining through attachment to the 'wrong' perspective is borne out in *Baby, It's You*'s many driving sequences. The car has, of course, been a potent symbol of the rock'n'roll teenager's new spirit of autonomy and desire for escape from parental control. In addition, a familiar trope of the teen movie has been to combine driving sequences with the pop music that is seen to voice teenagers' desires (the most celebrated example being *American Graffiti* (George Lucas, 1973)). The film's first such scene over-deter- mines the car as a vehicle for teen seduction and its association with rock'n'roll, to the extent that Sheik's attempts to impress Jill by taking her for a spin in the 'Ratmobile' take on the character of a well-rehearsed ritual.

The episode is prefaced by a protracted, playful discussion between the couple as to whether Jill can accept Sheik's offer of a ride – a negotiation about whether they should engage in this particular teen rite of passage. Once in the car, the Isley Brothers' frantic version of 'Shout' strikes up immediately as Sheik hits the drive button. The two shots that follow, of Sheik pressing down on the accelerator and the car racing towards the ground-level camera, come so quickly that they could be said to approximate the song's dramatic kicking into gear: both car and song explode out of the blocks.

This overplayed connection between music and machine is developed as the car skids to a halt past Jill's female friends, who are looking on at the action in an unnaturally static pose, in a shot that lasts longer than might be expected, thereby signalling an abrupt end to the energetic pacing of the scene up until this point (see overleaf). The girls look like a professional panel of judges, coolly appraising Sheik and Jill's performance. As the car stops dead, the song simply grinds to a halt, mid-flow. The framing of the sequence as an elaborate performance is further emphasised by Jill and Sheik's final words before she steps out of the car. With Jill framed in the open car window and Sheik outside, leaning on the hood, they engage in a deadpan exchange: Sheik – 'You like to drive fast?'; Jill – 'I love it'. Sheik then pulls open the door and Jill gets out, both maintaining eye contact as Sheik says 'I'll see you tomorrow then?', to which Jill replies with a cocky 'Don't count on it'. Both Jill and Sheik sounds like actors delivering lines and their movements appear equally predetermined.

Fig. 4.10

Fig. 4.11

I have identified the girls' singing of 'Chapel of Love', the second sequence to combine music with driving, as a moment where the film's questioning of pop's ability to match itself to the emotional situations of the film's characters is brought onto a diegetic level (that is to say, as a narrative element commented upon by the characters themselves). The third sequence, describing Sheik and Jill's drive to Astbury Park and stroll on the beach, to the strains of Ben E. King's 'Stand By Me', may, as already intimated, seem to be attempting just such an unprob-

Fig. 4.12

lematic match: Sheik and Jill demonstrate their determination to stay together by playing truant from school, the institution in which their social differences are most keenly felt. However, yet again, the sequence is marked first as a performance of transcendent coupledom, and then undermined as such by refusing to make the bodies of the lovers the focus of the mise-en-scène, whilst the song plays on regardless.

Sheik initiates the episode as a self-conscious testing of the strength of their love, stepping out in the path of Jill's car to persuade her to skip school. The powerful introduction of 'Stand By Me' non-diegetically on the soundtrack follows from this dramatic intervention, but the song is deliberately contrasted to the drab, unemotional details the film presents as a chronicle of Jill and Sheik's day together. The early part of the sequence places an emphasis on the effort it takes for them to get to the coast, rather than on the intimate pleasures of the journey (Ben E. King's voice is heard powerfully over a series of aerial shots of the car or signs by the side of the road). The song's celebration of transcendence is contrasted to the actual mundane presentation of Jill and Sheik's interaction. Subsequently, the sequence features banal shots of the sea and deserted pier, keeping Jill and Sheik, when they are shown, at long distance.

Fig. 4.13

Fig. 4.14

Fig. 4.15

The only exception to this is the camera's recording of their conversation in the car and as the music peters out, on the pier, about Sheik's admiration for Frank Sinatra. He explains to an amused and bemused Jill that he admires Sinatra because of his sense of style and continuing acknowledgement of his working-class roots. Like Springsteen's 'It's Hard To Be A Saint In The City', Sinatra's persona offers Sheik a model of dignified, class-specific, masculine performance to which he can aspire. However, this monologue actually serves to remind Jill of their different cultural backgrounds (she offers Sheik the ultimate insult to his musical tastes: her parents like Sinatra). The only closely observed interaction between the two during 'Stand By Me', then, undermines any hope that the escape from school could provide them with an opportunity to forget their differences and focus on the strength of their attachment to each other.

John Sayles, in conversation with critic Gavin Smith, has agreed that the final driving sequence of the film, with Sheik racing to Jill's college from Miami to the sound of Bruce Springsteen's 'Adam Raised A Cain', is the point at which his maintenance of a self-conscious pose is abandoned:

Smith: Sheik is gradually stripped of his identity during this sequence. By the time he finds Jill, he's become a real person for the first time, he's no longer playing a character.

Sayles: Yes. He doesn't believe that he is going to be the next Frank Sinatra anymore. As he says in the argument with her, 'I'm going to be a garbageman like my father'. He's gotten to that point. (Smith 1998: 99)

Both sections of *Baby, It's You* head towards their climax with Sheik driving frantically, accompanied by a Springsteen song. Each episode details a point of crisis in Sheik's keeping up of appearances. If the first section concentrates upon Sheik's self-styling of his own difference from the rest of the school and confrontation with authority (leading to his expulsion), it closes with a more serious clash: whilst the prom night from which he has been barred takes place, he and his friend Rat break into the town's costume-hire shop, leading to a car chase with the police and forcing Sheik to flee to Miami. The sequence, accompanied by Springsteen's 'She's The One', opens with a shot that comments in absurd fashion on the manner in which Sheik has stylised his 'otherness' throughout the high school section. The opening scene associates Sheik with 'Woolly Bully' to imply that he is a kind of wild animal in relation to the other school kids. The raid on the costume-hire shop begins with a slow pan from Rat, standing guard with a gun, to Sheik at the till, both wearing ridiculous plastic rat masks as disguise. In between them, as 'She's The One' begins, we see two sharply dressed mannequins displayed in the shop window, as if to remind the two thieves of the prom night to which they have been denied access. The shot visualises with 'real' masks and dummies Sheik's adoption of different poses to enact his difference in earlier sequences.

The sequence develops into a frantic car chase, the police coming into view at precisely the moment the song moves from its low-key verses, buoyed by a tinkling piano, which had been subdued under the screech of the Ratmobile and the conversation in Jill's car as a police siren wails past her. An electric guitar suddenly crashes out chords to a Bo Diddley beat, whilst Springsteen yelps, and the Ratmobile skids around the corner with the police car on its tail. The interest here is that the music's affective role in the sequence is purely percussive: the song moves into a more dramatic register at the same time that the car chase gets into full swing. There is none of the (over) careful choreography to narrative action or deliberate mismatching of music to narrative event that had characterised pop's use in the preceding sequences.

The same is true of the relationship built between 'Adam Raised a Cain' and Sheik's angry drive to Jill's college, and subsequent trashing of her room. Sheik has been sacked from his job miming to Sinatra and in a rage storms out of the restaurant, steals a car and heads for Jill. When he reaches the college, he impatiently demands to be shown to her room, where he is outraged by the visible signs of how much they now inhabit different worlds (he tears down a modish poster, pulls out the clothes from her drawers and discovers she is on the pill).

Fig. 4.16

The song is, in itself, conspicuously full of rage, at one point hitting an extended crescendo where the whole band just pummel one note, and resolving in a ferocious call and response between singer and backing band of the title line. It is displayed as unambiguously, and simply, the soundtrack to Sheik's aggression. It even stops completely when the film cuts mid-song to Jill, and re-enters as Sheik finally pulls into the college.

Fig. 4.17

As Gavin Smith notes, Sheik's identity is stripped down in the sequence. Motifs from the musical episodes of the first section are reprised without the same degree of stylisation: as in 'Woolly Bully', Sheik strides towards the camera as he storms out of the restaurant, but not, on this occasion, in time to the music. The driving montage recalls the 'Stand By Me' sequence, but this time the focus is on Sheik's face, rather than fetishising the car as a romantic symbol of rebellion in itself. Finally, Sheik's careful look at his own reflection at the beginning of the 'It's Hard To Be A Saint In The City' episode is re-enacted here, but now he surveys his weary, dishevelled appearance in a dirty truck-stop mirror. As John Sayles notes, the music acts to give a general sense of desperate energy to the scene:

Fig. 4.18

> I wanted this thing to actually build, to just push the thing forward so I used the Springsteen song 'Adam Raised A Cain' and it's very driving, percussive music. I just needed to keep his anger going through this whole sequence and have that feeling of 'I'm going to get there'. (Smith 1998: 99)

Both 'She's the One' and 'Adam Raised A Cain' are attached unironically to their action, yet this suggestion that the music is attuned to the emotional level of the events it accompanies also makes it relatively inarticulate in relation to the specific details of the scenes. Throughout *Baby, It's You*, pop's propensity to be used in the forging of identity is foregrounded and scrutinised. However, the notion that Sheik's 'true' emotions are finally being revealed in the closing sequences of each section requires that this interrogation into pop's role in self-display is temporarily suspended. The result is pop music that works in the manner of the conventional composed score, providing musical resonance to sensations already present on-screen. The consideration of pop as involved in a particular type of self-conscious social performance, a characterisation so fundamental to the music's representation in the rest of the film, must be suppressed if these two Springsteen songs are to achieve a degree of 'sincerity' in mapping on-screen emotions.

Conclusion

Baby, It's You ends with a return to the spectacle of pop music being used to enable a public performance of identity. After Sheik has confronted Jill in her room, and both have admitted to their disappointment at not having found a 'role' with which they feel comfortable, Jill convinces Sheik to be her partner at the college prom. The live 'garage' band respond to their unusual request to play 'Strangers In The Night' and, as they dance, the camera spirals up and away from them, Sinatra's own version taking over on the soundtrack, heard, at last, in its 'ideal' form. Sayles comments on this scene:

> What they finally do is a performance – a performance with each other so other people will see them. They could spend the night talking. Instead, what they don't do, because she understands him and how important display is to him, and she understands to a certain extent she has to make a statement in front of these other people, is sit in the room and talk all night – they go out and do a performance. (Smith 1998: 82)

The achievement of *Baby, It's You* is to identify, enact and provide a perspective upon the specific role of pop in the forging of identity. A popular model of the classic orchestral score relies on the music being characterised as operating from the 'inside-out': the score expresses musically what the characters are 'really' feeling. *Baby, It's You* explores the consequences of characterising its music as working determinedly from the 'outside-in': being taken on by its characters in their efforts of self-display.

John Sayles comments that Jill and Sheik are forced to face up to and reject 'some things in the romanticism of the songs' and that he uses 'the music to inflate something that is then deflated' (Smith 1998: 83, 101). The cultural assumption that pop music does offer its listeners potential ideal identities, as discussed in the previous chapter, means that the self-conscious, performative aspects of people's collusion with various types of music can be at the forefront of its representation in films, whether that collusion be romanticised or critiqued, as happens in *Baby It's You*. It is significant that the opening school hall sequence in *Baby, It's You* does not end precisely with the climax of 'Woolly Bully'. Sheik's pacing towards the camera may be synchronised with the final chords of the song, but continues after the music has stopped. Alone in a corridor suddenly evacuated of noise and bustle, Sheik looks in at Jill in her class, before continuing his walk along the empty hall. A strutting bull with the music, wandering alone without it, *Baby, It's You* is as interested in what happens to its characters when they are robbed of their soundtrack as it is in interrogating the music's role in their acts of self-display.

CONCLUSION

This study has been concerned with mapping out the potential in narrative cinema to provide a perspective on the spectacle of characters performing, responding or being linked to a pop song in a variety of ways, with varying degrees of awareness or non-awareness (ranging from singing a song on-screen to being accompanied by music which they cannot ostensibly hear). A final example, from Quentin Tarantino's 1997 film *Jackie Brown*, incorporates many of the strategies I have identified which attach pop songs to a particular character. The relationship between pop song and film character in this instance moves from one whereby the attachment between the two is initially very partial, to a much closer relationship by its conclusion, in which it is suggested that the title character deserves to be aligned with the ideal identity proposed by the song.

The credits sequence of *Jackie Brown* begins with the sounds of Bobby Womack's early 1970s soul track 'Across 110th Street', its wah-wah guitar and swooping strings intro heard over the logos for 'Miramax Films' and Tarantino's own production company 'A Band Apart'. The screen fades to black just as Womack is about to let out a melismatic

Fig. 5.1

'wooh', which actually finds visual accompaniment by a shot of a wall consisting of a chunky mosaic of pale and dark blue strips, arranged in a haphazard order. After a stab of strings, a second 'wooh' and another orchestral punch, Womack begins singing the first verse, which acts as a cue for the film's eponymous heroine, evidently an air-hostess, and played by Blaxploitation star Pam Grier, to enter the picture. With her upper torso profiled at the right of the frame, she is carried along by a moving walkway, the camera tracking by her side at its pace, so that Jackie remains at the frame's edge. At the end of the first verse, and on the cymbal splash that accompanies the movement to the chorus, the title of the film unfurls from screen left, rendered in big yellow bubble letters.

Five elements here may be offered as evidence that Tarantino is simply indulging the retro-hip tastes for which his films are renowned: the allusion to the similar opening shot of *The Graduate* (Mike Nichols, 1967), which features Dustin Hoffman being carried along on a moving walkway to the non-diegetic strains of 'Sounds of Silence'; the discernibly '1970s' combination of choppy guitar, orchestral swell and soulful black voice on the soundtrack; the chunky, somewhat garish (a rainbow of colours are revealed as Jackie glides past) mosaic on the wall; the presence of 1970s icon Pam Grier, 'rescued' from obscurity by the director's patronage; and the bright, bubblegum font selected to spell out the film's title.

However, the precise orchestration of sound and image and the subsequent action of the sequence work to put this somewhat posed opening into perspective. If Jackie is immediately associated with the lyrics of the song by the choreography of her entrance exactly as the first verse begins, it is also clear that there is a shortfall in the impact of this association. Bobby Womack moves from heavenly 'wooh-ing' to a declamatory vocal style for the verse, his words tumbling out in increasingly uneven metre, as if he is struggling to fit in a description of all the ills that surround him:

I was the third brother of five
Doing whatever I had to do to survive
I'm not saying what I did was all right
Trying to break out of the ghetto was a day to day fight
Been down so long, ain't nothing not crossed my mind
But I knew there was a better way of life that I was just trying to find
You don't know what you'll do until you're put under pressure
Across 110th Street is a hell of a tester

The urgency of Womack's delivery, with the music chattering insistently behind him, is contrasted to the curiously serene view of Jackie, penetrating the frame at first, but her features frozen thereafter, and her movement a matter of being conveyed by the walking pavement rather than by her forging through space.

The static pose of Jackie in the first shot does act as a statement of the film's 'off-beat' credentials, offering a concentrated view of a lead character in a Hollywood movie who is not only mature (*Jackie Brown* makes an issue of the age of its characters throughout), but African-American and female as well. Her immobile position on the right of the frame also allows the viewer to contemplate the star names listed on the left of the image (Bridget Fonda, Robert De Niro, Samuel L. Jackson, Michael Keaton). However, this exaggerated sense of Jackie's entrance precisely as an introduction (perhaps also to welcome Pam Grier back to the 'big time' after such a long absence), does jar with the song, which has descended from the heavens to the hurly-burly of life in the Harlem ghetto. The sudden halting of the tracking shot after the chorus, so that Jackie is carried off-screen by the moving pavement, adds to the impression that in her first shot Jackie is being offered as an object to be contemplated rather than as a character whose personality can begin to be judged. In this first shot, then, a certain distance is constructed between song and a film character who has yet to fully 'come to life'. However, the dramatic potential of creating such a distance can only be evaluated with reference to the sequence's subsequent progress.

A distance between 'Across 110th Street' and the events it accompanies continues to be contrived in *Jackie Brown*'s second shot. When, after the chorus, the song returns to the luscious between-verse 'wooh-ing' that punctuates Womack's grittily descriptive lyrics, the image conversely begins to engage with the quotidian detail of the film's opening location only previously apparent in Jackie's sporting of an air-hostess' uniform. Over the break between chorus and second verse are two shots detailing the airport's security checks: a shot of the X-ray machine screen and a pan down a woman's T-shirt as she is scanned by a metal detector.

The first shot of Jackie contrasts her stylised introduction with the plunging of the song into no-nonsense description; the shots of the X-ray machine and metal detector introduce the activities of the 'real world' at the same time the song takes respite from the world it describes in its verses. However, during the course of the sequence, this wilful mismatching between music and image becomes ever less apparent, as Jackie ceases simply to be an object of contemplation, her actions becoming more attuned to the bustling character of the song.

This process begins after the metal detector shot, with the camera pivoting from right to left to follow a now walking and talking Jackie moving past the X-ray machine and greeting its attendant, the shot taking in the whole of the room. This is choreographed with the bridge line to the second verse ('I got one more thing I'd like to talk to you all about right now'). At this point, Jackie is placed for the first time within the 'real' environment that had been withheld in her first shot.

The following three shots, each taking up two lines of the song, make Jackie's movement appear special within the frame, without freezing that special attention into spectacle as in the first shot. Jackie is first fully profiled in a side shot that places her in the centre of the image, in terms of width and depth, as she walks through the bright, marbled departure lounge, her steps traversing the luminous pools cast from the overhead spotlights. The frame is expansive enough also to take in the movements of those around her, all of whom walk in the opposite direction. A backward tracking shot follows, with Jackie viewed from just below waist up, swaggering towards the camera, before giving way to a profile shot of Jackie's face on the right of the frame, with blurred figures passing in the background on the left.

These three shots, capturing Jackie walking with assurance through her workplace, align themselves to the song's confident rhythmic swagger, the shots evenly edited and Jackie's movement poised. The increasing attachment between 'Across 110th Street' and Jackie's movement is part of the sequence's building of narrative momentum: as Jackie becomes more attuned to qualities audible in the song, her movement also becomes more integrated within a more 'active' (rather than posed, as in the first shot) type of fictional world.

In these three shots, Jackie's assured passage through the airport finds a correlation with the song's lyrics as well as its rhythm. Whilst Womack acknowledges the dangers of the ghetto, he also boasts of his superior perspective on the situation and his own ability to transcend it. This is particularly apparent in the six lines that accompany the shots:

> Hey brother, there's a better way out
> Surely that gold, shooting that dope, man you're copping out
> Take my advice, it's either live or die
> You've got to be strong if you wanna survive
> Your family on the other side of town
> 'll catch hell without the ghetto around

If these shots find Jackie becoming attuned to the singer's sense of self-confidence, she herself exhibiting sure-footedness in her day-to-day environment, the final two shots involve her with the equally prevalent 'hustling' tone of the music. The last two lines of the verse ('In every city, you'll find the same thing going down/Harlem is the capital of every good 'ol town') are predominantly covered by a tracking shot, again at some distance, following Jackie as she turns a corner, and for the first time in the sequence, loses some of her poise, hastening her stride as she evidently realises she is late. This faltering in her composure is measured by the shot, unlike any others depicting her in the sequence, not exactly occupying a measured unit of the song, giving way to the next image before Womack has sung 'town'.

The final action of the sequence is covered by a side-tracking shot akin to the one that first introduced Jackie, but now she is running with an anxious expression on her face (rather than gliding serenely), against a windowed wall which shows planes taxiing on the runway outside (rather than against an abstract mosaic of colour) and her body is no longer confined to one part of the frame (her movement is too erratic for the tracking shot to keep in one place and must eventually trail behind her as she runs towards the departure gate she is meant to be attending). Meanwhile, Womack sings the chorus for a second time, becoming ever more

Fig. 5.2

impassioned as the song comes to an end behind the sound of Jackie welcoming the passengers aboard:

Across 110th Street, just trying to catch a woman that's weak
Across 110th Street, pushers won't let the junkie go free
Oh, across 110th Street, a woman trying to catch a trick on the street, ooh baby
Across 110th Street, you can find it all, anything, yes you can, oh look around you,
look around you, look around you, ooohh

The development of this sequence involves a conscious 'closing of the gap' between off-screen music and on-screen action, whereby the partial attachment of the song in relation to the image suggested in the first shot is gradually replaced by Jackie's movement within the frame being made to associate itself with discernible elements of the music, without being laboriously literal about it (the action remains within the spacious surrounds of an international airport, rather than suddenly relocating to the inner city): like the singer, Jackie puts on a show of strength, offset by its locating within the daily grind, and her actions become more harried as the song works itself up into a climactic frenzy.

The song in this sequence, then, is ready and waiting for its 'meaning' to be elaborated upon by other elements of the narrative, but this sense of already containing a dramatic charge is in itself contained within the narrative as a whole by the enactment in Jackie's first shot of an 'unfulfilled' relationship between music and image. 'Across 110th Street' is repeated over the film's final frames, as Jackie drives towards the airport, in possession of the half-million dollars she has duped from Ordell and the police. Not realistically sited as emanating from her car stereo (the song actually begins over a shot of her accomplice, Max (Robert Forster), in his bail-bond office), Jackie nevertheless silently mouths the words of the chorus before the film cuts to its closing credits. The tentative attachment of the song in the opening sequence to Jackie is resolved in the film's final shot; Jackie, through her actions in between, having 'earned' the right to take on the singer's voice as her own. In this process, carrying the song from a position of distance from the character it accompanies to a much more complete attachment, *Jackie Brown* offers a particularly explicit example of the propensity I have described in various forms throughout this study: for pop songs in narrative films to be placed in relation to characters' bodies and minds, in a manner which reveals to the viewer their particular position in a film's fictional world.

NOTES

chapter one

1 For a good summary of these concerns, see Reay 2004: 37–41.
2 Descriptions of Beth Gibbons as a cabaret or torch singer, or chanteuse, abound in reviews, as do specific comparisons to particular female singers (most commonly Billie Holiday). These comparisons are supported by visual material released by the band which self-consciously presents Gibbons in a torch singer pose (for example, the live concert film *Portishead: Roseland NYC Live* and the promos for 'Over' and 'Tom the Model').

chapter two

1 For a subtle analysis of the utopian possibilities of the Hollywood musical see Dyer 1977.
2 It should be noted that McNally provides an interesting counter-reading to my account of *Pal Joey*, in which she claims that the playboy persona exhibits a number of 'cracks', both in the film itself and in the manner in which it was marketed.
3 'Pal Joey Review', *Variety*, 11 September 1957.
4 'Pal Joey Review', *Variety*, 11 September 1957.
5 See R. M. Morantz (1977) 'The Scientist as Sex Crusader: Alfred C. Kinsey and American Culture', *American Quarterly*, 29, 5, 563–89.

BIBLIOGRAPHY

Altman, R. (2001) 'Cinema and Popular Song: The Lost Tradition', in A. Knight and P. R. Wojcik (eds) *Soundtrack Available: Essays on Film and Popular Music*. London: Duke University Press, 19–30.

Clarke, D. (ed.) (1998) *The Penguin Encyclopedia of Popular Music* (second edition). London: Penguin.

Cohan, S. (ed.) (2002) *Hollywood Musicals: The Film Reader*. London: Routledge.

Douglas, S. (1994) *Where the Girls Are: Growing Up Female with the Mass Media*. New York: Times Books.

Dyer, R. (1977) 'Entertainment and Utopia', *Movie*, 24, 2–13.

_____ (1987) *Heavenly Bodies: Film Stars and Society*. London: Macmillan.

Feuer, J. (1982) *The Hollywood Musical*. London: Macmillan.

Frith, S. (1983) *Sound Effects: Youth, Leisure and the Politics of Rock*. London: Constable.

_____ (1987) 'Towards an aesthetic of popular music', in R. Leppert and S. McClary (eds) *Music and Society: The Politics of Composition, Performance and Reception*. Cambridge: Cambridge University Press, 133–51.

_____ (1996) Performing Rites: On the Value of Popular Music. Oxford: Oxford University Press.

Gorbman, C. (1987) *Unheard Melodies: Narrative Film Music*. London: British Film Institute.

Holden, S. (1995) 'Guide to Middle Age', in S. Petkov and L. Mustazza (eds) *The Frank Sinatra Reader*. New York: Oxford University Press, 64–9.

Mast, G. (1987) *Can't Help Singin': The American Musical on Stage and Screen*. New York: The Overlook Press.

McNally, K. (2002) 'Films for Swingin' Lovers: Frank Sinatra, Performance and Sexual Objectification in *The Tender Trap* and *Pal Joey*', *Scope*. Available online: http://www.nottingham.ac.uk/film/journal/articles/films-for-swingin-lovers.htm (accessed 15 January 2005).

O'Hara, J. (1952) *Pal Joey*. London: The Cresset Press.

Petkov, S. (1995) 'Ol' Blue Eyes and the Golden Age of the American Song: The Capitol Years', in S. Petkov and L. Mustazza (eds) *The Frank Sinatra Reader*. New York: Oxford University Press, 74–84.

Reay, P. (2004) *Music in Film: Soundtracks and Synergy*. London: Wallflower Press.

Reynolds, S and J. Press (1995) *The Sex Revolts: Gender, Rebellion and Rock'n'Roll*. London: Serpent's Tail.

Rockwell, J. (1995) 'From Sinatra: An American Classic', in S. Petkov and L. Mustazza (eds) *The Frank Sinatra Reader*. New York: Oxford University Press, 70–4.

Smith, G. (ed.) (1998) *Sayles on Sayles*. London: Faber & Faber.

Shaw, A. (1970) *Sinatra: Retreat of the Romantic*. London: Hodder Paperbacks.

Smith, J. (1998) *The Sounds of Commerce: Marketing Popular Film Music*. New York Columbia University Press.

1.3 READING BUFFY
Deborah Thomas

ACKNOWLEDGEMENTS

Warm thanks to my colleagues Susan Mandala and Neil Perryman for sharing some extremely interesting ideas about Buffy – on speech patterns and internet fandom respectively – and for their ongoing support and encouragement. I am also grateful to Natasha Smith and Catherine Jones for persuading me to accompany them to the 'Homecoming' convention in Glasgow in 2002 and for their unerring ability to point me to specific episodes and moments in the series on the basis of the vaguest of details from me, which saved me countless hours of research time. Their enthusiasm – as well as that of James Bell and Charlotte Evans – has been much appreciated. Natasha's thoughtful response to some of my ideas has been particularly helpful, and I dedicate this monograph to her.

1. Making the case

'It's time she had a chance to ... you know ... take back the night.'
— Interview with Joss Whedon on the DVD for Season One

It is well known amongst fans of *Buffy the Vampire Slayer* that its creator, Joss Whedon, was motivated to rethink the horror genre by his desire to see its typical victimised blonde female fight back. In the first shot of the series, a prowling camera positions us outside Sunnydale High School at night as the image goes on to dissolve to the darkened interior of the school. The camera continues to explore and, by means of some further dissolves, we enter what is clearly a science classroom. From off-screen right a man's arm in a black leather sleeve violently enters the frame, the fist smashing the classroom window from outside, and we cut to a face-on view of a cocky young man on the make with a pretty blonde woman, Darla, looking nervous and uncertain just behind him. As he climbs through the window, the image is filled by the blackness of his jacket, followed by a cut to an interior corridor, the camera moving left as both figures emerge from the background shadows. The woman hesitates when she gets to the foreground and then gives a start in response to a noise, but the young man assures her that no one is there. She looks around, sees that he is right, and turns back to face him, abruptly revealing herself to be a vampire and biting his neck as she pulls him down out of frame. The credits begin.

Whedon himself, in the DVD commentary on the episode (1.1: 'Welcome to the Hellmouth'), makes clear his own awareness that if Buffy is indisputably a blonde who fights back then so too is Darla, her vampire counterpart. Whedon goes on to state as a second component of his 'mission statement' that nothing is what it appears, with surprise and genre-busting as key elements in his grand design. The gist of the series is thus apparent right from the start and will be complexly shaded throughout its length in its repeated doublings of good and evil characters and in the shifting patterns amongst them, as well as in its ability to surprise us by undermining our previous too easy assumptions about the moral fabric of its world. A process of continual rethinking and regrouping is necessary to keep abreast of narrative events and their significance, the series inviting our alertness and rewarding our intelligent engagement with its project, as we shall see. Although Darla appears to be a minor character at this early stage, we will later discover that she is 'sire' to the vampire Angel, in other words the one responsible for having turned him into a vampire hundreds of years before by biting him and inducing him to drink her blood. Angel now has a soul, as the result of a gypsy curse which burdens him with remorse too deep-seated and entrenched ever to be expunged. However, his dark side is only suppressed, not destroyed, and, as a codicil to the curse, a single moment of complete happiness will be enough to remove his soul and let his *alter ego* Angelus resurface once again. When Buffy and Angel fall in love (providing a star-crossed and impossibly romantic mismatch of slayer and vampire), Buffy provides that moment of happiness and inadvertently becomes the instrument of his reversion to Angelus in Season Two. Thus, she walks in Darla's footsteps, effectively becoming Angel's second 'sire'. This thematic linking of Buffy and Darla, good blonde and bad, is imagined and extended in unexpected ways throughout the series while virtually every important character follows a path – or at least has striking moments – of devastating self-discovery and redemptive moral growth, even Darla (though, in her case, this occurs in the spin-off series, *Angel*, rather than in *Buffy* itself).

Thus, good and evil characters, as well as good and evil aspects of the same person, come to be progressively intermingled by such strategies so that no water-tight distinctions can be made between them. However, in addition to the unlikelihood of any straightforward triumph of goodness over evil, even the more modest hope that knowledge will still be able to triumph over the forces of unreason turns out to be over-optimistic. Season One begins, as we have seen, with a couple breaking into a science classroom at Sunnydale High School, and it ends with a vampire attack on the school library, workplace of Buffy's benevolent English 'Watcher' and high school librarian, Rupert Giles. Both places of learning – the science room and the library – are thus open to invasion by vampires, their vulnerability to such creatures providing a frame for the season overall. Rather than presenting Giles' alliance with Buffy and her friends as a confident commitment to such hard facts as science provides which, in the fullness of time, will inevitably defeat their enemies, the series increasingly comes to question mere book-learning divorced from complicating issues of moral substance and weight (for example, Buffy's knowledge that Angel has gone bad and that she has to kill him, in Season Two, is obviously complicated by her love for him, or at least for what he was). Even the bookish Giles concedes at the end of Season One that 'I don't like the library very much anymore', as the others head off to the local teenage club, the Bronze, a very different sort of place where they can relax and let off steam.

Concerns with knowledge and its value dominate the season, with relevant comments cropping up frequently throughout, though qualified to varying degrees by the intentions and intonations of their speakers. These range from Xander's deadpan remark, 'Everyone forgets, Willow, that knowledge is the ultimate weapon', when he tries to get out of helping Giles by convincing Willow that Giles will be fine on his own (1.5: 'Never Kill a Boy on the First Date') to Buffy's breezy retort, 'What am I, knowledge-girl now? Explanations are your terrain', in a gently sarcastic rejoinder to Giles (1.10: 'Nightmares'). Further, knowing and not knowing become ready sources of humour as the season progresses and more and more characters come to know – and casually accept – Buffy's supposedly 'secret' identity as a slayer, while even more humour is milked from the fact that Buffy's mother Joyce, as well as Buffy's date Owen in Episode 5 (1.5: 'Never Kill a Boy on the First Date') *fail* to grasp what everyone else so evidently knows. A final facet of this recurring thematic concern is that, along with the characters, viewers too come to know the series' particular brand of vampire lore as the season unfolds (for example, the way vampires disintegrate into dust when stabbed through the heart, and the way their faces scrunch up into 'vamp face' when they become roused to violent acts). At the same time, we need to familiarise ourselves with a large number of important characters, though it is not always clear which ones are to be the most important. Darla, for example, is 'dusted' by Angel in Episode 7 (1.7: 'Angel'), an apparently expendable bit-player, but she later re-emerges as a key player after all, both in flashbacks and in the spin-off series, *Angel*, when she is reconstituted and returned to the world. Our accumulation of this store of knowledge is vital both to the full understanding of later episodes and to our imaginative investment in the on-screen world.

Nevertheless, any initial assumption that this is an 'Enlightenment' text about the value and adequacy of much of this knowledge is largely broken down in the course of Season One. Episode 8 in particular (1.8: 'I Robot, You Jane') goes so far as to turn knowledge itself – or at least one particular version of it, an accumulation of facts alone – into the episode's monster. Giles and Jenny Calendar, a teacher of computing at Sunnydale High with whom Giles will eventually fall in love and who will be murdered by Angelus, now argue about the relative merits of books and information technology. What they fail to realise is that a recently arrived ancient text contains a demon who had been bound into its pages back in the fifteenth century, his body transmuted into arcane symbols. Willow unwittingly enters him onto the Internet when she scans the book into the computer, thus giving the demon – Moloch the Corrupter – enormous power and influence, not least over Willow herself when he hides behind a less sinister mask and chats seductively to her online. As Giles later puts it, 'The scanner read the book. It brought Moloch out as information to be absorbed', or in Buffy's more succinct account, 'He's gone binary on us'. In his final defence of books over computers (despite Jenny's reminder that Moloch came to them in a book), Giles argues for their *tangible* qualities, their specificity (ironically echoing Moloch's pleasure in being able to affect the world through touch when he is embodied by his followers in robotic form). As Giles haltingly tries to express this, 'The knowledge gained from a computer is … It has no … no texture, no context'.

In many ways, this episode is the crux of Season One, not only in its questioning of the value of knowledge as mere information – the episode thus preparing the way for later, contrasting presentations of knowledge as the recognition of moral worth – but in its juxtaposition of the technological and the occult (or, in generic terms, the clash between the narrative worlds of science fiction and of horror). However, more intriguingly, the episode and the season as a whole give us an early taste of the series' concern with less epistemological, more ontological themes and storylines. That is, the concentration on issues around knowledge begins to fall away and reveal a more enduring interest in issues around ways of being and alternative dimensions, providing dry-runs for some of the darkest episodes in later seasons. Thus, later stories about parallel universes are already prefigured in Moloch's entry into cyberspace, and the words which suddenly appear on the screen after he is scanned into the computer – a simultaneously chilling, yet unexpectedly poignant 'Where am I?' – will be echoed much more affectingly after Dawn and Buffy lose their mother to a ruptured aneurysm in Season Five (5.16: 'The Body') and Dawn asks in despair, 'Where'd she go?'

Explorations of what it is to be human, and the role of embodiment in making each of us one particular human being rather than another, will also dominate later episodes, where characters will switch bodies, become invisible, lose their sight, their memories, their ability to speak, even their most fundamental values, while some vampires, robots and other non-humans will appear to gain such things – and, alongside them, an affecting history and presence in the world – which endows them with a convincing humanity as well. Some of these themes get an early outing in Season One, often with minor characters in roles that will later be reprised by more central ones. For example, Marcie's invisibility in Season One (1.11: 'Out of Mind, Out of Sight') will be revisited in the form of Buffy's invisibility in Season Six (6.11: 'Gone') and then, with more edge, as Willow's invisibility to Buffy, Xander and Dawn – and theirs to her – in Season Seven (7.3: 'Same Time, Same Place'), reflecting their unreadiness to confront one another after Willow's destructiveness in Season Six and her off-screen rehabilitation in England. Similarly, the body-swap between Amy and her mother in Season One (1.3: 'The Witch') will be echoed by Buffy's body-swap with rogue slayer Faith in Season Four (4.16: 'Who Are You?'). Even Buffy's devastating death at the end of Season Five (5.22: 'The Gift') gets a preliminary more tentative try-out in the final episode of the first season (1.12: 'Prophecy Girl') when Xander revives Buffy from drowning.

For the moment, I merely want to lay the groundwork for the close analyses to come, making a case both for the seriousness of the series' concerns and the intelligence of their deployment, not least in visual terms. For it seems to me that *Buffy the Vampire Slayer* is television aspiring to the condition of film. Joss Whedon's degree in Film Studies, his declared enthusiasms (for example, in the DVD commentary to 'Innocence' in Season Two) for using long sustained takes and for directors like Max Ophuls who 'use the frame cinematically,' as well as his prior work in cinema, make such an aspiration unsurprising, though it was Whedon's confessed naïvety about television and its constraints which led him to put such preferences into practice where more experienced television hands might have faltered. His admiration for the medium of film is also evident in the series' widespread references to specific films. This does not so much take the form of explicit naming or parody and pastiche but rather, ideas from a range of films as varied as *Rebecca* (Alfred Hitchcock, 1940), *Johnny Guitar* (Nicholas Ray, 1954), *It's a Wonderful Life* (Frank Capra, 1946), *Kings Row* (Sam Wood, 1942), *The Stepford Wives* (Bryan Forbes, 1975), *Dark Victory* (Edmund Goulding, 1939), *The Touch* (Ingmar Bergman, 1971), *Meet Me in St Louis* (Vincente Minnelli, 1944), *The Red Shoes* (Michael Powell/Emeric Pressburger, 1948), *The Exterminating Angel* (Luis Bunuel, 1962), *A Matter of Life and Death* (Michael Powell/Emeric Pressburger, 1946), and others, are taken up as inspirational points of departure to be creatively reworked and elaborated with genuine freshness at numerous points throughout the series. In terms of the episodes we will be looking at more closely later in this study, *The Stepford Wives* and *Dark Victory* will prove particularly relevant to 'I Was Made to Love You' in Season Five (5.15), and *A Matter of Life and Death* to 'Normal Again' in Season Six (6.17).

Such evidence as I have given so far for *Buffy the Vampire Slayer* as cinematic television is largely anecdotal (Whedon's background and comments and the references to other films). Much more compelling are the ways that aspects of the mise-en-scène of the series are laden with meaning. In other words, the narrative world on our screens is visually weighted, not just presenting us with a world but with a rich and extended semantic text. For example, following Buffy's death at the end of Season Five, she is resurrected by her friends at the start of Season Six, Willow assuming with smug satisfaction that, through her own abilities as a powerful witch, she has pulled her friend out of an unspeakable hell dimension. She now anticipates Buffy's gratitude with both the eager desire to please that is her trademark in earlier episodes *and* some of the arrogance that will soon send her reeling off course in her growing addiction to dark magic. At the end of the third episode in the season (6.3: 'After Life'), in a scene examined more closely later, Buffy confides the bitter truth to the vampire Spike: 'I think I was in heaven.' However, we

Fig. 1.1

are actually *shown* this much earlier, shortly after the episode's midpoint, when Buffy walks through the cemetery past the statue of an angel. As she pauses for an instant in front of the stone figure whose head is blocked by Buffy's body but whose wings extend behind her as if they are her own, the image suddenly holds and displays her secret to us in an epiphany so delicately unstressed and fleeting that it barely registers until retrospectively confirmed by her later words to Spike. This delicacy and unpretentiousness

– the after-the-fact quality of much of the film's rhetoric which may often elude us the first time through – makes *Buffy* a series which abundantly repays a second visit.

Another example of how the series provides us with visual signposts to its intentions can be found in an episode mentioned earlier (7.3: 'Same Time, Same Place') when Willow returns from her rehabilitation under Giles' tutelage in England near the beginning of Season Seven. Unable to hook up with her closest friends, who appear not to have turned up to meet her at the airport, she finally locates Anya, a more peripheral member

Fig. 1.2

of their group, outside the demolished Magic Box, a shop which Anya ran before Willow's bad magic destroyed it. As they talk and Anya expresses her anxieties about the extent and reliability of Willow's cure, her feelings – and those of Willow's other more elusive off-screen friends – are expressed in the sign on the Magic Box wall behind Willow (which reads 'Unsafe'), just as Willow's fears that her circle of friends will not be emotionally receptive to her now that she is back in Sunnydale are reflected by

the sign on the door behind Anya ('Closed'). Both signs are perfectly understandable merely as aspects of the narrative world: the Magic Box *is* closed for repairs, its structure is unsafe. However, the double-meanings to which they lend themselves make what is a *world*, on one level, simultaneously a *text* to be read, on another.

Indeed, throughout the series, such double-edged signs and posters proliferate. For example, the high school has a poster which we may notice in Season Two (2.5: 'Reptile Boy'), warning its students that 'Not all drunk drivers die', underscoring the point with a picture of what appears at a distance to be a badly scarred teenage driver. So, the apparent meaning can be readily filled in: 'Not all drunk drivers die … Some of them survive but are scarred for life.' However, given that this is Sunnydale, an alternative reading is equally to hand: 'Not all drunk drivers die … Some of them return as vampires.' For the long-shot gives the *image* as much ambiguity as the *words* have, the scarred teenager easily reinterpretable from a distance as a vampire in characteristic 'vamp face'. Similarly, a sign inside the Magic Box which requires all shoppers to leave their bags and backpacks at the desk takes on new resonance when Tara's dreadful family turn up in Season Five (5.6: 'Family'), and we suddenly realise that Tara too needs to unburden herself of a considerable amount of unwelcome 'baggage' from her past. There are many more instances of such semantic layering – in terms of both themes and rhetorical devices – which have the effect of embedding a self-reflexive commentary on characters and events within the visual and verbal substance of their world. Sometimes elements from *outside* the narrative world, such as the titles of individual episodes, may exhibit a similar duality, or even multiplicity, of meaning. For example, an episode title in Season Four (4.12: 'A New Man') refers variously to Giles temporarily transformed into a Fyarl demon, to Adam as an android created from a combination of high-tech machinery and human parts, his presence retrospectively implied behind the door entered by Professor Maggie Walsh at the end of the episode, and to Riley both as the new man in Buffy's life and as a more sensitive version of masculinity, a 'new man' for our times.

Many of the aspects discussed so far are particularly pointed and pervasive in an aptly-titled episode from Season Six (6.12: 'Doublemeat Palace'). On one level the episode is about the (figuratively) soul-destroying and exploitative nature of casual work in the fast-food industry when Buffy – after her mother's death and her own death and resurrection – is forced to get a job to support herself and her sister Dawn, and it has the distinction of being, according to Whedon, the only episode which resulted in sponsors threatening to withdraw their patronage. The restaurant's specialty is the Double Meat Medley, which has patties of processed beef and chicken unappetisingly layered in the same double-decker bun. Significantly, the episode occurs in the midst of the graphically sexual relationship between Buffy and Spike which, in contrast to Buffy's earlier relationship with Angel or indeed to Spike's with Drusilla, is based almost wholly on lust, not romance, and fills Buffy with intense self-loathing and disgust. In a brief scene during one of Buffy's breaks at work, Spike backs her up against a wall (next to a sign reading 'Teamwork') as they form a 'double meat' sandwich of their own. The Double Meat Medley with its red meat and white meat slapped up against each other in unsavoury juxtaposition turns out to be a perfect metaphor for Buffy and Spike – one a red-blooded human, the other a vampire – and their purely physical relationship, while a sign inside the restaurant which proclaims enthusiastically, 'You're Part of the Double Meat Experience!' is, yet again, relevant to both aspects of Buffy's situation

Fig. 1.3

at once. Further, the episode's demon acts on Buffy by paralysing her, and this too reflects her sexually addictive relationship with Spike which deprives her of the will to resist him.

Finally, the episode occurs at a point when Buffy, having been brought back from the grave, is extremely worried that she may have come back 'wrong', with a bit of demon in her make-up. The episode's concern with the nature of the secret ingredient in the double meat patties – and Buffy's growing suspicion that it may be human flesh – is paralleled by her concern with what, if anything, is the new ingredient in her *own* constitution, and whether it is *non*-human. In both cases, Buffy's worries are unfounded, since she turns out to be fully human, and the scandalous secret ingredient in the meat patties, in a satiric twist, turns out to be vegetable. Nevertheless, despite this happy outcome, the episode is followed by another one (6.13: 'Dead Things') which is surely one of the darkest in this darkest of seasons, so any sense of reassurance we may feel is short-lived and readily undone.

The chapters that follow will concentrate on Seasons Five and Six for reasons which I hope will become clear. However, before we leave the early seasons behind us, I would like to take an extended look at an episode from Season Two (2.17: 'Passion') in illustration of the sorts of complexities of tone and point of view which are so characteristic of the series overall, but perhaps nowhere so disturbingly configured as here. If Season One introduces many of the central characters both to us and to each other, with most of the developing friendships and romances still tentative and unresolved, Season Two is much more insistent on pushing these relationships – as well as other new ones – to centre-stage (for example, the relationships between Xander and Cordelia, Willow and Oz, Joyce and Ted, though they all come unstuck at some point). The quirky vampire couple, Spike and Drusilla, are introduced to the series as old friends of Angelus who turn up in town, and Spike is increasingly undermined in his oddly touching devotion to the loopy Dru by Angelus' taunting attempts to insinuate himself between them, while Buffy struggles with the loss of Angel as a result of the brief happiness between them which has taken his soul after their one night together. Meanwhile, Giles hesitantly moves on from the intellectual sparring with Jenny Calendar in Season One to the verge of a real relationship. However, as Jenny works on her computer translating a ritual which might be able to restore Angel's soul (Giles having invited her to come round to his house when she has finished), Angelus appears at the school and brutally murders her, destroying her computer and print-outs before snapping her neck.

It is an audacious and shocking decision to get rid of a character who has become increasingly entwined with central aspects of the narrative, Jenny by this stage revealed to be not merely a techno-pagan at the interface of science and the occult but a descendant of the gypsies responsible for Angel's curse and sent to Sunnydale to keep him and Buffy apart. It is even more unexpected to get rid of her at the precise point when the romance with Giles is about to take off. We are thus *doubly* frustrated, as viewers, firstly in our loss of an attractive and feisty female character whose redemptive journey is not yet complete, as she works to win back Giles' and Buffy's trust. But, in addition, we are forced to relinquish the truly delicious prospect of seeing the fussy yet immensely sympathetic Giles simultaneously discombobulated and transported by love.

The pre-credits sequence of the episode opens with an overhead shot of young people dancing at the Bronze, and then cuts to ground level as we notice Buffy and Xander dancing amongst the crowd. At this point, Angel's voiceover kicks in: 'Passion. It lies in all of us … sleeping, waiting. And though unwanted, unbidden … it will stir, open its jaws … and howl.' I say 'Angel', rather than 'Angelus', because it is not absolutely clear which one we hear, producing an ambiguity to which we will need to return, though it is certainly Angelus whom we see, watching from the sidelines away from the dance floor as the camera cuts between him and Buffy and Xander. The two friends smile at each other as they dance, unaware of his presence, as Angelus continues to stare at them and then leaves. Soon after, Buffy, Willow, Xander and Cordelia themselves leave the building, walking left-to-right across the foreground of the screen, still oblivious to Angelus as he bites the neck of a woman in the background shadows as they pass him by. The camera stays on Angelus as his victim slumps to the ground dead, then it swivels to accompany him as he turns to watch Buffy and her friends walking off into the depths of the screen, with Angelus' head and back dominating the left foreground in near-silhouette. The pre-credits sequence draws to a close with stealthy camerawork in tune with Angelus' lurking presence outside Buffy's house, as she uneasily looks out the window to camera, then gets ready for bed and falls asleep, the sequence ending after we glimpse Angelus' shadowy face outside the window and then see him sitting by Buffy's side as she sleeps. Although I want to concentrate on the much later scenes after Jenny's murder, these opening moments are worth pausing over for several reasons.

First, we are given a great deal more information than Buffy and her friends, by our much closer alignment with Angel/Angelus, through the voiceover, the voyeuristic camera and the access to his actions that we get. This is a pattern that will be especially disturbing in the aftermath of Jenny's death. Second, and related to this, a strong impression is produced of people being out of each other's visual range, in their own separate spaces while events (for example, the killing of the woman outside the Bronze) go on around them unobserved. This will have a humorous reprisal a few scenes later in the high school library, where Buffy, Xander and Cordelia are meeting with Giles to discuss Angelus' behaviour, the library serving as an ongoing private space for the gang's meetings with Giles throughout the first few seasons until the high school itself is destroyed at the end of Season Three (3.22: 'Graduation Day', part 2). For now, in 'Passion', two students come into the library to get some books, interrupting the group's discussions and generating the following comic exchange:

Xander [annoyed]: Does this look like a Barnes & Noble?

Giles: This is the school library, Xander.

Xander: Since when?

The two bemused students go off to the stacks while Giles and the others leave to continue their meeting elsewhere. When one of the students, Jonathan (who will emerge as a central character later in the series), steps out of the stacks to ask for help ('Hello?'), he finds to his surprise that everyone is gone. Both Xander's and Jonathan's bewildered reactions in such rapid succession register and reinforce the way their fields of vision are tightly circumscribed, blinding them to what is happening in the wider world outside their own activities and concerns.

Indeed, in *Buffy the Vampire Slayer* more generally, flurries of narrative activity often appear to be carrying on beyond the main events and outside the spaces occupied by the lives of the main characters. This may take shape in humorous background business visible only to us, as when Spike is reluctantly living in Xander's basement and tries to hit him from behind with a wrench but is overcome with pain before the blow connects, in Season Four (4.11: 'Doomed'). A playful and more extended exploration of this idea of 'narrative marginalia' becomes the focus of an episode in Season Three (3.13: 'The Zeppo'), where Xander single-handedly saves Giles, Buffy, Willow, Angel and Faith from a bomb in the boiler-room beneath them while they carry on their own business upstairs, without ever becoming aware of their danger. In that instance, we stay predominantly with Xander, his 'secondary' story edging the season's main storyline largely off-screen. Once the spin-off series, *Angel*, comes into being several seasons into *Buffy*, this sense of characters operating in disparate parts of the narrative world becomes even more acute, especially in crossover episodes when Buffy goes off to Los Angeles (cropping up in a simultaneous episode of *Angel*) or Angel himself comes back to town. However, it is a strong tendency simply from the perspective of *Buffy the Vampire Slayer* itself, with various central characters (Spike and Drusilla, say, or Faith, Willow, Riley or Giles, or even Buffy herself) going off elsewhere for long stretches of narrative time and then returning in later episodes, their off-screen experiences often recapitulated for us at some later stage. The series structure with its breaks between seasons may also encourage speculation as to what has happened in the interim. Of course, all film and television narratives must give some degree of acknowledgment to characters' off-screen moments, allowing, at the very least, that their lives carry on away from the camera, but *Buffy* goes further in looking at the interaction (or *lack* of interaction) between central and marginal storylines simultaneously unfolding in different parts of the *on-screen* world, as well as across the boundaries of the frame.

Jonathan, whom I mentioned earlier for his transient appearance in the library, is the main example of a character who continually appears in the margins of the Buffy world. He is first introduced in Season Two (2.4: 'Inca Mummy Girl'), when about to be kissed by a revivified mummy princess who stays alive by sucking the life from her victims, though she is interrupted in time for Jonathan to walk off safely, unaware of his lucky escape. In the following episode (2.5: 'Reptile Boy'), we may notice him bringing coffee and a muffin to Cordelia at the Bronze, and he is briefly taken hostage at a school Career Day five episodes after that (2.10: 'What's My Line?', part 2), though he assumes that it is only a demonstration and is once again amusingly unaware of his peril. Although he begins as little more than an extra, the humour and unpredictability of his reappearances eventually give them the feel of cameos, as regular viewers come to know him and find him sympathetic, while the play on his *narrative* marginality underlines his *social* exclusion from the circles of vampire hunters and normal teenage friends alike. Fittingly, he finally takes on a more prominent narrative role at the point when his social isolation pushes him to a thwarted attempt at suicide (3.18: 'Earshot'), an attempt misinterpreted by Buffy as an intention to shoot other students from the tower where he has gone to shoot himself. At the prom two episodes later (3.20: 'The Prom'), we catch a gratifying glimpse of him with a pretty woman on his arm as his story continues to play out on the periphery of the main narrative events, his short-lived background appearances reminding us that there are other stories unfolding somewhere else. Jonathan does eventually achieve an episode whose story revolves completely around himself (4.17: 'Superstar'), even transforming the credits sequence of the episode to feature himself and his exploits, though its narrative world turns out to be an alternative universe he has conjured up precisely in order to re-invent himself as a star. Finally, he becomes a reluctant villain in Season Six, and ends up murdered by Andrew, one of his co-conspirators, in the final season of the series (7.7: 'Conversations with Dead People').

We will return to some of this much later. For the moment, it is enough to note the way Jonathan weaves in and out of the narrative from its margins to centre-stage, embodying a range of roles from sympathetic loser to illusory superstar to villain to victim. This is typical of the way the series presents the centrality of its on-screen events as *provisional*, subject to the gaze and interest of its camera, reminding us from time to time that, if it were to swerve and poke amongst the shadows, it might find all sorts of alternative narratives to pursue. Joss Whedon's previously cited enthusiasm for long takes is well suited to the display of such shifting spatial relationships between the camera and the nooks and crannies it explores, allowing characters and the spaces they occupy to move in and out of the spotlight in a single shot. So, along with the series' thematic interest in multiple dimensions which co-exist with the narrative world we see on-screen, and which are regularly evoked, are a dizzying number of alternative characters and their stories, all located within the world of Sunnydale itself, whom the series silently acknowledges (and occasionally moves to on-screen prominence), even though its central characters remain largely ignorant of their presence in the margins around them.

It is time to return to Giles' discovery of Jenny's death. Our terrible knowledge of what Giles has yet to discover produces a deeply felt and unbridgeable gap between us and him as he arrives home with his face in shadow and finds a rose on the weather-beaten wooden door, the strains of *La Bohème* faintly audible through the door. What he takes to be Jenny's creation of an inviting setting for romance appears to us with sickening clarity as Angelus' work. The lush music, candles and blood-red roses strewn on the stairs leading up to the bedroom, where we anticipate Jenny's dead body on the bed, contribute to an atmosphere of Gothic excess in the overly stage-managed theatricality of the scene. Poor Giles appears thoroughly out of his depth in his tweeds and spectacles, inappropriately dressed for a night of romantic passion and hopelessly unprepared for the revelations signalled so clearly to us by the cloying morbidity of the mise-en-scène.

The air is thick with double-edged promise when we first find ourselves inside, ahead of Giles. However, after this cut to the interior of his house, with the camera moving slowly left, all of a sudden we are reminded of the much earlier scene in the library which now seems a world away, as Giles pokes his head around the door and repeats Jonathan's bewildered 'Hello?' to the empty room. Trying to get his bearings as he hesitates politely on the threshold of what is, after all, his own domain, his discretion makes him seem all the more vulnerable as he steps into Angelus' grim set-up, blind to its meaning, despite some uncertainty on his part at its overblown tone. Frowning slightly

as he finds a note on what we recognise as Angelus' cream-coloured paper (but which Giles does not), he reads its single word ('Upstairs') and gives a tentative smile. In a touching series of gestures, he removes his glasses, tidies his hair and briefly covers his mouth with his outspread left hand, smoothing his face rapidly downward, as if he cannot quite believe his luck yet feels inadequate to his allotted role in the romance, though eagerly determined to have a go. His hesitancies are at odds with the swelling romantic certainties of the music and the stately

Fig. 1.4

camera movements throughout the scene, and our hearts surely sink as he begins to climb the stairs.

The culmination of the sequence – the revelation of Jenny's dead body maliciously laid out on the bed – is accomplished in a series of cuts between Jenny and Giles: from the first shot of Jenny as the sweeping camera leads us in, we cut to a close-up of Giles, his smile slipping away as he takes in what he sees and prises it apart from what he's been led to expect, dropping a bottle of wine and two glasses which shatter on the floor in a quick inserted shot, then back to her, then him, then to a closer shot of her, then, finally, back to Giles, staring off-screen. 'O soave fanciulla', from *La Bohème*, continues to be heard throughout, though the aria has been slightly rearranged to allow its culmination to coincide more ironically with the culmination of the scene. Thus, a later section of the music, where Mimì and Rodolfo sing in alternating succession, had accompanied Giles' entry into the house. Now, Rodolfo sings alone as Giles climbs upstairs, ending with '*In te ravviso il sogno ch'io vorrei sempre sognar*' ('In you I see the dream I'd like to dream forever'), but then leading into a melodious mingling of the voices of *both* Mimì and Rodolfo in mocking counterpoint to his loss as Giles drops the bottle and glasses and takes in the fact of Jenny's death, with its ruthless dashing of all his hopes. The uneasy combination of romantic lyrics with the onset of Giles' grief makes explicit the links between love and death implicit in Angelus' scenario throughout (and, indeed, implicit in Buffy's love for Angel which unleashed Angelus in the first place: the present mise-en-scène is much more appropriate to *that* relationship than to Jenny and Giles).

With the final shot of Giles facing the camera and staring fixedly off-screen, the camera pulls back to reveal that he is, in fact, no longer upstairs, and we now notice police and ambulance men removing Jenny's body through the front door to Giles' left (on the right of the screen, that is, as he faces in our direction), some time having evidently passed since the final shot of Jenny. So, having been placed in a position of privileged knowledge throughout the previous bits of the sequence, we abruptly find ourselves misled and momentarily disorientated, at the precise moment when Giles regains his orientation, as the painful realisation of how Angelus set him up is sinking in. When Giles is invited to the police station to answer some questions, he asks to make a telephone call first, and, with a short decisive nod to himself as he shores up his resolve, he walks off-screen.

At this point the troubling voiceover returns – 'Passion is the source of our finest moments…' – over a cut to a shot of Buffy's dining room, seen from outside through net curtains, as Buffy and Willow enter in the background on the right, the camera tracking left to keep them in shot, while Angel continues: '…the joy of love … the clarity of hatred…' (Here we cut to a close-up of Angelus, facing right, then turning towards us as the telephone rings in Buffy's house) '…and the ecstasy of grief.' We cut to Willow and Buffy in the far backgound of the shot, facing the camera as Buffy hurries towards it to answer the telephone. The camera remains outside with Angelus, and slowly moves left around the house, past walls and windows which alternately make the screen go black and then provide us with another view inside, so we can intermittently follow Buffy's progress as she reaches and answers the telephone. We again cut to Angelus, then to a shot of Buffy half hidden by blackness on the right of the screen (giving the effect of a hand-held camera looking in) as we hear her say 'Giles', though her voice is indistinct. From an extreme close-up of Buffy as she listens, we return to Angelus watching intently, then back to Buffy reacting without words and handing on the telephone to Willow, with both of them in medium long shot, Buffy sliding down the wall to a sitting position on the floor. Willow, now in extreme close-up, can only manage a few words ('Hello? Really? No … no…') before she starts to sob, and we cut back to Angelus smiling. Finally, we see Joyce hugging Willow, Buffy lowering her head to her knees, and Angelus smiling more broadly and walking away.

Fig. 1.5

The combined effect of the muffled interior sounds, intervening curtains and blacked-out portions of the screen, the initial long shots of Willow and Buffy, and our lack of access to what Giles is saying on the other end of the telephone, is to distance us from them all despite our intense emotional involvement in their reactions, both seen and (in the case of Giles off-screen) merely imagined. In this way, we simultaneously care deeply about what is happening while being encouraged to understand it from a multitude of perspectives at once, without being swamped by a sentimental over-indulgence in any one. We can remember the cold resolve of Giles' final stares in the earlier scene, as well as his grief, and we understand the way Buffy's compassion is complicated by her guilt at having unleashed Angelus on her friends, while the voiceover in its intimate address makes more sense than we might wish in our efforts to cut ourselves loose from Angelus' perspective at a point when he could hardly be less sympathetic. Not only does much of the voiceover commentary ring true, but the sentiments and the tone of voice alike seem at least as characteristic of Angel as of Angelus. Thus, for example, the assertion in the voiceover of 'the joy of love' is met two episodes later (2.19: 'I Only Have Eyes for You') by Angelus' disgust when he is taken over by a ghost whose love story he is forced to act out and experiences such love for himself, reacting by washing himself over and over to dispel his feelings of violation by the love that was in him, rather than experiencing any joy. Even though the two competing aspects of Angel/Angelus have been temporarily split apart through the loss of Angel's soul, the voiceover provides a reminder of a side of Angelus which is not completely destroyed, but still remains suspended out there in the ether somewhere, just as voiceovers themselves are often uneasily located in an undefined off-screen space when their address is to the viewer, as is the case here, rather than to a character within the narrative world.

As Giles returns home from the police station to collect his weapons, the camera sweeps quickly round the room, independent of his movements, which are mainly outside its field of view, and ending up on a drawing of Jenny, as Giles leaves unseen. After a cut to darkness, we fade in on the door opening inward, as Buffy, Willow, Xander and Cordelia arrive and Xander repeats Giles' earlier 'Hello?' in the same doorway and from the same viewpoint as in the earlier scene, though Buffy knows exactly what to make of Giles' absence and has none of his earlier bewilderment (or, indeed, of Jonathan's before him): 'He'll go to wherever Angel is.' Her confidence is not the result of any factual evidence alone (though the missing weapons are noted), but of a deeper and more intuitive recognition of Giles' character and an understanding of his state of mind. I will not dwell on the action scene that follows, except to remark on the bickering between Spike and Angelus that precedes Giles' arrival and Buffy's subsequent rescue of him, and the fact that Spike keeps Dru from intervening to help Angelus, thus consolidating our growing sympathetic allegiance to Spike which will be so crucial to the episodes we will be looking at in the following chapters. After Spike, Dru and Angelus slip away, Buffy angrily punches Giles ('Are you trying to get yourself killed?'), and then tearfully embraces him ('You can't leave me! I can't do this alone'), and it now looks as though *their* relationship – the relationship between the Slayer and her Watcher – is at the emotional heart of the episode, rather than hers with Angel or his with Jenny.

When Buffy first cost Angel his soul a few episodes back, the series distinguished itself from run-of-the-mill teenage horror films by refusing to turn this into a punishment-for-sex scenario, even when Buffy herself insisted it was all her fault. Its words of exculpation are, crucially, given to Giles, in one of the most morally and psychologically satisfying moments of the entire series, as they sit side by side in his car and talk (2.14: 'Innocence'). At this point, we hear Giles tell her firmly: 'The coming months are going to be hard … I suspect, on all of us. But if it's guilt you're looking for, Buffy, I'm not your man.' He furrows his brow and slowly shakes his head repeatedly as he speaks, looking straight ahead and then turning to face her, his gaze steady as he concludes with the following words: 'All you will get from me is my support … and my respect.' His steadfastness here is all the more impressive in its contrast to his earlier stammering perplexity when he failed to grasp that Buffy had slept with Angel: 'Bu… but how … how do you know you were responsible for…' Giles breaks off as Buffy turns her head and stares at him wordlessly and the truth finally sinks in ('Oh…'), with Giles unable to sustain the look between them as he removes his glasses and averts his eyes.

With Giles' subsequent offer of unwavering support and respect, the series furnishes additional proof, if any were needed, that it weighs its characters less by the facts that they know than by the moral choices they make in light of whatever they happen to know at the time. 'Innocence' ends with Buffy and her mother watching a film on television together, in which we catch a glimpse of Robert Young. On the heels of his earlier film work, Young became well known to American television audiences in the 1950s for his role as the eponymous father in *Father Knows Best*, a popular series with a cosy view of middle-class family life. His appearance here brings to an appropriate conclusion an episode in which Giles offers Buffy his unconditional backing, not in any endorsement of the claim that father-figures *do* know best, but as an *antidote* to such claims, acknowledging her right to make her own mistakes and standing by her all the same.

These moments from 'Innocence' hang over the events that we have been examining in 'Passion' three episodes later, when he is far more personally affected by the results of her earlier behaviour, which makes their continuing relationship, now tangled up with Buffy's guilt and Giles' grief, even more moving. As Giles returns home once more, Angel resumes his voiceover commentary: 'It hurts sometimes more than we can bear. If we could live without passion, maybe we'd know some kind of peace, but we would be hollow: empty rooms, shuttered and dank. Without passion, we'd be truly dead.' Earlier in the episode, Giles warned Buffy that 'as the Slayer, you don't have the luxury of being a slave to your passions', and now he learns that he too must relinquish his desires, producing a further bond between them – an enforced stoicism to underpin their common moral purpose – at a point when they could so easily have been driven apart. Together they visit Jenny's grave, and Buffy tells him she is now ready to kill Angelus.

In a coda to the episode, we cut from Buffy's conversation with Giles to the computing class that Willow is temporarily teaching in Jenny's place, Buffy's words bridging the cut. After Willow greets the class, Buffy continues to speak about Angel off-screen: 'Nothing's ever gonna bring him back.' We then cut to Jenny's bright yellow back-up disk (containing the spell to restore Angel's soul), as it falls to the floor between desk and filing cabinet when Willow sets down her books. That the disk – and, by extension, the task of returning Angel to what he was – is destined for *Willow* is suggested by the fact that she wore bright yellow in one of the episode's early scenes, which both literally matches her to the disk and yet also captures something of the misplaced optimism she – and Jenny before her – place in technological solutions, rather than face-to-face encounters. So 'Passion' leaves us with two alternative future scenarios: either Willow will give Angel back his soul or Buffy will end up killing him. What we do not yet know is that they will both happen at once, in the final episode of Season Two (2.22: 'Becoming', part 2).

My reason for examining 'Passion' at such length is to further my case for *Buffy's* seriousness of intent and intelligence of execution. I wanted to bolster the earlier examples offered of thematic complexity and semantic layerings of words and visual imagery throughout the series with a more concentrated look at aspects of point of view, narrative structure, off-screen narration, tone, performance, and so forth in a single episode, though I found myself needing to make reference to the earlier episode, 'Innocence', as well. In the course of the discussion, the undertakings of the episode were found to be ambitious and wide-ranging: (i) to explore the limitations of its characters' abilities to see beyond their own activities and desires, (ii) to play with narrative marginality and the relationship of the camera to the narrative world it explores, (iii) to raise questions about romance by fortifying its links with darker passions and exploring its blind spots, (iv) to relate Angelus to his narrating off-screen self and the contrasting spaces they occupy, (v) to complicate our responses to various characters (for example, Spike), while making unexpected links between others (such as Jonathan and Giles), (vi) to reinforce the bonds between Buffy and Giles through their deepening appreciation of each other's moral worth and steadfastness, and, finally, (vii) to balance viewers' simultaneous awareness of a multiplicity of points of view with experiences of intense emotional involvement.

There is no doubt that the series makes heavy demands upon its viewers, our reactions to characters and events continually in need of revision and development in a parallel process to the experiences of the characters themselves as they change and develop. For example, Giles' declaration of unwavering support to Buffy – the firmness of his commitment, come what may – gives him a moral heft which makes it impossible to see him merely as a befuddled figure of fun, despite frequent gentle humour at his expense. Any such moments will always be tempered with respect and affection, his essential dignity a given, from the end of 'Innocence' onward, though future developments may add further inflections to the mix. This continual weathering of the characters as they try to find their way through a complicated ethical and aesthetic landscape is essential to the 'adult' tone of the series which offers viewers of all ages the same respect that Giles offers Buffy. This is undoubtedly a key factor in the loyalty of *Buffy's* fans. It is difficult to come into the series midway or to dip in and out of it without a proper sense of overall storylines and relationships. It is even more difficult to write about it coherently in a study of this length without feeling overwhelmed by the richness of the material, the sheer quantity of significant detail. I will take two different tacks in the next two chapters: first, to concentrate on some of the details, with close readings of very specific moments from three episodes in Seasons Five and Six; second, to make a much broader sweep across these seasons in order to look at some key narrative strategies, in particular by considering what happens when we *re*-read Season Five in the light of Season Six. Naturally, it will be impossible to keep these two approaches completely distinct. In the final chapter I will confront the fact of academic fandom head-on, since it is so central an aspect of academic writing on the series, not least my own.

2. On being human

...the development of a healthy, secure, coherent structure of personality depends in the first instance upon the child's repeated experience of being recognised and sustained...
– Anthony Storr, *Solitude* (1997)

The scenes I have chosen to look at in this chapter involve Buffy in three quiet encounters, first with the robot April, as she runs down and 'dies' (5.15: 'I Was Made to Love You'), then, in the remaining two scenes, with Spike (5.18: 'Intervention' and 6.3: 'After Life'), as she respectively discovers he can be trusted and then comes to confide in him when she cannot share her thoughts with anyone else. There is no action to speak of in any of the scenes, and no other characters appear, but the three moments taken together provide a modest progression in the series' meditations on what it is to be human, as well as in Buffy's relationship with Spike. Despite his physical absence from the scene with April, his activities elsewhere in the episode are closely related to the issues being raised in that scene, just as our sympathy for him more generally, despite his lack of full humanity, relates to our capacity to be touched by April's 'death'.

We saw in our discussion of 'Passion' in the previous chapter that the nature of the connection between Angel and Angelus (the vampire with and without his soul) is difficult to pin down, though the ambiguous voiceover suggested that Angelus's better self was somehow hovering outside him rather than destroyed. (This separability of the soul is confirmed in Season Four of *Angel* – A4.11: 'Soulless' – when Angel's soul is removed and we see it as a wispy bright light in a jar.) Other episodes make clear that, conversely, when Angel *has* his soul, Angelus continues to persist *within* him: thus, earlier in Season Two before Angel goes bad, when Willow figures out that the demon Eyghon will try to escape danger by hiding in the nearest dead or unconscious person, Eyghon is tricked into entering Angel's body, where Angel's own 'inner demon' fights and defeats him, his body providing the battleground for this internal struggle (2.8: 'The Dark Age'). So souls appear to be more easily detachable than demonic alter egos which, however powerfully they may be subdued, remain very much in residence.

Yet possession of a soul is no guarantee of absolute and abiding goodness, as Dawn at least believes when she points out that 'Xander had a soul when he stood Anya up at the altar' (7.6: 'Him'). Further, it is not the case that all signs of humanity are destroyed in its absence, as we will see with April. For more hard-headed evidence than that offered by Dawn to support the claim that those with souls may be morally flawed, one has merely to look at flashbacks of the human version of Angelus before he lost his soul in the first place and became a vampire (2.21: 'Becoming', part 1). A hedonistic womaniser ready to steal from his father and proud of his aversion to 'an honest day's work', he is more than willing to have Darla 'sire' him, and he speaks in tones nearer to the honeyed sarcasm of Angelus than to Angel's intonations. Indeed, when Willow meets her vampire self (3.16: 'Doppelgangland') and Buffy reassures her – 'Willow, just remember, a vampire's personality has nothing to do with the person that was' – Angel interrupts to correct her: 'Well, actually…', until they stare him down and he decides not to contest the point. Of course, at least one of Willow's observations of herself as a vampire in this episode – 'I think I'm kinda gay' – *will* turn out to be true of her non-vampire self as well, and to be very clearly in evidence as a *positive* development from her meeting with Tara in Season Four onward. Finally, Cordelia's friend Harmony, who is killed at the end of Season Three (though we do not discover she is a vampire until Season Four), remains completely and humorously unchanged after her transformation into a vampire, an incongruous 'mall girl' wandering the world of the undead (4.3: 'The Harsh Light of Day').

Spike appears to be the odd one out in this pattern of continuities between vampires and the people they once were. His present 'bad boy' image as a vampire is wildly at variance with his previous human identity as a devoted mama's boy and figure of fun within his upper-class circle of acquaintances: ironically, his nickname of 'William the Bloody' turns out to refer not to his evil deeds as a vampire, but to the 'bloody awful' poetry he wrote while alive. But even in Spike's case, the discrepancy can be resolved by seeing his post-mortem identity as an aspirational pose. Drew Z. Greenberg develops this idea in his DVD commentary on one of the episodes he wrote in Season Six (6.9: 'Smashed'). Spike has just discovered that, despite the government chip in his head which normally causes him excruciating neurological pain whenever he strikes out at humans, he is now somehow able to hit Buffy without doing himself any harm, so he rushes off to try it out on someone else. Greenberg describes the next scene as the most controversial in 'Smashed', presumably even more controversial than the rawness of Buffy and Spike's first sexual encounter later in the episode (when a building comes crashing down around them in symbolic collusion): 'I guess it goes to the nature of Spike and what's happened to him since his chip was implanted. Is he evil? Is he good?' Greenberg goes on to note that 'if you pay attention you can see that he has to psych himself up to do the biting. So the question becomes, does he *want* to bite the girl or does he *want* to want to bite the girl? He has to do a lot of convincing of himself.' Thus we hear Spike telling himself, 'So here goes', to fire up his resolve before he attacks.

In fact, we see the full process of his change from sentimental poet to punk vampire in incremental stages, and not only the end result, beginning with a flashback to 1880 (5.7: 'Fool For Love') when he is still human and foppish, with an upper-class English accent, spectacles and floppy hair, besotted with the inaccessible Cecily, who finds him beneath her. This sentiment will be echoed later by Buffy, which I presume evokes viewers' pity for Spike and puts us firmly on his side in wanting their relationship to develop. The version of his past that he narrates to Buffy is not quite so humiliating as the one we *see*: thus, in the flashback, Drusilla discovers William shedding 'unmanly' tears before she sires him, and when he then tells Buffy, in the present, how he had to get himself a gang, what we *actually* see is Angelus throttling him. Nevertheless, when Angelus calls him William, he insists 'It's Spike now' (in revenge for others' earlier mockery of his poetry, when he overheard someone boasting that he would 'rather have a railroad spike through my head than listen to that awful stuff'). Spike is talking tougher now, and large helpings of swagger, sarcastic humour, peroxide and black leather eventually complete his change. The instability of this version of himself is underlined by the ease with which it appears to drop away. This may be seen when he puts on other clothes, for example Xander's Hawaiian shirt and Bermuda shorts when Spike has accidentally shrunk his own clothes in the wash (4.11: 'Doomed'), or when he loses his memory and thinks he is Giles' son, only to then take on the details of Angel's identity instead when he finds out he is a vampire inexplicably fighting on Buffy's side (6.8: 'Tabula Rasa') and improvises an explanation: 'I must be a noble vampire, a good guy, on a mission of redemption. I help the helpless. I'm a vampire with a soul.' Of course, this description *will* later turn out to apply to himself as much as to Angel, though we do not know it yet.

The point is that Spike's particular identity as a vampire is a deliberately constructed *image*, and we *know* it, so that we remain aware of the vulnerable third-rate poet beneath the unexpectedly moving tough-guy act, and, even without a soul, Spike remains a sympathetic character throughout, never again quite so foolish as when he was a living human, but never fully evil either, unlike Angelus. In fact, after Spike seeks and regains his soul, any moral improvement in him beyond what he has already achieved *without* one is barely perceptible, though the retrieval of his soul certainly causes him torment and pushes him to the edge of madness. Buffy's reply when Dawn asks her what it means that Spike now has a soul is a simple 'I don't know' (7.6: 'Him').

'I was made to love you'

April is a construction too, though not of her own making. Carefully programmed by the nerdish Warren with no other purpose than to love him unconditionally and serve his needs, April now proves a liability as he tires of her devotion and single-minded pursuit of him, abandoning her for a living woman, Katrina, with a will of her own (though he will eventually tire of that as well, especially when she opposes her will to *his*, setting Warren on a course of attempted rape and then murder). The sequence where April's

Fig. 2.1

batteries run down is two minutes and forty seconds long, consisting of twenty shots, as Buffy and April sit on adjoining swings in a deserted playground and talk. It begins with a high-angle shot of the empty playground as the camera moves slowly downward to include the swings and the two figures in long shot, their shadows extending towards us on the ground in front of them, and it ends in a reversal of this shot with the camera now rising above them, but this time keeping them both in the final framing.

In between these two long shots which enclose the sequence as a whole are alternating medium shots of Buffy, April, and Buffy (shots 2–4), then a close-up shot of April and a matching one of Buffy (shots 5–6), a two-shot (shot 7), a series of alternating medium shots, beginning with April and ending with Buffy (shots 8–15), another close-up of April (shot 16), followed by alternating close-ups of Buffy, April, and Buffy again (shots 17–19), before we end with the final long shot rising above them both (shot 20).

There is a strong sense of symmetry between Buffy and April in the editing of the sequence, which parallels and reinforces their equal weighting *within* the shot when they appear together in the frame, all of this underpinning Buffy's recognition of aspects of herself in April (in particular, the way April's identity is over-invested in her need to please Warren, which leads to Buffy's decision that she herself should try to manage without a man in her life for a change). The episode relates April to other female characters as well. For example, Buffy's mother Joyce is in the early stages of dating a new man and nervously chooses an outfit she thinks will make a good impression, while Anya amusingly says of April that 'She speaks with a strange evenness and selects her words a shade too precisely', failing to appreciate that this description applies to her own idiosyncratic use of language too. Another aspect of the scene is that both of the two runs of alternating close-ups (shots 5–6 and 16–19) are initiated by shots of April, in moments which intensify our emotional involvement with her. In the first case, she notes that 'It's getting dark. It's early to be dark', and we realise she is about to 'die', and in the second instance, she tries to put on a brave face while having been programmed only to fall back on clichés: 'When things are sad … you just have to be patient. Because … because every cloud has a silver lining', adding cheerfully, 'And … when life … gives you lemons … make … lemonade.'

April is thus clearly shown to be Warren's creation – a mechanical girlfriend with no mind of her own – and yet, simultaneously, she seems to transcend this, both in her links with other characters and in the effects on us of witnessing Buffy's attempts to comfort and reassure her throughout their conversation (clearly treating her as if she were human, and even defending her to Xander in the following scene: 'She wasn't crazed'). Even more telling are April's own expressions of existential doubt which exceed her programming and imply a limited degree of self-consciousness: 'I'm only supposed to love him. If I can't do that, what am I for? What do I exist for?' Further, as we have seen, the visual style of the sequence gives April considerable dignity and moral weight by balancing her with Buffy through the shot/reverse-shot symmetries and maintaining an equivalent camera distance from both April and Buffy within each run of shots. And finally, the privileging of April's thoughts and perceptions by allowing them to generate each set of close-ups, makes her the subjective centre of her own demise, and not just a mindless *thing* for Buffy to react to and deal with before moving on.

However, April's vulnerability – her capacity to evoke our sympathy – is also partly to do with her *difference* from normal humans. Thus, whereas Buffy leans back against one of the chains of the swing so she can remain turned towards April and face her directly, April's posture is more chaotic and less purposeful, her legs splayed at the knees and her arms dangling. Her skimpy dress with its bright floral print contrasts not only with Buffy's dark trousers and leather jacket but with everyone else's more weatherproof clothing elsewhere in the episode, April's outfit making no concessions to practicality or ease. Although her serenity suggests she is insensitive to cold and discomfort, an earlier conversation between Buffy and Warren as they try to track down April makes clear the robot's ability to feel something like pain (and in a manner that has obvious parallels with Spike's implanted chip):

> *Warren:* '…I made it so that if she heard me and she didn't answer, it causes this kind of feedback.'
> *Buffy* [incredulous]: 'Wait … If you call her and she doesn't answer, it *hurts* her?'

So Buffy at the same time recognises that April is a mechanical object and yet also responds to those aspects of her speech and behaviour that make her seem much more than this. Buffy's response to April's reliance on clichés, mentioned earlier, is to echo April's words – 'Clouds and lemonade, huh?' – in even tones, without making any judgements. Through the non-committal repetition of April's words, without either openly challenging the triteness of her outlook *or* hypocritically pretending to endorse it, Buffy offers her a sort of validation, or at least acceptance. It is an act of kindness towards an innocent in a wicked world beyond her understanding.

This is very different from the attitude to its robots taken by Bryan Forbes' 1975 film, *The Stepford Wives*, where the men in the small town of Stepford have replaced their wives with robots every bit as complaisant as April, but without her vulnerability and her puzzlement at the bad behaviour of her man. The horror of *The Stepford Wives* lies in the husbands' treatment of their *human* wives, whereas April is the focus of our sympathy in 'I Was Made to Love You'. Thus, the comparable playground scene, filmed in a single shot, where Joanna (Katharine Ross) and her friend Bobby (Paula Prentiss) approach and then sit down on adjoining swings while deciding to investigate the strange goings-on in Stepford, takes place *before* either one is murdered and replaced by her robotic twin. The robots in the film are completely lacking in the sorts of human qualities that April possesses in the *Buffy* episode, with all warmth and personality belonging to the women of flesh and blood.

The other film that feeds into the *Buffy* episode is Edmund Goulding's 1939 melodramatic 'woman's film', *Dark Victory*, which has no robots, but does feature Bette Davis's character, Judith, dying in similar circumstances to those in which April finds herself, at least up to a point, though with no precise equivalent to Warren. Judith's husband, Dr Frederick Steele (played with hang-dog sincerity by George Brent), with whom she falls in love after she thinks his surgery has saved her life rather than merely prolonging it a little, is a well-meaning idealist, but his behaviour in keeping the truth of her condition from her is patronising nonetheless. He tells her best friend Ann (Geraldine Fitzgerald) that Judith will, at some point, experience 'a dimming of vision', then, after a few hours at most, she will die. Judith discovers the truth but has a chance to keep a secret from *him* in return, when the onset of blindness arrives and she packs him off to an important board meeting in New York, her husband unaware of her deterioration, while she remains behind to die resolutely alone.

Her words to Ann when her vision starts to fade – 'Look how it's clouding up. It's getting darker every second. It's funny, I can still feel the sun on my hands' – provide an obvious reference point for April's words to Buffy quoted earlier: 'It's getting dark. It's early to be dark.' However, unlike Judith, April has no idea what her loss of vision signifies, and she 'dies' abruptly in mid-sentence, a smile on her face, from a very unglamorous running down of her batteries, with Buffy by her side in quiet fellowship. There is none of the drawn-out sentimental overkill of Judith's staging of her solitary death as an ennobling spiritual triumph while the film joins its purpose to hers by providing 'inspirational' music on the soundtrack in a facile attempt to stir up our emotions. Judith's words to her husband before he leaves – 'Have I been a good wife?' – and his reassuring hug, in response, again are paralleled when April insists to Buffy in some bewilderment, 'I was a good girlfriend', and Buffy reassures her, 'I'm sure you were'. However, in contrast to the uncompromising condemnation of Warren's behaviour that the *Buffy* episode offers, *Dark Victory* never questions the idyllic marriage Judith and Frederick appear to have achieved. Her post-operative claim that, as his obedient patient, 'I've practically been your slave' is never taken as seriously by the film as perhaps it needs to be. In both cases, another woman acts as mediator for the couple (Buffy for April and Warren, Ann for Judith and Frederick) when they are no longer able or willing to communicate directly, each relationship based on a suppression of the truth, though for very different reasons.

So *Dark Victory*'s transfiguration of Judith through her embracing of the role of perfect wife meets *The Stepford Wives*' icy vision of wifely perfection as monstrous. Out of this incompatible mixture comes April, a manufactured 'ideal' girlfriend who is grotesquely programmed to do Warren's bidding and whom he unfeelingly throws away, yet who remains more than the sum of her material parts and very touching in her efforts to fulfil her designated role. In contrast, Buffy, who has also been dealt a hand she has not chosen for herself, will finally be given a chance to change her destiny and free herself from her special role as Slayer, though it will take until the final episode in the final season (7.22: 'Chosen') for this to emerge. It has been clear all along, in any case, that the series rejects essentialism. People are to be understood as what they do and experience, not as what they *are* in any permanent and pre-determined sense. Whedon's comment about Tara in the DVD overview to Season Five – that 'family are the people who treat you like family … and not necessarily the people that you're related to by blood' – is relevant to April too: to be human is to think and behave as human, not necessarily to be made of living flesh and bone. Equally, by being compelled by the implanted chip in his head to stop behaving badly, Spike eventually becomes as good as he is forced to act: to behave like a good man is no longer distinguishable from being one.

The most concentrated and explicit example of this scenario is when Faith switches bodies with Buffy to escape the police after killing a man in Season Three (3.14: 'Bad Girls'), then being stabbed by Buffy and falling into a coma (3.21: 'Graduation Day', part 1), and eventually reviving and escaping from the hospital in Season Four (4.15: 'This Year's Girl'). In order to pass as Buffy in the episode immediately after the body switch, which follows its consequences (4.16: 'Who Are You?'), she has to learn to behave like her, practicing in front of a mirror and self-consciously repeating to herself what she sees as Buffy's mantra: 'You can't do that, because it's wrong.' She later makes a play for Spike at the Bronze, confusing him by the unfamiliar sexual explicitness of her offers, but laughingly adding, as she walks away, that she will not be following through: 'And you know why I don't? Because it's wrong.' However, when she kills a vampire in order to maintain the ruse of being Buffy, she herself is thrown into confusion when she is thanked by the woman she has saved. Ironically, Tara is able to sense the body swap (just as Faith picks up earlier on Tara's relationship with Willow), where Willow (Buffy's best friend after all) fails to do so, but Faith herself continues to grow into Buffy's values through playing her part. Eventually she stops a killing spree by a group of vampires not just to convince others that she thinks it is wrong, repeating the mantra once again, but because she means it this time. When she heads out of town in her own body again, at the end of the episode, her expression is serious as the implications of this – and perhaps the stirrings of guilt they provoke – sink in.

In Season Six (6.9: 'Smashed'), Buffy will tell Spike 'You're not a man. You're a thing,' immediately before he discovers, to his puzzlement, that he can hit her without pain, and later in the episode it seems that the reason may lie with *her* being not quite human since her return from beyond the grave. The evident hurtfulness of her remark makes it easier to sympathise with Spike than with Buffy, and, given Buffy's kindness to April in 'I Was Made to Love You', it suggests that she has suppressed her earlier generosity out of some sort of defensive denial of her growing feelings for Spike (indeed, as we have seen, the walls of her resistance to him come tumbling down – *literally*, as the building collapses around them – by the episode's finale). The series is consistent in its criticism of those who treat people – and robots and vampires who take on human vulnerabilities – merely as *things*.

A scene in 'I Was Made to Love You', just over halfway through the episode, provides a small reminder that Spike is more than this. In several shots, we see a restroom sign on the wall behind him in the Magic Box. Above the word 'Men' is the usual symbol for

disabled access (a figure in a wheelchair) next to the usual male icon (depicting the standing figure of a man). Together these figures unobtrusively insist on Spike's humanity – the fact that he is a man as much as a vampire, or at least that he deserves to be treated as one – while, at the same time, recalling one of the most sympathetic shots of him, from Season Two (2.14: 'Innocence'), when he is confined to a wheelchair after his injuries in an earlier episode (2.10: 'What's My Line?', part 2). In 'Innocence', as

Fig. 2.2

Angel, Dru and the Judge go out without him, walking off-screen in the foreground of the shot, Spike is suddenly revealed in long shot in his wheelchair, a small figure isolated and still in the middle of the frame. We see the restroom sign in the Magic Box, in 'I Was Made to Love You', just as Spike finds out that April (who had earlier thrown him through a window) is a robot. This eases the humiliation he had felt at her hands, though he now faces the combined hostility of Giles, Willow, Xander, Anya, Dawn and Tara, all of whom know about his feelings for Buffy and uniformly reject him in response, one after the other. Giles is the most adamant, shoving Spike roughly against a cabinet and speaking with cold deliberation, his words measured and full of menace:

> *Giles:* We are not your friends. We are not your way to Buffy. There is no way to Buffy. Clear out of here. And, Spike, this thing … get over it.

Narrowing his eyes, Spike challenges him with a tight smile:

> *Spike:* I don't know what you mean.
> *Giles:* Yes, you do. Move the hell on.

Following Spike's enforced departure, hunched under a blanket to shield him from the sunlight, we cut from a close shot of Giles' grim face and from the dull colours of the Magic Box scene to April in her pink floral-patterned dress against the brightly coloured pink and orange mise-en-scène of the coffee shop where she is looking for Warren, the editing emphasising the links between Spike and April in their unreciprocated attachments to Buffy and Warren respectively. So the restroom sign, with its reminder of Spike's bad treatment at the hands of Angelus and Dru in Season Two (now echoed in the unfeeling coldness with which he is treated by Giles and the others), and the present links between Spike and April in their thwarted searches for love, are mutually reinforcing. Similarly, the remembered sight of Spike in the wheelchair and the current one of him hunched under the blanket work together to present him as an exposed and beleaguered figure, undeserving of his fate.

Given all of this, our sympathy for Spike – already very strong – is buttressed even further in 'I Was Made to Love You', but then uncomfortably complicated near the end of the episode, when he turns up at Warren's house with a carton of Buffy memorabilia that he has accumulated (photographs, bits of clothing, a blonde wig, and so on) and insists that Warren make him a robot of his own in Buffy's image (the Buffybot). If Spike was previously linked to April in their shared ambiguity (their emotional expressiveness appearing to give each of them an effective human identity despite their biologically non-human bodies), it is a shock to see him suddenly step into Warren's shoes and put a twinned version of Buffy in April's. However, it is not quite so straightforward: whereas Warren constructed April because he preferred a girlfriend he could treat as a thing, it is very clear that a robotic version of Buffy falls far short of what Spike really desires and that it is Buffy's rejection of him (her refusal to treat *him* as more than a thing) that pushes him to go for second-best. His resorting to a robot seems sad, rather than villainous, and in its undoing of the earlier links between Buffy and Warren in their respective objectifications of Spike and April, it can be taken with some sympathy as an understandable retaliation. In any case, our memory of Giles' recent advice to Spike to 'Move the hell on', which Spike has now done, lingers over Spike's actions and may encourage us to push some of the responsibility in Giles' direction.

The relationship between persons and things which is explored through our shifting perceptions of characters like April and Spike leads us to the conclusion that they and the more fully human characters throughout the series are never purely one or the other. This realisation hits us with a visceral punch in the final moments of the episode, when Buffy returns home and finds her mother dead, an event whose painful effects will

run their course and be studied with almost clinical precision in the subsequent episode (5.16: 'The Body'). The 'thingness' of Joyce's unanimated body is palpable, with its legs bent outward below the knees in a recumbent mirroring of April's dying pose. However, Buffy's grief-stricken reaction shows how impossible it is for her – for all of us – to separate the person that was from the body that remains. Her regression to childish desperation as she starts to take in her mother's death with rising panic ('Mom?

Fig. 2.3

… Mom? … Mommy?') may well evoke the earlier childhood setting of the playground where April expired, but the low-key register of Buffy's sympathy for April has now been replaced by gut-wrenching and irrecoverable loss.

'Intervention'

Many of the events in 'I Was Made to Love You' continue to reverberate in subsequent episodes, especially the death of Buffy's mother and Spike's requisition of the Buffybot. The completed robot in Buffy's image first appears three episodes later (5.18: 'Intervention') in one of the most narratively complicated episodes of the series, the one we will be considering next. This complexity is reflected in the unusual length of the pre-credits sequence, which is almost seven minutes long overall and brings together several important plot developments in thirteen extracts from previous scenes in less than the first minute-and-a-half alone. We are reminded, first, that the season's crazy villain Glory, a glamorous and utterly self-centred god-in-exile trying to get back to her own dimension by finding the mystical Key to unlock the portal, now knows that the Key is in human form, though she does not yet know that it is embodied in Buffy's sister Dawn, who was created for that purpose. Second, we revisit Spike's dream in which he is kissing Buffy, and witness his horror when he wakes up and takes this in ('Oh, God, no'), followed by his declaration to Buffy of his feelings for her and her rejection, and then the appearance of April which inspires him to order a robot of his own. And, third, we again see Buffy finding her mother dead, followed by Joyce's funeral and Buffy talking with Angel as he helps her get through the night after the burial.

The episode continues to interlace and develop these strands, with a couple of significant themes emerging across them all, especially those relating to vision and its impairment, and, connected to this, the ways emotional vulnerabilities may be hidden behind misleading and defensive surfaces. The first pre-credits scene to follow the edited bits from previous episodes takes place in Buffy's kitchen, where she, Dawn and Giles are doing the washing-up and making weak jokes as they put on brave faces for one another in the wake of Joyce's death and funeral. Buffy tells Dawn that 'if there are any plates in your room, let's have them before they get furry and we have to name them', and her sister replies in a manner that cannot help but pull us up: 'Hey, I was, like, five then.' The poignancy implicit in her reply derives from our knowledge that Dawn has only existed since the start of Season Five, and her memories of being five years old, as well as the others' memories of her past existence, are implanted and illusory, and they all know it. So right away we are given a clear impression of an unspoken agreement amongst these characters – at least at this particularly difficult time – to pretend to accept surface realities as the whole story. Despite Dawn's earlier desperation when she discovered the truth about her origins (5.13: 'Blood Ties'), Joyce's death two episodes later and Glory's ongoing menace have shelved her existential crisis, and the scene conveys both a protective 'armour' being put in place and its fragility. The theme of defences going up continues as Dawn leaves the room and Buffy and Giles move into the living room and begin to talk more openly. Giles takes on the role of a kind confessor, and the fact that his white T-shirt is visible above the top of his gray sweater, encircling his neck, gives him a priestly appearance to match. When Buffy expresses her worry that she is getting hardened by her slaying – 'I'm starting to feel like being the Slayer is turning me into stone' – Giles counters her feelings of emotional shutdown by offering to take her on a quest to a sacred place nearby in the desert for a day or two.

After Buffy tries to make up for her emotional containment by telling a bemused Dawn how much she loves her (Dawn responding that Buffy's 'Gettin' weird'), we then move into the next pre-credits scene by means of Buffy's reply to Dawn that 'weird love's better than no love'. Unerringly, this leads us to Spike collecting the Buffybot from Warren, and it is difficult not to smile at the segue. Indeed, the shifts of tone throughout the episode are so frequent as to keep us constantly on our toes, as we move from serious issues of grief and emotional debilitation to affectionate humour at the expense of characters we care about (like Spike and Giles) and those to whom our allegiance is much weaker (like Glory's hapless minions), and back again. Yet far from being mere comic relief, even the humour produced by the excessive fawning of the minions is instructive in the staggering insincerity they display – another example of how the episode foregrounds such defensive façades – as the minions address Glory in ever escalating hyperboles in the misplaced hope of escaping her displeasure.

The humour derived from the enthusiastic grovelling of Glory's minions is partly an accumulated effect from their appearances earlier in the season, drawing on a continuing vein of humour that will be mined in later episodes as well. For example, in the episode immediately after 'Intervention' (5.19: 'Tough Love'), as Glory luxuriates in a bubble bath, three of her obedient minions kneel blindfolded by the side of the bath, waiting on her with loofah, chocolates and a drink in hand, and her accusation that they never bathe is met by one of them rhapsodising eagerly: 'Oh, but we do, Your Scrumptiousness. We bathe in your splendiferous radiance…' until Glory interrupts to insult them. It is not

Fig. 2.4

just the outrageous excess of their words that may make us smile, nor the way the minions occasionally run out of steam through constantly having to excel themselves with ever more flattering praise. Equally telling is the fact that Glory is perfectly aware of their insincerity, referring to it as 'lame toadying' in the episode which precedes 'Intervention' (5.17: 'Forever'), and yet she requires their tributes to continue all the same. Appearances matter to Glory (which is why Spike will find it easy to arouse her anger by insulting her physical appearance – her hair, figure and clothes – when she is torturing him near the end of 'Intervention'). Glory's superficiality, as well as the zealous toadying of her shameless minions which joins them to her in an openly acknowledged masquerade of willing servitude, is an extreme version of the episode's thematic interests. Even Willow will be depicted as being amusingly and excessively obsessed with the outward look of things when we overhear her lending a set of notes to a fellow student later in 'Intervention', advising him anxiously: 'And, uh, don't write in it, or … or … uh … put a coffee mug down on it or anything. And … and don't spill. OK. Oh, and don't fold the page corners down. Bye!'

Spike's relationship with the Buffybot might seem like more of the same: an interest in perfected surfaces regardless of the emptiness or disorder that may lie beneath (the emptiness in the robot, that is, and the disordered emotions in himself). Just as Glory is not bothered by whether her minions mean what they say, as long as they throw themselves into their roles with a convincing display of vigorous devotion, so too might Spike's acquisition of the Buffybot appear to imply that all he needs is an illusion of Buffy, as long as the robot plays her part with relish. Thus, although he initially complains to Warren that 'She looks a little shiny to me' (that is, the surface she presents to the world is too obviously artificial, the illusion too openly declared), he changes his mind when the robot opens her eyes, greets him and kisses him forcefully as if she really means it: 'She'll do.'

However, in contrast to the self-conscious joking noted earlier amongst Buffy, Giles and Dawn, or the openly inauthentic relationship between Glory and her 'boys', Spike's need to believe it is Buffy herself he is with begins to take him over. Thus, after the robot holds a stake to Spike's heart in what is clearly a pre-programmed mock 'fight' in his crypt, and he kisses her, the throaty intensity with which he says her name and the intimacy of the camerawork produce the effect of Spike succumbing to his fantasy. So too do his words in a later scene as they lie naked on the floor – 'You're mine, Buffy' – until the robot abruptly breaks the illusion with her reply, asking if she should start the program over again. Spike quickly replies (as we cut from a shot of them together to a close-up of Spike alone in the frame, his brow furrowed): 'Shh. No programs. Don't use that word. Just be Buffy.' However, even as she smiles back at him, it is with far too big and bright a smile. Her hoop earrings – and, elsewhere, her high heels and pleated skirt – are not quite right (indeed, Buffy will later call the robot 'Skirt Girl' to emphasise how unlike Buffy's clothes the outfit is). The make-up too is over-polished, the illusion unsustainable.

The episode veers into a broad comedy of errors as Buffy's friends prove unable to distinguish the Buffybot from the real thing, despite the facility with which, in 'I Was Made to Love You', they had recognised April to be a robot at first sight. The Buffybot's oddities, far from alerting them all to her being a robot, produce either mild bewilderment or, in Anya's case, immense delight. As an ex-demon, she has not quite mastered the art of being human herself and does not recognise such quirks as being in the least bit odd. Thus, when the Buffybot, having been programmed to know that Anya is a committed capitalist, asks her how her money is, Anya replies – 'Fine. Thank you for asking' – and turns pointedly to Xander with a smile on her face, nodding with pleasure, as if to suggest to him that he might well take more interest in such things himself. At the same time as Buffy's friends fail to realise they are dealing with a robot, Glory's minions lurk around the periphery of various scenes (suddenly revealed peering through windows, around corners, and so on) as they follow Glory's instructions to watch Buffy and her friends: 'Find out who's new in her life, who's … special, who's different.' In a double dose of mistaken identity, they see the Buffybot protecting Spike while out on patrol and conclude that, as *she* is the Slayer, then *he* must be the Key, triumphantly capturing him and bringing him to Glory. The two minions who are holding Spike between them, each by one of his arms, spread their free arms wide and present him to Glory with a flourish, their faces beaming, though she is quick to sniff him out as a vampire, realising at once that he has insufficient purity to be the Key.

While Buffy's friends and Glory's minions alike wander through the narrative in happy ignorance, providing numerous examples of faulty vision in the face of the misleading appearances of the objects in their world, Buffy continues her quest in the desert – what Xander will refer to as her '*vision* quest experience' – and selected scenes from this are intercut with events back home. The desert scenes begin by poking fun at Giles after he drives Buffy to the sacred location in his red convertible (bought earlier in Season Five), another shiny surface in this episode of false displays. In an episode from Season Six mentioned earlier in this chapter (6.8: 'Tabula Rasa'), when Spike loses his memory and thinks he is Giles' son, he comments sarcastically that 'Dad' probably has 'some classic midlife-crisis transport', correctly imagining it as red, shiny and phallic. This interpretation of the car is certainly open to us as we see it edge into view around a bend in the desert road in 'Intervention': a false presentation of self which may well have stemmed from Giles' need to divert his attention from such midlife turmoil within himself, as Spike will later imply.

The gourd-shaking jumping-in-and-out ritual Giles has to enact in aid of Buffy's quest is gently ridiculed by Buffy as a kind of hokey-pokey (Buffy adding quietly in mock-serious tones as he finishes, 'And that's what it's all about'). It is performed with self-conscious embarrassment by Giles himself, well aware of how preposterous it looks. However, Buffy's comments throughout the more serious stages of the quest itself – 'I know this place', then, later, to the figure who appears to her, 'I know you. You're the first Slayer' – suggest a clarity of vision lacking elsewhere in the episode so far, which gives a validity to the first Slayer's enigmatic words: 'Love is pain … Love will bring you to your gift … Death is your gift', even though Buffy herself is at a loss to understand them at this point. Though we may not know it yet, the way is being prepared, in the midst of significant amounts of humour in the episode, to Buffy's death in the season finale (5.22: 'The Gift').

If 'Intervention' is thus a crucial stage in Buffy's journey, it is no less important for Spike, and his self-sacrifice at the end of Season Seven is also being more distantly prepared. In fact, even as early as the end of 'Intervention' itself, Spike is ready to die rather than betray Buffy. The scene we will be examining in detail – the final scene in 'Intervention' – is where she comes to know this. It is the only time in the episode we see Buffy and Spike interact (after the opening visual 'quotes' from previous episodes, that is), though Spike does lie bruised and battered on the sidelines after his escape from Glory while Buffy fights the minions in the lobby of Glory's building (along with Giles, Xander and the Buffybot). However, Spike and Buffy only briefly share the frame throughout the fight, with Spike a small unmoving figure in the background of the action whom Buffy never appears to notice (though the Buffybot does). In other words, until the episode's final scene, Buffy's and Spike's journeys are almost completely separate, though the fact that almost all of Spike's scenes contain Buffy's robotic double makes it *seem* as though they are barely ever apart. The most important narrative strand of the episode, winding its way through and around its other concerns, is the bringing together of Buffy and Spike, with Spike forfeiting his fantasy version of Buffy, while Buffy in turn is forced to relinquish some of her earlier prejudices about *him*, leading them both to a more authentic relationship with each other based on mutual trust.

The theme of trust which is so crucial to Buffy's developing relationship with Spike, like so much else in 'Intervention' – and indeed in *Buffy the Vampire Slayer* more generally – is reflected to varying degrees of prominence in other plotlines. I mentioned above that *almost* all of Spike's appearances prior to the final scene show him interacting with the Buffybot: the only exceptions are his scenes with Glory. However, there are striking parallels between his treatment at Glory's hands and at the robot's. Thus, in the first scene of Spike alone with the Buffybot in his crypt, she throws him onto the bed on his back, straddling him and ripping his black T-shirt before pretending to stab him in the heart. Similarly, in the first scene of Spike with Glory, she throws him onto her bed and straddles him as well, before torturing him by sticking her finger in his gut to 'read' him and see what is inside. Although his black T-shirt is intact when he is brought to her (Spike evidently having a good supply of such clothes), it is shown to have been torn across the chest by the time we reach a later scene, when he is still in Glory's custody, his appearance deteriorating from scene to scene as he becomes more beaten up and bruised.

What may thus appear as a link between the Buffybot and Glory, and may even be taken to imply a masochistic wish on Spike's part to be punished by them both (since he is, after all, the one who instructed Warren on the 'special skills' he wanted him to include in the robot's programming) can more usefully be read as a contrast. As we will see in more detail in the following chapter, the series distinguishes between situations where characters are unwillingly tied up or chained and at the mercy of their enemies, on one hand, and those where willing partners play at relinquishing power in safe and trusting collusion, on the other. Spike's programming of the Buffybot is a prelude to his relationship with Buffy in Season Six, where many of the same playful features will prevail, and it sets in relief the one-sided and unacceptable torture which Glory inflicts on him against his will, where trust is absent.

At the present stage, of course, the fact that the Buffybot has been programmed according to his own instructions makes it impossible for them to interact playfully in this way in any authentic sense, since that would require two free agents willingly ceding their power on a basis of trust, so the best he can hope for is a simulation of such a relationship. Its inadequacy is forcefully conveyed just before Spike is captured and delivered to Glory, when we cut to a medium close-up of Spike alone in the frame in the wake of his various sexual encounters with the robot in earlier scenes. Indeed, it seems more than likely that another such encounter has taken place off-screen immediately prior to *this* scene as well, as Spike's dishevelled hair and the cigarette hanging from his mouth would seem to suggest. Wearing one of his customary black T-

Fig. 2.5

shirts, he leans back against the wall, a picture of emotional detachment and alienation. The door handle rattles, Spike hurriedly buckles his unfastened belt, telling the Buffybot to hide, and Xander enters.

Xander tells Spike he saw him with Buffy (or so he thinks), and Spike begins to realise the game is up, though he appears unsure how to respond. Making a small show of sullen defiance, he tries to brazen it out, but the fact that this comes so soon after the close-up conveying Spike's disillusionment with the Buffybot makes him seem defenceless and wary, rather than genuinely spoiling for a fight. The relationship with the Buffybot is already played out, and Spike seems to be walking through his part in the confrontation with Xander, sparring more out of habit than anything else, as he follows Xander's lead and prolongs his mistaken assumption – and Spike's own fantasy – that it *was* Buffy whom Spike was 'comforting' in the cemetery when Xander saw him. Shortly after Xander accuses Spike of being a monster, Glory's minions arrive and take him to be the Key. Spike is thus having to defend himself in all directions – denying that he is a monster to Xander, denying that he is the Key to Glory's minions – while not quite knowing who he is or should become, nor how to put the robot behind him without being caught out by Xander and the others. His perplexity persists throughout this scene, and his attempted bravado now appears as the thinnest of covers. There is a notable echo of the progression that we saw in Giles in our consideration of 'Innocence' above, where he stammered in confusion when trying to grasp precisely what it was that made Angel go bad, yet went on to achieve genuine moral stature in his unconditional commitment to Buffy, despite the consequences of what she had done. Spike too will rise above his own confusions to discover his moral centre when he refuses to betray Buffy to save himself.

The final scene in 'Intervention' is comparable in length and number of shots to the scene examined from 'I Was Made to Love You': approximately two minutes and thirty seconds long and made up of twenty-five shots. The sequence of shots is structured around a run of five shots more or less in the middle which have no dialogue at all (Shots 12–16). This wordless segment is framed by two bits of dialogue, first the more extensive conversation between Spike and Buffy when he takes her to be the Buffybot (Shots 3–11), and, afterward, by further dialogue between them when Spike is fully aware that it is Buffy he is talking to and not the robot, though Spike speaks only twice (Shots 17–18), while Buffy speaks at greater length (Shots 18, 20 and 22), interspersed with wordless close-ups of Spike (Shots 19, 21 and 23). Finally, these two conversations either side of the silent centre of the sequence are themselves further framed by Buffy's wordless arrival at Spike's crypt at the beginning (Shots 1–2) and her wordless departure at the end (Shots 24–25). So silence plays an important part in the scene, whether on its own or in its interplay with dialogue, an interplay between talking and taking in the presence of another person, both by listening in the dialogue segments and by silent observation throughout the scene.

Of all the characters in *Buffy the Vampire Slayer*, Spike is probably the one whose relationship with Buffy is most movingly defined by their moments of stillness together, often involving silence as well (as we will see in the scene to be examined later, from 'After Life'). Although Spike is frequently a man of many words, especially when cornered or under threat, and is in command of a range of intonations from sarcasm to indignation, swagger, seductiveness and beyond, he can also show himself to be a man of *few* words when he forgets his defensiveness and puts someone else's needs before his own: this 'someone else' tends to be Buffy (or, occasionally, Dawn). For example, eleven episodes earlier in Season Five (5.7: 'Fool For Love'), Buffy finds out her mother has to go into hospital overnight for a CAT scan, and she goes out on the back porch alone and cries. Spike arrives with a gun, determined to kill her after she had expressed her disgust for him earlier and cruelly told him he was beneath her, though, as usual with Spike, his dramatic gesture undoubtedly has more bark than bite. Now he becomes aware of her distress, and the sinister point-of-view shot as he first approaches her is quickly replaced by more open and sympathetic shots which balance what he sees with how he reacts. He lowers the gun and asks if there is anything he can do. Receiving no reply, he tilts his head to study Buffy quizzically, then sits down on the porch steps beside her and hesitantly pats her on the back. Buffy never seems to notice the gun nor to feel at all threatened by his presence, perhaps sensing more clearly than he does that he could never do her serious harm. The camera moves slowly to the right as they continue to sit together quietly in the evening stillness, no longer speaking or touching or looking at each other anymore, just remaining side by side and sharing the shadows. Such moments represent Spike at his best.

Fig. 2.6

In the final scene of 'Intervention', its organisation around its silences and their interplay with the two conversations inserted within the sequence draws on our memories of such earlier moments, and, once again, shows how much better Spike is than Buffy's friends at sensing her presence and picking up on subtle changes in her moods and behaviour. In line with this, there is much more emphasis on his silent reactions than on anything he has to say once he realises that this is Buffy and not the robot. The focus on Spike and his experiences throughout the scene, rather than on what Buffy is going through, is accomplished through a number of strategies. First, Buffy has come along with a very specific purpose in mind: to find out whether Spike has put Dawn in danger by revealing her identity to Glory (though we may not be aware of this at first nor appreciate that it is really Buffy arriving at Spike's crypt and not the robot). The immediately preceding scene both makes clear that Buffy is appalled at the prospect that the broken robot might be fixed and also lets us know that Willow could easily repair it if Buffy wanted her to, with even Xander expressing some sympathy for Spike after his beating and the loss of his 'toy': '...the guy was so thrashed.' Thus, we are simultaneously prepared for two possible outcomes – the robot either abandoned in its present state of disrepair or restored to Spike in full working order – without finding out for sure which one takes place off-screen after the end of the scene.

However, regardless of whether we immediately realise that it is Buffy impersonating the Buffybot's speech and movements and wearing her clothes, any uncertainties disappear with the first close-up of Buffy (Shot 10) and her response, after Spike insists she can never tell Glory who the Key is: 'Why?' The close-up underlines the importance of this question to Buffy, imposing a sincerity on her delivery of the line which is wholly lacking in her imitation of the robot's programmed chatter up to that point. Yet despite our being in on Buffy's purpose, at least from the close-up onward, our sympathies appear to be directed more strongly towards Spike, partly because, unlike Buffy, we already know he stood up to Glory. We can thus afford to be critical of Buffy's deception and the lack of trust in him that it reveals (especially given the evidence of his battered body): for us, if not for her, Spike's trustworthiness is already beyond dispute.

Further, the camera places us inside the crypt with Spike before Buffy arrives, and we remain there with him after she leaves. Her comings and goings as she moves into and out of the scene take place in the background, whereas Spike is consistently located in or near the foreground of the image in every shot in which he appears. Thus, there are a greater number of close-ups of Spike, whereas Buffy's more variable distance from the camera makes our intimacy with her more patchy. The close-up shots of Spike have little depth of field, with plain, dull-coloured walls and windows out of focus behind him, which encourages us to concentrate more fully on him. In contrast, in the close-up of Buffy when she asks Spike why Glory must not find out about Dawn, we see various details and objects in the background. For example, a statue of a woman just behind her may remind us of Buffy's confession to Giles earlier in the episode that 'being the Slayer is turning me into stone'.

Thus, Spike's emotions are much more 'visible' throughout the scene than Buffy's, with a number of reaction shots of his face as he tries to make sense of what is going on. Though Buffy and Spike ask three questions each, Buffy's are either a rhetorical performance to convince him she is the Buffybot ('Do you wanna ravage me now?'), or a straightforward trawl for information ('Why did you let that Glory hurt you?'), or, finally, in the close-up mentioned earlier, a final need to reassure herself of Spike's continuing reliability when he tells her Glory can never find out who the Key is ('Why?'). In other words, they are all part of her calculated plan to gain information vital to her and Dawn and are intellectually motivated rather than emotionally revealing. Spike's questions, on the other hand, are spontaneous reactions to a series of perplexing events: the unex-pected arrival of what he takes to be the Buffybot ('Where've you been?'), the fact that she has not been destroyed ('Will fixed you?'), and the realisation that the robot is Buffy after all, which Spike makes clear when he asks about the Buffybot's fate. They increase our sense of his emotional vulnerability as he falls for Buffy's ruse and as his struggle to understand what is going on puts him at so clear a disadvantage. The third and final question ('And my robot?') is an acknowledgment of the success of her deception – with, perhaps, a quiet note of token defiance to cover his humiliation at her knowing about the Buffybot – rather than exposing a genuine desire to reclaim it. Indeed, he lowers his head when Buffy reprimands him, and, after a few broken words ('It wasn't supposed to…'), he says nothing further, unable or unwilling to mount any sort of self-defence or justification.

Our emotional involvement with Spike is thus assured by all these elements: (i) Buffy's deceptiveness and lack of trust in him (and the fact that we know better), (ii) her accurate impersonation of the robot's superficiality, as well as the visual links between her and the stone statue, both of which block our access to her feelings and suggest a certain 'hardening' and emotional inaccessibility in Buffy, (iii) our physical affiliation with Spike as Buffy arrives and leaves, (iv) Spike's greater intimacy with the camera through his consistent placement in the foreground of the image, (v) the emphasis, through choice of camera distance and shot duration, on Spike's reactions, as he tries to puzzle out what's going on, rather than on what he says, (vi) the emotional and physical pain he is in and the touching hints of defiance with which he endures them both. Buffy's kiss, when she comes to know that Spike has been true to her and Dawn in the face of Glory's torture, generates the scene's single close-up view of them together in the frame, cut around an inserted reaction shot of her from somewhat further away (though, in the close-up shots that surround it, we get much more access to *his* face than to hers). At the same time, the kiss motivates the wordless sequence of shots at the heart of the scene.

The five shots that comprise this sequence (Shots 12–16 in the scene as a whole) follow Spike's admission that he would die for Buffy, and they unfold as follows:

12. Cut to Buffy over Spike's shoulder in medium close-up as she moves in towards him. [4 seconds]

13. Cut to Spike over Buffy's shoulder in close-up as she kisses him. He looks puzzled and pulls back slightly, frowning, as he figures out what's going on. This is the middle shot of the scene as a whole, though in terms of expired time, the mid-point occurs in Shot 11. So there are two competing centres to the scene: Buffy's recognition of Spike's trustworthiness (Shot 11) and Spike's recognition of Buffy (Shot 13). [9 seconds]

Fig. 2.7

14. Cut to Buffy over Spike's shoulder in medium close-up as she holds his gaze and silently confirms her identity by the steady intensity of her look. As the central shot in the five-shot sequence, the sustained look between them is another crucial pivot around which the scene's multiple symmetries revolve (a third mid-point to add to those mentioned above). [4 seconds]

15. Cut back to Spike over Buffy's shoulder in close-up again, with Spike characteristically tilting his head to study her, as we saw before in 'Fool For Love'. [4 seconds]

16. Cut to Buffy in medium close-up over Spike's shoulder (though he is nearly out of frame on the left), as Buffy turns to go. [1 second]

Spike's reaction to Buffy's kiss as being recognisably different from the Buffybot's is further evidence of the robot's inadequacies as object of his desire, and, for a brief moment, his fantasy comes true, as what he takes to be the Buffybot is 'magically' transformed into Buffy herself. However, Buffy's choice of a kiss as his reward for standing up to Glory for her and Dawn is double-edged: it both expresses her knowledge of his yearning for her and, at the same time, encompasses the fact that the kiss means something different to him than to her. Thus, the kiss, though freely given, can only ever fall short of what he wants, since Buffy acts out of gratitude, and not reciprocating desire. In this way, she is kind to him while simultaneously remaining uninvolved, as with her quiet sympathy for April in 'I Was Made to Love You', and nothing much is at stake for her in terms of commitment or emotional risk.

Earlier in the scene, Spike contrasts the Buffybot with Buffy, describing the latter as 'the other, not-so-pleasant Buffy', thus pinpointing his essential difference from Warren in Spike's preference for a woman with a will of her own, even if it makes her 'unpleasant'. The downside of this is that her affection cannot be forced, and Spike is left more lonely than ever as she leaves. Following Shots 13 to 15, with their intense shared looks into each other's faces – their mutual recognition of each other's fundamental human qualities – Buffy tells him what she thinks of the Buffybot in response to his final question about its fate ('The robot was gross and obscene ... it wasn't even real'). Spike lowers his head in apparent shame or defeat, and Buffy too averts her gaze as she walks away. Turning her head slightly, but still facing away, she tells him that what he did for her and Dawn 'was real' (Shot 20). Spike lifts his head in close-up (Shot 21) and, in an answering close-up, Buffy turns her head fully to meet his look (Shot 22): 'I won't forget it.' Another close-up of Spike (Shot 23) is followed by another of Buffy (Shot 24), still looking at Spike and then turning away and walking off, with the camera remaining stationary as she closes the door behind her in the background. The scene finishes with a close-up of Spike looking at the door in silence and stillness (Shot 25), then the end credits start to appear.

The sequence as a whole represents a further step in the exploration of what it is to be human which is so central to the series as a whole. However, unlike the treatment of April in 'I Was Made to Love You', the humanising of Spike has ramifications for Buffy herself which will prove more difficult for her to put aside. At this point, although she recognises Spike's basic goodness, she lacks the attraction to him which the camera already displays (and the audience presumably share). There are two self-conscious camera movements in the scene which exemplify the way Spike seems to fascinate the camera: first, after Buffy enters Spike's crypt near the beginning of the scene and walks briskly forward, her arms swinging by her side as she imitates the Buffybot, and we then cut to Spike lying still with his eyes closed, the camera rapidly closing in on him, independent of Buffy's movements (Shot 3); second, when the camera circles around him in close-up as he asks about the fate of the robot (Shot 17). These examples of how the camera gravitates to Spike and is unable to tear itself away provide a contrast to the ease with which Buffy detaches herself and walks away at the end of the scene. Although she has certainly come to recognise him in some deeper and more accurate way – granting him moral qualities which make it impossible to treat him with a clear conscience as no more than a monstrous *thing* – she has yet to recognise *herself* in Spike. That will come later. So too will her own enthralment as she enters into a sexually addictive relationship with him in Season Six where she appears to forfeit her will to resist him, despite the self-loathing she experiences as a result. However, before that can happen she has to die, although her death at the end of Season Five will not be examined until the following chapter. For now, we need to skip forward to the third of Buffy's brief encounters to be looked at here.

'After Life'

This episode takes place shortly after Buffy's friends have brought her back from beyond the grave, and its final scene shows her escaping from their eager interest in her to spend some time on her own, only to discover Spike in the shadows behind the magic shop. The relationship between Spike and Buffy builds on the trust established at the end of 'Intervention', but now Buffy is the one who is emotionally raw and vulnerable and taken to the edge. Another difference from 'Intervention' is that, as noted earlier, Spike and Buffy only come together there in the final scene, having followed separate narrative paths until then. 'After Life', in contrast, is punctuated by a series of quiet scenes between them interspersed with chattier scenes of Willow, Tara, Xander and Anya, sometimes with Buffy present and sometimes without her, with little overlap between the two. Spike tends to keep his distance whenever the others turn up, and Xander is particularly quick to speed him on his way. Besides Buffy herself, only Dawn seems caught in the middle, initially appearing alone with Buffy, but welcoming Spike without hostility when he turns up and joins them, and sharing scenes with the others as well. So the battlelines are drawn.

Willow, Tara, Xander and Anya are intimately bound together by having conspired to bring Buffy back without telling either Dawn or Spike of their intentions, and they now appear to experience little guilt – at least not consciously – about the dangers they were courting nor the damage they may have done, though they keep reassuring one another that everything is all right. Willow in particular is far too self-satisfied at her own achievement, with far too much riding on a successful outcome, to show much interest in Buffy's feelings or to confront her own moral failings openly. Further, their pact to resurrect Buffy seems to have bound and isolated them within the episode's narrative structures as well as its plot, just as Buffy's growing trust in Spike opens up narrative spaces and journeys for the two of them to share away from the others, where they can confide in each other and be understood. One way of formulating the difference amongst the characters is that Spike and Dawn devote themselves to reassuring Buffy, while the others are much more concerned with reassuring themselves. In fact, even Dawn ultimately reveals her own neediness when she tells Buffy wistfully, 'Don't worry about me', in the course of Buffy leaving to patrol on her own without a thought for Dawn whose words may be seen as a direct response to Buffy's blatant *lack* of worry over her. Nevertheless, the touching indirectness with which her vulnerability is exposed testifies to her brave attempt to put Buffy's needs before her own, thus confirming her deeper links with Spike, rather than with the smug egocentricity of the others.

The episode as a whole feels less complicated than 'Intervention' in its narrative structure and concerns. First of all, the pre-credits sequence which edits together bits from previous episodes is more focused on a single plot strand: Buffy's death and resurrection (with a reminder of Spike's unrequited love for Buffy and the intensity of his grief when she dies, his legs giving way beneath him as he sinks to the ground in despair). Secondly, each scene follows on the heels of its predecessor with a much firmer sense of temporal continuity, at least at first: events are followed across a couple of nights and days, with the first post-credits scene displaying its tight sequentiality with particular force.

The scene begins with a fade-in on Dawn and Buffy entering their darkened house at night. Soon Spike arrives and is effortlessly eased into the scene, followed by the arrival of Willow, Tara, Xander and Anya as Spike talks with Buffy downstairs. This interruption causes Spike to leave, while Buffy goes upstairs to bed, pleading tiredness. A little later, when Xander and Anya leave the house, Xander notices Spike still hanging around outside. Following their confrontation, Spike drives off on his motorcycle, and we cut to Buffy upstairs in her room, still dressed as before, which emphasises that little time has passed across the cut. She turns her head with a start when she hears Willow in the hallway outside her room as Willow returns to her own room after phoning Giles, and we then listen in on a conversation between Willow and Tara, once Willow is back in their room, in which Willow decides to telephone Xander. This, in turn, motivates a cut to Anya and Xander together in bed, and their telephone ringing a short time afterwards. Thus we see the characters grouped together in various combinations and locations, reinforcing our sense of the separation of each person or couple or group from all the others, but with the strong temporal continuity of the whole thing fixing and sealing all these separate encounters and conversations into a seamless and unified sequence of events. By the time we cut to Xander in bright sunlight the following day, we are nearly halfway through the episode, yet it seems as if we have only watched a single scene in an approximation of real time which feels only minimally compressed.

The episode quickly begins to map out its thematic territory throughout this extended opening sequence, most importantly in the contrast it sets up between the tact and gentleness that Dawn and Spike offer Buffy and the insensitivity of the others, above all Willow and Xander. When Spike first arrives at the house to check on Dawn, unaware that Buffy has been restored, Dawn reassures Buffy at the sound of the door opening downstairs:

> Dawn [to Buffy]: It's OK. It's OK.
> Spike [shouting offscreen]: Dawn! Dawn! Are you there?
> Dawn [to Buffy]: It's … it's just Spike. [Turning in Spike's direction] I'm here!

As he scolds her for worrying him, she interrupts with quiet embarrassment as she attempts to adopt a convincingly cheerful tone: 'Spike … Look.' Buffy walks slowly down the stairs, her shadow accompanying her on the wall beside her, but Spike remains unperturbed: 'Yeah? I've seen the bloody bot before. Didn't think she'd patch up so…' Suddenly, he stops, and the camera moves in to a medium close-up of him, followed by a cut to Buffy returning his look and moving towards the camera into close-up as well. It is another powerful moment of mutual recognition, as in 'Intervention', but now all the more extraordinary both because Spike has no reason to believe Buffy to be anything but dead and buried, and because not so much as a touch has passed between them to tip him off this time, much less a kiss as before.

In an unexpectedly moving gesture, Buffy lowers her eyes, notices her shirt (which was unbuttoned earlier when Dawn was cleaning the graveyard dirt off Buffy's neck) and starts to button it up, continuing her reluctant attempt to think herself back into the world and its proprieties. (Another example of Buffy's difficulty remembering how the world works, and of the touching innocence and vulnerability this seems to confer on her, occurs when Dawn tells her earlier that someone will telephone Giles, and Buffy wonders, 'What, um ... will you say to him?') Buffy's awkwardness continues when the gesture of buttoning up her shirt causes Spike to notice her bloodied knuckles and she quickly hides them. The close-ups between them carry on, and Spike immediately understands – as Dawn did not – that Buffy has had to claw her way out of her coffin. Spike gently tries to counter her shame and emotional disconnectedness by telling her that he once had to do the same thing himself. Although Dawn lacks Spike's insight into Buffy's experiences, she is equally alert to her needs, and Spike's promise to Buffy – 'We'll take care of you' – acknowledges his common purpose with Dawn.

While Dawn goes off for bandages, Spike and Buffy sit facing each other in the foreground in the first of their three meetings alone with each other in the episode as he holds her hands and they talk. His body language when he leans in slightly to hear her and nods in affirmation is of a kind with Dawn's earlier tenderness as she had guided Buffy in and washed her. Suddenly, Willow rushes in with the others, asking, 'Is she here?' The disorderly intrusion of all four of them arriving at once abruptly shatters the peaceful haven created by Dawn's and Spike's more sensitive approaches to Buffy, and both Willow and Xander (whose idea of consolation is to offer to get Buffy a pizza) have never seemed more crass. Meanwhile, Spike walks off in the foreground, his departure unremarked. Xander's comment to Spike when he spots him outside as he and Anya leave – 'I hope you're not gonna start your little obsession now that she's around again' – reveals a streak of vulgar mean-mindedness all the more shocking in its contrast with Spike's own generous behaviour to Buffy, where all traces of his own desires were subsumed to her needs.

Spike grabs Xander by the collar and slams him against a tree, furious that the others brought Buffy back and did not tell him, reminding Xander pointedly: 'I worked beside you all summer.' The way the light shines on Spike's face in close-up, just under his eye, suggests the appearance of tears without their actual presence, so Spike can be both vulnerable and strong at once. His moral censure of Xander and the others for accepting his help while excluding him from their trust is extended to a condemnation of their irresponsible use of black magic in his final comment as he drives away: 'That's the thing about magic. There's always consequences. Always!' It is an observation worthy of Giles. Indeed, in Giles' absence, Spike unexpectedly fills the moral vacuum left by his departure, and the act of slamming Xander against the tree may recall the moment in 'I Was Made to Love You' examined earlier when Giles shoves Spike himself against a cabinet to make a point about his leaving Buffy alone.

The following morning, Willow, Tara, Xander and Anya discuss the demon that seems to have accompanied Buffy back from hell, not yet realising that he is *their* creation: one of the consequences of meddling in black magic that Spike warned Xander about. When Buffy arrives wearing a black shirt that makes her stand out from the others and the bright daylight around them, they try to tell her what her resurrection means to them. However, their words are empty and bland (the best Xander can do is to tell her that having her back is 'so important'), and the absence of soundtrack music adds to the sense of a lack of emotional connection between them and Buffy that permeates the scene. As they continue their researching indoors, Buffy remarks that she misses Giles, which provokes Willow's equivocal response that she knows she is 'a kind of poor substitute', thus clearly expressing her resentment at being so under-appreciated and her wish to be assured that she is not a poor substitute for Giles after all. This implicit arrogance will become explicit when Giles returns in the following episode (6.4: 'Flooded') and Willow coldly directs her anger towards Giles himself when he criticises her for bringing Buffy back at such risk and calls her a 'rank, arrogant amateur', rather than congratulating her as she expects.

The awkwardness of the scene – the emotional coldness of its tone – pushes Buffy to go off on her own to patrol, without a backward glance at Dawn and the others, leading straight to Dawn's possession by the demon, who has no solid body of his own. It is all too easy to see the demon as a vehicle for Dawn's suppressed anger at Buffy for her apparent indifference. After all, the demon's earlier manifestations (first, disguised as Buffy verbally abusing Willow and Tara, then as Anya taunting Xander) and its later one (in the body of Xander as they discover together that killing Buffy will keep the demon from dissipating) can readily be taken to reflect the brew of ill-feeling amongst them that cannot be owned up to and dealt with in the open. As Xander reassures Dawn that the demon is gone, Anya qualifies his optimism: 'Yes, but where did it go? I mean, evil things have plans. They have things to do.'

We cut from this to Spike pacing in his crypt, punching the wall until his knuckles bleed. Presumably the point of the cut from Anya's words to Spike is less to suggest that Spike actually *is* an evil thing than to highlight the discrepancy between the gang's condescension towards him and the more sympathetic view we are being encouraged to adopt. On hearing the door opening, Spike goes upstairs to find Buffy there, the two of them immediately linked together in the dialogue between them, providing a further basis for resisting the superficial implications of the cut to Spike from Anya's words.

Buffy: Your hand is hurt.
Spike: Hm. Same to you.

So Buffy's wish to patrol by herself is a flimsy concealment of a deeper wish to return to Spike for the second of their three encounters in the episode, in preference to remaining with her 'friends'. Both she and Spike are wearing black tops, and both blend in with the darkness of the surrounding mise-en-scène. This growing affinity for the concealing cloak of darkness which Buffy displays is seen earlier too in the way she enters rooms without turning on the lights, leaving others to do so on her behalf (for example,

Dawn is the one to turn the lights on both upstairs and down when she first brings Buffy home), and in the way her shadow accompanies her downstairs in the first meeting with Spike.

Spike and Buffy sit facing each other as he does all the talking, essentially apologising for failing to prevent her death, though he did save her later: 'Not when it counted, of course, but ... after that. Every night after that.' The camera cuts from close-ups of her to medium close-ups of him, with a couple of long shots of them sharing the frame. His open acknowledgment of his failure to save her contrasts with Willow's more covert desire for praise and thanks (though Tara does get Willow to admit her disappointment in Buffy, at least to her, by prompting Willow gently in an earlier scene, after Willow's telephone call to Giles: 'You thought she'd say thanks. Be more grateful.'). Further, the way Spike and Buffy face each other and look directly into each other's faces is very different from the conversation between Willow and Tara which begins, at least briefly, with Tara looking off-screen right towards Willow, who is only seen on-screen in the mirror behind Tara, her face turned away in the depths of the frame, behind the reflection of the back of Tara's head. So we have an over-determined image of non-communication, with Tara looking away from the mirror, and both women seen from behind in the mirror itself, until Willow turns around. Shortly after, in bed with Tara, Willow owns up to her vanity in wanting Buffy's gratitude (as Tara had suggested): 'Would I be a terrible person if I said "Yes"?'

Such veerings between honesty and miscommunication are obliquely represented early in the episode by a word game Anya tries to get the sleeping Xander to play with her when she cannot fall asleep (and before he is awakened by Willow's telephone call): 'OK, I'm gonna describe an adjective with accurate but misleading clues, and then you have to guess what it is.' Unfortunately, we never get to hear her do this, though the prospect is intriguing, both because her usual literal-mindedness makes it hard to imagine her being any good at wordplay, but equally because her quirky use of language is insensitive to shadings of tone and meaning so that, despite its literal accuracy, it often inadvertently leads its listeners down the garden path. Anya's tendency to miss the point in her single-minded quest for literal accuracy is shown at the start of the second day (after Buffy's solitary patrol and nighttime visit to Spike's crypt) when Willow discovers the demon is a side-effect of Buffy's resurrection, 'Like a price.' Anya quickly corrects her: 'Well, technically, that's not a price. That's a gift with purchase', thus combining her literalness with her capitalist zeal.

In the end, it is Buffy who does what Anya suggests, after the demon is defeated and Dawn tells Buffy that the only thing the others want is to see her happy. Turning up at the Magic Box, Buffy chooses her words with care as she finally thanks Willow and the others for having brought her back. She begins by lying that she was in hell, as they have all assumed, but then continues more truthfully: 'I, um ... I can't think too much about what it was like. But it felt like the world abandoned me there. And then suddenly ... you guys did what you did.' (Here Tara insists it was all Willow's doing, and Buffy continues.) 'OK. So you did that. And the world came rushing back. Thank you. You guys gave me the world. I can't tell you what it means to me. And I should have said it before.' A cut to Willow in close-up makes her gratification evident, as she completely misses the 'accurate but misleading' phrasings that Buffy uses, especially the ambivalence that hangs so heavily in the air around Buffy's penultimate sentence: 'I can't tell you what it means to me.' Further, Buffy's comment on how 'the world came rushing back' is reminiscent of the way that Willow and the rest of the gang came rushing in so intrusively during Buffy's initial conversation with Spike. It may also recall the way the camera rushed in on Willow as she threw her head back, surrounded by light, and cast the spell that turned the demon from an insubstantial figure to a solid one that Buffy could defeat, thus associating the camera rush with Willow's power. So this image of the world rushing back is likely to be a negative and disturbing one for the audience, but one whose implications are completely lost on Willow, prepared as she is to have her actions vindicated and affirmed, but not seen critically.

From this we cut to the third encounter between Buffy and Spike, and the final scene in the episode, a scene that lasts three minutes and 48 seconds and is made up of 28 shots, as Buffy emerges from the back door of the Magic Box to find Spike waiting for her in the shade, having heard her inside 'exchanging a special moment' with her friends and, once again, preferring to remain outside their circle. When he asks her sarcastically whether she is not 'leaving a hole in the middle of some soggy group hug', she tells him she just wanted some time alone and walks over to sit down beside him. The scene is deceptively simple: all that happens is that Buffy tells Spike she thinks she was in heaven, not hell. Buffy's admission becomes a virtual monologue, with Spike saying nothing after Shot 12 in the sequence, when Buffy cuts off his offer of help and his attempt to empathise ('...I do know a thing or two about torment') by suddenly undermining his assumptions and confessing: 'I was happy.' Spike's function in the long series of intercut close-ups between them (Shots 8–11 and then Shots 13–27) is to be the one person she can confide in, and they take up well over half the scene. As Buffy says, 'I can be alone with you here', making him not so much a nobody as an intimate part of herself, a quiet sounding-board for her own thoughts. The close-up reaction shots of him that bind him to her throughout her extended confession give the scene an intimacy more fully reciprocal than in the final scene in 'Intervention', when Spike was the emotionally fragile one and Buffy remained emotionally detached. Here, Buffy is the fragile one, but Spike hangs on her every word.

At the start of the sequence, everything seems back to normal (that is, to the way things were before Buffy's death). Wearing neither her funeral dress nor the plain white or black blouses of earlier scenes, her hair no longer wild after the climb from her grave nor carelessly tied back as before, Buffy is dressed with much more care and attention to detail. Her outfit is beige and stylish, she wears a locket and bracelet, and her hair is loose and clean. Spike too seems back to his usual attempts at sarcastic banter, after their earlier more authentic moments together. Nevertheless, Buffy's appearance, juxtaposed with the immediately preceding scenes where she sends Dawn off to school and then thanks her friends in the Magic Box, seems part of an attempt to put on a brave face for them all which is betrayed by details of her performance and facial expressions throughout those scenes. Similarly, Spike's sarcastic manner is quickly dropped when he notices her present unease, studying her closely in Shot 5 as she fiddles with her hair, folds her hands in her lap, and lowers her eyes, Spike responding by asking gently: 'Are you OK?' Buffy's choice of solitude and shadows is matched by Spike's willingness, as a vampire vulnerable to sunlight, to wait for Buffy outside during the day (though he reassures her, 'Sun's low enough. It's shady enough here'), as they take tentative steps towards each other's worlds, meeting up in a gray place in between them.

The imagery of the episode as a whole finds its culmination here. For example, Willow and the rest of the gang can be seen to be on the side of solidity and light, while Buffy herself feels insubstantial and prefers the dark. Thus, Willow performs a spell to make the demon solid in order for Buffy to be able to defeat it, and, although the demon is able to possess the actual bodies of Anya, Dawn and Xander in turn, it can only take on the *appearance* of Buffy while Buffy herself lies asleep in bed. When they fight each other, the demon confirms Buffy's experience of physical insubstantiality by telling her: 'You're the one who's barely here, set on this earth like a bubble.' Similarly, we have noted how Buffy prefers to stand in darkened rooms, while others (like Dawn and Tara) are seen turning on lights. Now, in the final scene with Spike, Buffy explains distastefully how 'hard, and bright, and violent' she finds the world. This violence is reflected in her description in the Magic Box scene of how 'the world came rushing back', as well as in her present words to Spike of being 'torn' out of heaven by her friends, descriptions which contrast with the quiet stillness Spike offers her here and elsewhere, as they talk.

Her choice of clothing in the episode's final scenes may now be taken not just as an indication that she is getting back to normal (or at least pretending to do so for the sake of her sister and friends), but as a reflection of her attraction to the amorphous gray areas that Spike inhabits and their shared suspension between life and death, both in the flimsiness of the fabric and in its pale beige shades (as opposed to the heavily textured fluffy red top that Willow wears in the scene where Buffy thanks her, as well as in contrast to Buffy's own blouses earlier in the episode, one all white, the other completely black). Buffy's growing closeness to Spike and her estrangement from Willow provide moral markers of the very different trajectories Spike and Willow are now embarked upon: where Willow is starting down a path of arrogant abuse of her magical powers, Spike (who momentarily takes on Giles' role by pointing out that magic always has consequences) is on a path to redemption, ultimately regaining his soul at the end of Season Six and closing the Hellmouth in Season Seven. Even at this earlier stage, Spike seeks forgiveness for having failed to keep Buffy alive, while Willow seeks gratitude and praise for having saved her from hell, though she has actually done no such thing. Buffy's first close-up in the final scene (Shot 9) is generated by Spike's genuine concern (offering his help if she is in any pain), the word 'pain' providing a bridge across the cut to Buffy's close-up, where she briefly returns his look before lowering her eyes.

The structural oppositions of the season's storyline are thus laid out with extreme clarity, and it is equally obvious where we are encouraged to direct our sympathies. The grayer, less physically substantial terrain on which Buffy and Spike come together in trust and mutual understanding at the end of the episode is reflected in the more uncertain sense of space and time we are given as viewers, compared to the tight continuity we noted earlier in the opening scene. Buffy's confrontation with the demon takes place around daybreak after a sleepless night during which the gang research the demon, and Buffy visits Spike in his crypt. From Buffy's beheading of the demon in the early hours between night and day, we cut to a shot of Sunnydale in bright sunlight, followed by Dawn heading off to school, Buffy turning up at the Magic Box, and the final scene with Spike. However, whether this day is the same one as when the demon is killed (and thus a mere couple of hours later) or whether there has been an intervening day of rest and recovery, there is no way of knowing. The location behind the Magic Box is also disorientating: only Spike's comment about overhearing Buffy 'exchanging a special moment with her friends' lets us know where we are, since the space just outside the back exit from the shop is not a familiar series location.

The final scene of 'After Life' is thus appropriate to Spike's and Buffy's developing relationship as equals occupying a shadowy middle-ground between their two contrasting worlds. Unlike 'Intervention', where Buffy arrives and leaves in the background and Spike is the focus of our emotional involvement in the scene, the final shot in 'After Life' (of Buffy in the foreground and Spike a smaller figure behind her as she leaves) reverses the scene's opening shot where a smaller Buffy in long shot comes out of the Magic Box to discover Spike entering the foreground in medium close-up. The long series of alternating close-ups between them which forms the bulk of the scene reinforces the balancing of our sympathies between the two. Such things as Buffy's diaphanous blouse, whose fabric moves delicately in the breeze as she and Spike share a patch of shade, the lack of firm anchoring of the scene in a familiar space and determinate time, and the overlap of the words of Buffy's extended confession across alternating close-ups of them both, produce a sense of boundaries being dissolved and of the hard, violent imagery of Willow's world giving way to something more tentative and with softer edges. Buffy's longing for such a space is apparent when she tells Spike that 'Time didn't mean anything. Nothing had form', after her death, and that she was '...happy. At peace.' Although Buffy keeps her eyes lowered or averted for virtually all of her monologue (despite Spike's intense looks at *her*), there is no longer any need for the moments of recognition which punctuated earlier scenes and episodes. By now, each of them knows and trusts the other. In 'After Life' they have moved on from this to recognise *themselves* in each other, as this boundary too, between self and other, begins to fall away. Of course, the series is by no means over at this point, with just over forty more episodes to go, and their relationship will continue to evolve in unexpected ways.

An account of any aspect of such a long and complex series as *Buffy the Vampire Slayer* can only be partial and provisional, given the way its characters both drive the narrative and continually change and develop in response to its events and to their interactions with other characters who are themselves following equally complicated paths. My choice of scenes has depended heavily on a sense of the moral weight and integrity of the series and the way this plays out in a range of thoughtful explorations of the distinction between persons and things. Rejecting essentialism, the series gives many examples of characters who achieve a convincing humanity simply by behaving like humans, and thus acquire a certain right to be treated as human by others, despite their robotic or vampiric forms. April's final moments in 'I Was Made to Love You', and Spike's requisition of the robot in Buffy's image later in the same episode, were used to set the scene for various encounters between Buffy and Spike in 'Intervention' and 'After Life' either side of Buffy's own death at the end of Season Five. These Buffy/Spike encounters provide a delayed payoff for Season One's exposure of the inadequacies of mere information on its own – surely an over-rated commodity in the present age of information technology – by presenting us with moments of recognition between Buffy and Spike which have profound moral qualities and implications which far transcend the characters' generic roles as vampire and slayer and the acquisition of factual knowledge alone. The final scenes of these two episodes are meditative codas to all that has gone before.

3. *Re*-reading *Buffy*: 'Normal Again'

> *Dawn*: Everything about me is made up.
> — 5.13: 'Blood Ties'

In examining some of *Buffy*'s thematic preoccupations in the previous chapter, we looked at a diverse range of decisions, some deliberate and others no doubt more intuitive on the part of the creators of the series, their happy confluence generating a wealth of meanings around these issues. Details of script, performance, costume, set decoration, lighting, camerawork, editing strategies, visual imagery and motifs and thematic structures have all shown themselves to be rich and productive sources of such meanings, mutually reinforcing one another or pulling against each other in dynamic interaction. Further, the semantic plenitude of the *Buffy* text (the way that everything in it seems so full of meaning) becomes, itself, an object of self-examination for the series. In other words, *Buffy the Vampire Slayer* is not only about the characters and events within its narrative world, but about its own origins as a collective product of the imagination, about its processes of making meaning, about its identity as a text. This will be the subject of the present chapter.

We have seen that *Buffy the Vampire Slayer* plays with narrative by means of strategies such as allowing us glimpses of characters and events in the margins of the on-screen world or weaving in and out of more central storylines, or by orchestrating coordinated crossovers between contemporaneous episodes of *Buffy* and *Angel*. For example, one of the characters in Season Four of *Angel* rings up Willow for help, and Willow receives the telephone call on *Buffy* (7.17: 'Lies My Parents Told Me'), afterwards telling Buffy she has to go away for a day or two and subsequently turning up in Los Angeles on *Angel* (A4.15: 'Orpheus'), leaving Los Angeles at the end of the same episode and arriving back in Sunnydale on *Buffy* once again, with Faith in tow (7.18: 'Dirty Girls'). Angel himself turns up in Sunnydale a few episodes later (7.21: 'End of Days' and 7.22: 'Chosen') with a mystical amulet for Buffy which he acquired in the final episode of Season Four of *Angel* (A4.22: 'Home'). These crossovers go beyond mere guest appearances by characters from one series on another where all significant action is contained within the series they visit (for instance, when Woody from *Cheers* turned up on its spin-off series, *Frasier*). Rather, they imply that important narrative events of each series intersect with those of the other one, generating a larger space encompassing them both. Thus, although parts of the narrative of *Buffy* play out in the margins of the frame or are explicitly indicated as happening off-screen by on-screen references, other events related to those in *Buffy* take place wholly outside the visible portions of its narrative world and without being acknowledged in any detail by the series itself, though they are clearly visible as part of the on-screen world of *Angel*. To understand these events fully, both series need to be seen, so there is no longer just a *Buffy* text and an *Angel* text, but a *Buffy/Angel* text as well.

Another less frequently used strategy which binds the two series together is when the same events are presented in both, but with the experiences of different characters being emphasised in each. Thus, in a *Buffy* flashback to 1880, we see Spike before his transformation into a vampire, being rejected by the woman he loves, then sired by Drusilla a short while later (5.7: 'Fool For Love'). In the corresponding flashback in *Angel*, we see Spike just after Cecily rejects him and before Drusilla sires him, but with both these framing scenes missing from the episode, as Spike bumps into Angelus when passing him, Darla and Drusilla in the street (A2.7: 'Darla'). This street scene occurs in 'Fool For Love' as well, but without our seeing the faces of Angelus, Darla and Drusilla, since the episode concentrates on the experiences of Spike, who barely notices them, whereas in 'Darla', which concentrates on the shared perspectives of Angelus and Darla, we remain with them and Drusilla as Spike walks off. Each series fills in details missing from the other, and a more rounded understanding is only possible through watching them both. This strategy continues later in both 'Fool For Love' and 'Darla' with their respective flashbacks to the Boxer Rebellion in China in 1900 as well: once again, the two episodes have a scene in common when Drusilla tells Darla and Angel (whose soul is now restored) that Spike has 'killed himself a Slayer', though the scene of the actual killing is only included in *Buffy*, not *Angel*. In both series we see all four of them – Angel, Darla, Spike and Dru – approach the camera side by side as a fire burns behind them, but 'Darla' gives us a slow-motion shot of Angel singled out in the frame, while 'Fool For Love' gives us one of Spike on his own instead.

Beyond *Buffy*'s narrative playfulness and experimentation at the level of characters and events, we have also noted how the series is consistently concerned with presenting its narrative world as a densely packed and meaningful text whose rhetoric is no less important than the events it depicts, and not just as a complex but believable universe in its own terms. At times, even the characters themselves present their experiences as if fancifully picturing themselves to be embedded in carefully constructed scenarios that need critical interpretation, as when Giles tells Buffy, 'I believe the subtext here is rapidly becoming a ... a text' (2.11: 'Ted'), or when Buffy herself says, 'I'm still needing backstory here' (2.13: 'Surprise'), or Oz responds to Willow mistaking something he says to mean he finds her boring, by countering, 'I'd call that a radical interpretation of the text' (3.16: 'Doppelgangland'). Indeed, when Andrew makes a video in Season Seven (7.16: 'Storyteller') it becomes precisely this sort of construction, placing an extra layer of representation between us and the episode's narrative world as we see it through the eyes of Andrew's camera and with his voiceover commentary.

Such self-reflexive aspects achieve their most extreme formulation in Season Six (6.17: 'Normal Again'), when they threaten to undermine the narrative world built up so painstakingly throughout the entire series and to make it come tumbling down around us. Suddenly the possibility is raised that everything we have seen so far is a mere figment of Buffy's imagination, a literal and thorough-going construction from *outside* the imagined world, rather than the fanciful conceit of a character from *within* a world otherwise intended to be taken as 'real'. That is, the 'textness' of Sunnydale (its imaginary made-up aspect) may become so salient that Buffy herself is forced to take notice, its constructedness no longer merely an obvious fact for *viewers* of the series who necessarily balance their involvement with characters and events with the realisation that they are watching them on the television screen.

The plot of 'Normal Again' appears deceptively uncomplicated at first: Buffy is infected by a demon she kills, which causes her to hallucinate that she is in a mental hospital where her parents and a well-meaning psychiatrist try to convince her that her life as a slayer is the product of an over-active imagination, her friends, vocation and adventures all illusory. However, from the perspective of what we may call the 'Buffy universe', the assertion of its own illusoriness – what we have been calling its textness – is *itself* an illusion. Both worlds – the one where Buffy is a deluded young woman imagining herself into an extraordinary role, and the one where she really *is* the Slayer, hallucinating that she is *not* – are filmed with the same verisimilitude and visual clarity. The cuts back and forth between them slice what we see into narrative segments with equally compelling claims on our belief and demands for our allegiance. However, by the

Fig. 3.1

end of the episode, our belief seems to lead us one way and our allegiance the other. Thus, the final shot is in the mental hospital, not in the Buffy universe, as the psychiatrist regretfully tells Buffy's parents, 'I'm afraid we lost her.' In the end Buffy rejects the psychiatrist's advice to free herself from her delusions and regain her sanity by temporarily entering the world she has imagined and killing off her friends. The camera pulls back from a now catatonic Buffy who has refused to return to 'normal' at her friends'

expense. Instead she commits herself to the Buffy universe forever. Surely we share this commitment, despite the devastating evidence of the final shot.

The episode's strategies are reminiscent of those used in *A Matter of Life and Death* (Michael Powell and Emeric Pressburger, 1946), whose alternative spaces represent heaven and earth. In this fim, Peter Carter (David Niven), a British pilot during World War II, is forced to bail out of his burning plane without a parachute, after explaining his situation over the two-way radio to an American servicewoman, June (Kim Hunter), and promising to come and visit her as a ghost. The opening title of the film proclaims that 'This is a story of two Worlds … the one we know and another which exists only in the mind of a young airman whose life and imagination have been violently shaped by war.' Heaven is at first presented in black and white, and one of its inhabitants – 'Conductor 71' (Marius Goring), who lost Peter in the fog when he jumped from his plane and has now been sent back to earth to retrieve him – comments, after his arrival in the 'real' world: 'One is starved for Technicolor up there.' The everyday world is thus shown as a cinematic space, as much a product of the imagination as is heaven, and the film moves back and forth between the two worlds as the authorities in heaven hold a trial to determine Peter's fate, though he has by now met up with June, after washing up on the beach (having apparently fallen safely into the sea). The trial in heaven takes place at the same time as surgery on Peter's brain to try to save him back on earth, the two worlds appearing to merge when Peter and June are themselves called as witnesses by the heavenly court who descend on a celestial staircase to the operating theatre to interview them (with all the characters filmed in colour at that point).

Despite some ambiguity in how we are to take the film's alternative worlds, since both are explicitly shown throughout and several characters travel between them with ease, the film is careful to let only Peter 'see' Conductor 71 during his various visits to earth, when everyone else around him is frozen in time for their duration. Further, the trial scenes occur when Peter is either asleep or under anaesthesia. In this way, we are offered the strong implication that all the supernatural scenes are the product of Peter's unconscious mind. Accepting that this is the case in the Powell and Pressburger film, however, is far less disturbing than accepting the possibility that the Buffy universe is all in Buffy's mind. In *A Matter of Life and Death* our emotions are on the side of Peter's and June's burgeoning romance on earth. We stand to lose very little if we accept that Peter has merely imagined the scenes in heaven and those with Conductor 71 on earth, since they have no great hold on us. In contrast, the possibility of losing the world Buffy may have imagined from her hospital bed in 'Normal Again' is much more traumatic.

If we assume that those of us who have made it as far as the final stretches of Season Six are likely to be devoted viewers of the series, we have an obvious stake in the 'worldness' of the Buffy universe even as we are made aware in 'Normal Again' of its textuality (not only as a television series, which we have known all along, but within the terms of its own narrative world, at least that version of it seen from the perspective of the mental hospital). Thus, our commitment to the illusion of Buffy-as-Slayer (and all that goes with it) rests upon an extremely knowing and self-conscious decision on the part of viewers at the end of the episode. Buffy's own decision (as mental patient) to return to her friends while knowing they are figments of her imagination is also presented as a deliberate choice, a celebration of generosity and creative abundance over ordinariness and disempowerment. By the time Andrew makes his video in 'Storyteller', Buffy's words to him ('Stop telling stories. Life isn't a story') confirm her commitment to the 'reality' of the narrative world in which she chooses to remain at the end of 'Normal Again', even as its final shot implies the illusoriness of her choice. Thus, one consequence of Buffy choosing the imaginary world of Sunnydale over the real one of the mental hospital is that she has to suppress her knowledge of its imaginariness and to take it as real, while dismissing the hospital as a mere hallucination.

The effect of ending the episode in this way is to let its implications cast their net over the rest of the series. The possibility that a mentally ill Buffy is generating all the remaining episodes meshes with the series' preoccupations both with parallel universes and with the provisionality of the on-screen world – its concern, that is, both with relationships which stretch across narrative worlds and those that extend beyond the boundaries of the frame – and it is hard to completely suppress our knowledge that a catatonic Buffy may continue to exist unseen and unacknowledged in a discontinuous off-screen space outside the Buffy universe. One specific instance where a later event makes sense as the product of Buffy's continuing authorship of the series relates to the psychiatrist's comment that Warren, Jonathan and Andrew – Season Six's so-called villains – are unworthy monsters, mere kids playing with toys. This unkind implication that Buffy's imaginative powers are running out of steam may well be what is behind Warren shooting Buffy and accidentally killing Tara in the process two episodes later (6.19: 'Seeing Red'), Buffy thereby vindicating her continuing creative vitality to the psychiatrist and proving him wrong. In an even more ingenious twist, the demon that infects Buffy in 'Normal Again' turns out to have been set on her by Warren, Jonathan and Andrew as part of their plan to undermine her. If Buffy has conjured up the trio in her head, as the psychiatrist insists, it is a fitting revenge on the psychiatrist that she has imagined the trio as the cause of her hallucinations. Buffy does not just show the psychiatrist to be wrong about the depth of the trio's villainy (and, thus, about the extent of her own creative powers), as has already been suggested. She reduces the psychiatrist himself to no more than an illusory product of their evil deeds.

Two details in 'Normal Again' are particularly relevant to re-reading the series in its terms. The first is when the psychiatrist tells Buffy to be wary of the things she wants in the Buffy universe that keep attracting her, because the previous summer, *when she had a momentary awakening*, 'it was them that pulled you back in'. The second detail for us to keep in mind occurs during the camera's final retreat from a close-up of Buffy, withdrawn and unresponsive, in the corner of her hospital room: as the camera pulls further and further back through the window in the door to Buffy's room, it keeps the empty bed with its leather wrist and ankle restraints in view, as Buffy herself is edged off-screen. We will return to this later. Turning our attention to Buffy's momentary awakening the previous summer, we see, from what the psychiatrist says, that this was a time when she was able to put her supposed delusions out of her mind, abandoning the Buffy universe for several months, perhaps even to the extent of being well enough to leave the hospital and enjoy some time at home with her parents. The corresponding period, from the perspective of the Buffy universe, is, of course, the time between her death at the end of Season Five (5.22: 'The Gift') and her resurrection near the start of Season Six (6.2: 'Bargaining', part 2), the time she will later describe to Spike as like being in heaven.

Fig. 3.2

In light of the psychiatrist's remarks in 'Normal Again', Buffy's leap to her death can now be reinterpreted as a leap out of the fictional landscape of Sunnydale into her hospital bed, and thence into the embrace of her parents – her mother still alive and her parents' marriage still intact – for a short spell of ordinariness and sanity. It is a leap away from being the star of her heroic adventures to being their admitted author, an identity that must be disavowed once she commits herself to the 'reality' of the Buffy universe at the end of the episode, and to her slayer role within it.

Indeed, Buffy's death is presented visually not as a simple suicide but as a leap out of the Buffy universe into another dimension somewhere else – a chasm seeming to open up in mid-air and swallow her into itself long before she would have hit the ground – so that it is a real shock to find her dead body lying on the rubble at the end of the scene, so thoroughly does she seem to disappear into thin air as she falls.

Buffy's initial abandonment of her Sunnydale friends when she jumps from the tower, and her forced re-entry when her friends pull her back (events occurring either side of the interface of Seasons Five and Six) are reiterated, in 'Normal Again', by less dramatic back-and-forth crossings between its two incompatible worlds. These alternating sequences end in a moment of deliberate and decisive commitment based on Buffy's fleeting ability to hold both worlds in her mind at once and square up to the consequences of her choice, only to then forget where she has returned from for the rest of the series. Her stay in the hospital is dismissed from then on as no more than a passing hallucination of demonic origin, a one-off event rather than the underpinning (and at the same time the *un*pinning) of the entire series. If Buffy now suppresses her knowledge of her point of origin as she returns to the Buffy universe for good, then, conversely, in her earlier leap from the tower, she knows nothing of her *destination*, and her decision to jump is intended solely as a means to save the world she is leaving, not to deny its reality.

It is certainly notable that what endangers that world is that all the portals between it and other dimensions have begun to open, letting all manner of monsters spill into it from elsewhere. This interdimensional breakdown which Buffy sacrifices herself to undo – the threatened instability of parallel universes merging into one unholy mess – reflects the confusions between worlds (the 'Buffy world' of vampires and slayers, and the more prosaic world of the hospital) and the unstable traffic between them that 'Normal Again' retrospectively projects back onto Season Five. 'Normal Again' allows us to read the climax of Season Five not just as a seepage between 'real' dimensions of equal status, but just as much as a seepage between all such dimensions (now explicitly coded as fictional), taken as a whole, and the contrasting world where Buffy is in the mental hospital. In other words, the various dimensions opening up at the end of Season Five all exist to the same degree, though normally compartmentalised and inaccessible to one another except by travelling through portals by extraordinary means. In contrast, the supposed reality of all these dimensions together may now be seen as completely subsumed within the world of the hospital, these dimensions proliferating as imaginary products within the primary reality that generates them.

The opening of portals between alternative dimensions *within* the Buffy universe may be seen as punching holes in the fictional world itself (or at least what counts as the fictional world from the perspective of the real world of the hospital), threatening to leave it in tatters. Indeed, even in its own terms, Season Five produces a strong impression of alternative fictional worlds in collision, from the appearance of Dracula – most famous of fictional vampires whose visit to Sunnydale is as unlikely as it is brief – in the first episode of the season (5.1: 'Buffy vs. Dracula') through to the arrival of the Knights of Byzantium, who equally seem to come from an altogether different fictional world to Buffy's, particularly in the scene where we see them in chain-mail and on horseback chasing the caravan in which Buffy and her gang are making their escape (5.20: 'Spiral').

An explicit fiction of another sort is introduced into the Buffy universe at the end of the Dracula episode in the form of Buffy's 'sister' Dawn. Suddenly she is there as if she were always present, Joyce telling Buffy to take her sister with her to the movies, and both girls protesting in unison: '*Mom!*' Although we are given no explanation for her extraordinary introduction to the series, we find out later that she is 'the Key', a concentration of mystical energy able to open up the portals between dimensions and sought by the season's powerful villain, Glory, to allow her to return to her home dimension, though Glory has no idea at first that the Key is disguised in human form. It turns out that some monks embodied the Key in the form of Buffy's sister to ensure it a powerful protector, implanting false memories of Dawn's past in an innocent Dawn herself and in everyone around her. This is the truth about Dawn in the terms provided by Season Five's story arc. Buffy kills herself in her sister's place so that the portals between dimensions, which Dawn's blood-letting has opened, can close again before Dawn dies, the substitution of Buffy for Dawn made possible by their having the same blood in their veins, as sisters. So, in the terms of Season Five, Dawn really is human at the same time as she really is a mystical key.

However, once again our reading of all this gets a further gloss with the help of Season Six. For if Dawn is the key to unlocking dimensional portals, she is also the key to Season Five in another sense: her fictionality – her constructedness in the guise of Buffy's sister – brings dangerously close to the surface the possibility for the characters that they and their world are fictions as well. It is almost as if she has been placed in the fictional world as a retrospective reminder – or a prospective forewarning – of the lessons held in suspension in the final devastating shot of 'Normal Again'. The psychiatrist in 'Normal Again' himself comments on the oddity of Dawn's introduction to the Buffy universe with an alternative explanation: 'Buffy inserted Dawn into her delusion, actually rewriting the entire history of it to accommodate a need for a familial bond.' From the perspective of the hospital world, the monks embodying the Key in human form as Buffy's sister Dawn are representatives within the Buffy universe of Buffy's catatonic self outside it, the means by which Buffy creates Dawn as a fictional sister in an imaginary world.

Nonetheless, despite the serious undertones of Dawn's brief introduction to the series at the end of 'Buffy vs. Dracula', her first extended appearance in the following episode (5.2: 'Real Me') is lighthearted and affectionate in tone. The use of her voiceover as the camera moves around her room and ends up on her writing in her diary gives us direct access to her private thoughts, endowing her with a substance and interiority that belie her origins: 'Nobody knows who I am. Not the real me.' Her words appear to reverse Buffy's own concerns, expressed in a pre-credits conversation with Giles ('I need to know more. About where I come from'), in Dawn's confident assertion of knowing herself better than anyone else. Despite her complaint that 'It's like nobody cares enough to find out', her comment that, if she had superpowers like her sister, she would 'wear a mask to protect my loved ones', suggests she takes some pride in hiding herself from others. The irony, of course, is that her implicit claims to self-knowledge and self-possession – to a 'real me' within her grasp – are built on an illusion of selfhood. In a later episode, when she visits her mother in hospital, a madman will point at her and proclaim: 'There's no one in there' (5.9: 'Listening to Fear'). However, when we first get to know her in 'Real Me', we do not yet realise the extent to which her 'real self' is utterly absent as a product of any genuine memories or experiences of her own. Thus, although we certainly do not yet know who she is and are aware that some sort of explanation for her sudden arrival is required, we are still likely to assume that there *is* a self 'inside' her to be known. That is, we mistake what is a profound ontological deficiency in Dawn for an epistemological deficiency in ourselves.

Still, she has been fitted out with an illusory self that does service for the real thing, and it gives her a workable version of a teenage girl's sensibility. Both her innocence about sex (in missing the implications of Tara's and Willow's relationship, for example) and her schoolgirl crush on Xander are presented with considerable charm and sweet-ness. Thus, when Dawn tells us in voiceover that she feels Xander sees her 'as I am. As a woman', we cut to Dawn smiling goofily in his direction, oblivious to the chocolate ice-cream all over her mouth. Additional humour derives from the use of Harmony and her disgruntled minions in the episode (a sort of incompetent equivalent to Glory and *her* minions), as we see the fruits of Harmony's search for self-esteem since her break-up from Spike in Season Four. Having now got herself a gang of sorts, she

Fig. 3.3

tells Spike unconvincingly: 'You just can't stand the fact that I'm my own person now … I've found the real me and I like her.' Although humorous music is used from time to time in order to underline the gentle satire at her expense, she is often touching in her inept attempts at self-assertion and, like Dawn, is a kind of innocent bolstering up her uncertain sense of who she is with brave words. Despite being a vampire, Harmony is not very good at being bad, and she is often caught out unawares, like Dawn with the chocolate ice-cream on her face. Thus, the vacuousness at Harmony's centre, coupled with her lack of self-awareness, reinforce the season's more serious concerns with *Dawn's* illusory selfhood and resultant misplaced confidence in her knowledge of herself.

Such issues around Dawn and her place in the Buffy universe are reflected and given their own particular spin not only in Buffy's curiosity about her own origins ('where I come from'), but in Harmony's attempt to re-make herself in a braver image, and even in Giles trying on a couple of new versions of himself (as illustrated by the red car he has just acquired and is eager to show off to Willow and Tara, and by the interest he takes in the profit margins of the Magic Box, whose owner has been killed by Harmony's minions, and which Giles takes over by the end of the episode: 'It'll give me focus'). Tara, too, worried about being an outsider, gives hints of harbouring a darker version of herself from the world when Willow hugs her from behind, calling her 'one of the good guys', and Tara's smile abruptly drops away. This will be explained and developed later in

Fig. 3.4

the season (5.6: 'Family'). Thus, in spite of the light-hearted tone of much of the episode, a darker thread winds its way through and implies that more serious issues are yet to come, most notably when Dawn is approached by a madman outside the Magic Box (while the others examine the dead body inside) and he warns her ominously: 'I know what you are. You don't belong here'.

The implications of Dawn's final voiceover go well beyond her intended meaning in ways she cannot begin to imagine, as she manages a last dig at Buffy: 'She still thinks I'm Little Miss Nobody, just her dumb little sister. Boy, is she in for a surprise!' As we see her write these words in her diary and hear her speak them in voiceover, the camera pulls back from a medium close-up to a somewhat longer shot, peeling us away from too intimate an alignment with her perspective and implying a vantage-point outside the narrative world from which to observe it. Elsewhere, Dawn's voiceover itself is occasionally allowed to persist across cuts between shots of her writing in the diary and shots of what she is describing, often with Dawn as a character immersed within the scenes she describes. So she too alternates between being an active participant embedded in the Buffy universe and a disembodied voice commenting upon it from the ambiguous space outside its boundaries where voiceovers seem to originate. In other words, although her commentary is anchored in the narrative world by the shots of her busily writing, the persistence of her voice across other shots as well makes her seem to have one foot inside the narrative world before us and another outside it.

In a series so full of various texts to explain the workings of the world (from Giles' ancient tomes and the websites accessed by Willow to Andrew's home video in Season Seven), it is significant that Dawn uses diaries to create a coherent version of herself. However, some of the diaries which purport to chronicle her earlier life (before she came into existence as the embodied Key a mere six months previously) turn out not to be her own work after all: her life has thus been 'authored' from elsewhere, though she does not know it yet. Significant, too, is the fact that she discovers her identity as the Key from Giles' notes in the Magic Box, provoking Buffy's anger at Spike when she discovers he accompanied her there: 'How could you let her find out like that? From books and papers? You hate me that much?' (5.13: 'Blood Ties'). Along the same lines, near the beginning of this episode, when Dawn correctly senses that the others are talking about her behind her back, she storms off in a huff before sneaking out of her room to go to the Magic Box, telling them, 'Fine. I'm just gonna go to bed. That way, I won't accidentally get exposed to … like, words.' Finally, once she learns what she is, her response is to tear up her diaries and burn them in a bin, eliciting a poignant reaction from the others when they find out:

Buffy:	She burned all of her diaries.
Xander:	The Dawnmeister Chronicles?
Willow:	She's been keeping those since … I mean…
Buffy:	Since she was seven. I remember too, Will.

The concentration on writing and words – the alternative versions of Dawn authored by Giles, by the monks who installed her in her present life (complete with diaries from the past), and by Dawn herself – feed into our revisionist account of her from the perspective of 'Normal Again' in Season Six, when Buffy herself will be retrospectively exposed (if we take the hospital scenes as the ultimate reality within the series overall) as the overarching author of Dawn and all the others.

Many of Dawn's responses, while they may be taken simply in the terms posed by Season Five, are equally resonant in light of Season Six, and Dawn thus becomes emblematic of *all* the characters who are taken to be products of Buffy's imagination. Her desperate plea – 'What *am* I? Am I *real*? Am I *anything*?' – applies to everyone in the Buffy universe. Similarly, when she talks with Joyce and Buffy, after the others have gone home, and says, 'I'm just a key, right? Everything about me is made up', Buffy's response makes *her* emblematic, in turn, of all of *us*, caught up in a fictional universe whose characters move us despite the fact that we know they are not real: 'Dawn, Mom and I know what we feel. I know I care about you, I know that I worry about you.' Dawn's story not only relates to the issues around personhood raised in the previous chapter, but to the series' self-reflexive concern with what makes it possible for acknowledged fictions to touch us so deeply.

Three-quarters of the way through 'Blood Ties', Dawn turns up in the mental ward at the hospital, having earlier remembered the way a couple of crazy people had seemed to know who she was. Her appearance in the ward disturbs the patients, all bound to their beds by wrist constraints, and one of them – Orlando, a Knight of Byzantium driven mad by Glory – recognises Dawn as the Key, calling forth from her a torrent of questions about her origins: 'Where did I come from? Who made me?' and so on. If we now consider the final shot in 'Normal Again', mentioned earlier, a startling link with the present scene leaps out at us. Then, as now, we are in a psychiatric ward, and then, as now, leather restraining cuffs are prominent features in the scene. If our re-reading of Season Five depends on the assumption that Buffy has authored it from her hospital bed outside the normal narrative world of the series, it is perfectly plausible that the madness and physical constraint she has occasion to experience in the hospital would be salient features of the world she conjures up.

The claim attributed to Giles in his notes – 'Only those outside reality can see the Key's true nature' – is an equally understandable scenario for her to invent, and the lunatics who recognise Dawn provide an equivalent within the Buffy universe for a catatonic Buffy outside it. They are the representatives of her disempowered self, just as the monks who created Dawn in the first place were seen earlier to provide an equivalent for her creative side in inventing Dawn. Further, if Buffy as the Slayer represents her fantasised compensation within the Buffy universe for the less heroic reality of her position outside it, then the text that Buffy authors allows her to express her disempowerment, her creativity and her fantasies of power all at once, through the madmen and the monks in Season Five and the Slayer herself throughout the series. As the psychiatrist explains to Buffy's parents, 'Buffy's delusion is multi-layered. She believes she's some type of hero ... but that's only one level.'

More broadly, madness and physical constraint – especially in the form of bondage – are themes which cut a broad swathe through the series as a whole and implicate most of the major characters in one way or another and to various degrees of seriousness, though Season Five is probably where they get their most extended and explicit treatment. After all, the season is centred on a crazy villain, Glory, who gets her energy by draining the minds of ordinary people, who go mad as a result, a scenario which is causing a notable increase in the number of mentally unstable people in Sunnydale and filling its mental wards to overflowing. Thus, there is a lot of literal madness in the season: Glory, of course, and those she drives mad (including Tara), Joyce, who begins to say crazy things due to a tumour pressing on her brain, and even Buffy, after Glory takes Dawn away and Buffy withdraws into a catatonic state until Willow enters her mind through a spell and brings her out again.

Beyond this rampant literal craziness, the season is characterised by metaphors of madness that colour virtually all of the relationships and characters' perceptions of themselves and each other. For example, Riley confides to Xander how lucky he feels with Buffy: 'Half of me is on fire, going crazy if I'm not touching her ..' (5.3: 'The Replacement'), and Willow reassures Tara that families always make one crazy, with Buffy reiterating this later in the same episode when she talks to Riley about how Dawn drives her mad (5.6: 'Family'). Four episodes later, Xander warns Buffy she is 'actin' like a crazy person' after Riley tells her he is going away (5.10: 'Into the Woods'), while Warren tells Buffy that April was too perfect: 'I thought I was going crazy' (5.15: 'I Was Made to Love You'). In addition, when Spike hits Buffy to rouse her to action from her catatonic state, Xander asks him: 'Are you insane?' (5.21: 'The Weight of the World'). In the end, it is Glory herself who is given the most extended statement on the proliferating madness around them, both literal and more metaphoric. Having earlier told her minion Jinx that Ben, with whom she shares a body, is driving her insane (5.12: 'Checkpoint'), she later asks the capitve Dawn how people cope with their feelings: 'Call me crazy, but as hard-core drugs go, human emotion is just useless!' Glory looks at the world 'and all I see is six billion lunatics looking for the fastest ride out. Who's not crazy? Look around' (5.21: 'The Weight of the World').

If the re-reading offered here of Buffy's death from the vantage-point of 'Normal Again' is plausible, then it is not surprising that at the end of Season Five Buffy prefers to leap out of such a world gone mad on all fronts in order to return to the comparatively restrained insanity of her hospital room, though her emotional needs draw her back to Sunnydale in Season Six. Willow's efforts to pull Buffy out of her short-lived catatonic state in 'The Weight of the World' provide a preview of Buffy's later returns to her friends in Season Six (both when they resurrect her at the start of the season and when she willingly opts to commit herself to their world for good in 'Normal Again'). Their conversation inside Buffy's head, after Willow does a spell to enter her psyche in order to convince her to emerge and retrieve Dawn from Glory, is instructive:

> *Buffy*:   I killed Dawn.
> *Willow*: Is that what you think?
> *Buffy*:   My thinking it made it happen.

Even though Willow tells her to get past her guilt and snap out of it, for an instant Buffy seems to be aware – at least in the depths of her unconscious – of the instrumental power of her thoughts. So even within the Buffy universe itself, Buffy has moments of 'madness' which allow her to half-acknowledge her position outside it.

Going even further, there is a suggestion, in 'Normal Again', that the mental hospital where Buffy finds herself is itself ambiguously located, and not so clearly placed outside the Buffy universe as we may have assumed. Buffy confides in Willow that she *was* in a mental institution for a couple of weeks after she saw her first vampires six years earlier, adding in despair, her eyes filling with tears: 'What if I'm still there?' So the world which we have taken her to have created as a fantasised escape from her incarceration in a mental hospital outside the Buffy universe turns out to have a mental hospital within it in which she has been a patient in the past, and it is a part of the fantasy – at least for a moment – that she is a slayer who may herself have generated Sunnydale and all her friends not from outside the world of slayers and vampires but from within it. This complex layering of fantasies within fantasies is difficult to grasp, for viewers and characters alike. Indeed, only Spike seems perfectly happy with the possibility that he is a product of Buffy's imagination, telling Xander that it explains a lot if they are all in Buffy's brain: 'Yeah. Fix up some chip in my head. Make me soft, fall in love with her, then turn me into her sodding sex slave…' As the last bit of this is news to Xander ('What?!'), Spike adds dismissively: 'Nothing. Alternative realities', leaving it at that.

The episode in Season Five with perhaps the most obvious possibilities for a re-reading in terms of 'Normal Again' (5.12: 'Checkpoint') has the Council of Watchers coming to town to submit Buffy to a barrage of tests of her physical and mental fitness, providing an apt displaced representation of the tests she is undoubtedly subjected to in the hospital (indeed, we see the psychiatrist peering into her eyes with a small flashlight at one point, as if to underline the way she is an object of scrutiny there). Quentin Travers himself, the unsympathetic head of the Council, has a trim graying beard similar to the one sported by the psychiatrist, though the psychiatrist bears an even stronger physical resemblance to Principal Wood in Season Seven: both he and Wood are

Fig. 3.5

Fig. 3.6

African-American, both bald, both wear an earring in the left ear, and, once again, both have small, neatly trimmed beards, though Wood's is black, not gray. By Season Seven, when most of the issues raised in 'Normal Again' have long since been resolved, it makes sense that the psychiatrist can be represented by a more likable authority figure (Principal Wood) than in Season Five (Quentin Travers), since in 'Checkpoint' Buffy is less than half a season shy of leaping back to the psychiatrist's world, rather than free of it forever, so he remains a potent off-screen threat, despite his good intentions.

Even Giles, the most fatherly and benevolent authority figure in the series, betrays Buffy briefly back in Season Three (3.12: 'Helpless'). On the instructions of Travers, he injects her with a drug to weaken her and test her resourcefulness, as part of a time-honoured 18th-birthday rite of passage for slayers (a rite which Giles describes as cruel even though he carries it out). Although he ultimately confesses all this to Buffy – and Travers fires him as Buffy's Watcher, as a result – she continues to feel the betrayal keenly (in an episode where her *actual* father lets her down as well). Accepting that Buffy is in a psychiatric hospital thus allows us to re-read earlier episodes with a new understanding of their ramifications, though we may also choose to continue to read them in their own terms without such retrospective layerings.

Like madness, bondage is a recurrent theme across the series, taking both a menacing form and a more playful one. Almost all the major characters are shown in chains or manacles or with ropes around their wrists at one point or another: Angel, Spike, Drusilla, Willow, Xander, Giles, Dawn, Faith, Oz, Amy, and Buffy herself, as well as the various anonymous mental patients who are kept under restraint. In addition, most of the heterosexual relationships take a lively interest in such things. This latter aspect of the series is regularly seen as the contribution of co-executive producer and writer Marti Noxon (for example in her own DVD commentary to 2.10: 'What's My Line?', part 2 or in Joss Whedon's DVD commentary on 2.14: 'Innocence'), though her concern with the relationship between love and pain – and their thematic links with issues around trust and power – is so integral to the series as a whole that it is extremely unlikely that this is simply a maverick interest of her own with no substantial connection to the concerns of other series collaborators, in particular Joss Whedon himself.

Fig. 3.7

In her commentary to 'What's My Line?', part 2, Noxon points out: 'This may be one of the first episodes that I wrote where we started to go to the scary place of S and M with these two. It became one of the things that at least Joss likes to say is my hallmark. It's one of the things that I'm proud to say I have contributed to on the show greatly, which is a really perverse sense of sexuality.' (She laughs.) 'Can you blame us? Really. Look at that guy. Look at her.' Although Spike and Drusilla are on-screen for much of this, Noxon seems to be referring to Dru and *Angel*, who is bound, gagged, and bare-chested nearby and whom Dru will go on to torture. In any case, all three are implicated by Noxon's 'hallmark contribution', just as Noxon implicates her collaborators by her use of words like 'us' and 'we'. In Whedon's commentary to 'Innocence', he, in turn, refers to Noxon's contribution: 'the idea of love and torture and pain and power – and bondage – and all of these things working together in the minds of these people. Marti really brought a lot of cool, twisted sexuality to the characters *that fit really well'*, Whedon once again stressing the consonance between Noxon's intentions and the requirements of the series, as Whedon sees them.

The more playful instances of bondage generate humour as much as they raise serious issues like those just mentioned. For example, when Buffy's mother and Giles regress to the condition of amorous teenagers after eating some candy whose manufacture is overseen by Ethan Rayne, a former friend of Giles from the darker days of his youth, and Buffy later asks them to find something with which to tie Ethan up, Joyce gives an apologetic smirk and pulls out a pair of handcuffs from inside her coat (3.6: 'Band Candy'). Buffy convinces herself at the end of the episode that, 'At least I got to the two of you before you actually did something.' However, when she temporarily gains the ability to hear other people's thoughts, twelve episodes later, Buffy discovers that her mother and Giles did 'do something' after all. Buffy suddenly sits upright in bed,

Fig. 3.8

as Joyce unsuccessfully tries to keep her distance so Buffy will not read her thoughts, and asks her mother with escalating disbelief: 'You had sex with Giles? *You had sex with Giles?!* ... On the hood of a police car? ... Twice?' (3.18: 'Earshot').

In Season Four, when Buffy and Eddie, a fellow student at the University of Sunnydale, chat about how difficult their college courses have turned out to be, she again seems to find out more than she really wants to know, after confiding to him that she sometimes feels like carrying a security blanket around with her. Eddie concurs, citing his favourite book as his example of one: '*Of Human Bondage*. Have you ever read it?' Taken aback, Buffy replies politely, 'Oh, I'm not really into porn. I mean I'm just ... I'm trying to cut right back', until Eddie explains that it is not about actual bondage at all (4.1: 'The Freshman'). In the following episode, Xander comments, 'Why couldn't Giles have shackles like any self-respecting bachelor?' (4.2: 'Living Conditions'), and he goes on to give a memorable speech about the uses of rope well into the final season (7.14: 'First Date').

By Season Six, when Buffy's relationship with Spike has itself taken a rough and masochistic turn for her, we see them naked together under a rug on the floor as Spike asks her if she even likes him (6.13: 'Dead Things'):

Fig. 3.9

Buffy: Sometimes.

Spike: But you like what I do to you. [He pulls out a pair of handcuffs and lets them dangle in the air as if to illustrate his words, in a shot of the two of them together, following a run of close-ups of each of them alone in the frame in turn, which comprise the immediately preceding ten shots of the scene.] Do you trust me?

Buffy [looking at him steadily]: Never.

The scene occurs in one of the bleakest episodes in the series, where Warren murders his ex-girlfriend Katrina after putting her under a spell and trying to rape her, later convincing Buffy that *she* killed Katrina instead. Buffy takes out her growing despair on Spike, beating him up viciously as he refuses to fight back, his face swollen as he tells her, 'You always hurt … the one you love, pet,' a line she more or less repeats after she finds out that Katrina was killed by Warren, not herself. Horrified at the nature of her relationship with Spike, Buffy confides in Tara, asking her, 'Why do I let Spike do those things to me?' and begging Tara not to forgive her.

So, in Buffy's own experience of bondage and sado-masochistic sex, any sense of fun has long since given way to much darker currents by the time of the episodes leading up to 'Normal Again'. As viewers, we may smile at the double entendres around Buffy's relationship with Spike, but she herself remains more troubled. For example, when Buffy apologises for not having been around more, Willow tells her innocently, 'It's OK. We know you've been all tied up' (6.13: 'Dead Things'). Similarly, in a later episode, Willow points out a grass stain on Buffy's jacket when she joins Buffy and Dawn in the kitchen (6.15: 'As You Were'):

> *Dawn:* Some vampire get rough with you?
> *Buffy:* He's not getting any gentler.
> *Willow:* He?·
> *Buffy:* They. Them.

Buffy herself is not able to take such things as lightly as we do, and her desire to free herself from what she experiences as an addictive and degrading relationship is surely at odds with the enormous sympathy for Spike that the series has engendered in its audience, and thus the likelihood that most viewers will want the relationship to work out. Our greater access to an ongoing strain of playful humour around bondage throughout the series contributes to the split between Buffy's viewpoint and our own.

What has been argued throughout this chapter is that the implications of 'Normal Again' extend both forward and back across the series as a whole, layering additional significance upon it which goes beyond the meanings of narrative events in terms of the Buffy universe alone. The worries and concerns experienced in the mental hospital by the version of Buffy located outside the world of Sunnydale may be seen to be reflected in events and characters inside it through scenarios which work and re-work a central core of preoccupations around such things as personhood, madness, power and trust. Further, the proliferating worlds and dimensions within the Buffy universe, as well as the breakdown of barriers between them, allows the series to reflect upon its own creative processes and the ways we come to care so deeply about a fictional world we know to be unreal. In the course of this, two episodes have emerged as crucial anchors for our reading: 'The Gift' in Season Five and 'Normal Again' in Season Six. Each one provides a resolution to the series up to that point, and each is equally devastating in its way, with one a mirror-image of the other: thus, the leap out of the Buffy world in the former is reversed by Buffy's definitive return to it by the end of the latter.

It is well known that the creators of the series were often in a kind of limbo over whether the series would be renewed from one season to the next, which is a problem for any long-running series whose ambitions are unconventional enough to be seen to threaten the creation of a commercially successful product. Another difficulty in mapping storylines coherently across future seasons is the question of how long key actors and other creative personnel would want to carry on. For example, when Kristine Sutherland, who plays Buffy's mother, told the show's producers that she would be out of the country for Season Four, Whedon replied, as Sutherland recounts it, that she would have to be back for Season Five, since he was planning to kill her then (DVD overview to Season Five). Finding ways to draw each season to a satisfying conclusion without foreclosing the possibility of a longer storyline and more permanent closure at a later stage must have posed a considerable challenge whenever such uncertainties arose. With 'The Gift', for instance (the 100th episode in the series), Whedon comments in the DVD overview to Season Five: 'I think originally I had thought about the idea of ending the series then.' Buffy's leap out of the fictional world, separating herself from Dawn and the entire Buffy universe – from her imaginative creations, if we accept the psychiatrist's premise in 'Normal Again' – was thus paralleled by the very real possibility for Whedon himself of ending the series and abandoning the products of *his* imagination at the very same point. Instead, the series goes on to surpass and reinvent itself in Season Six.

Following Joyce's death from a ruptured aneurysm at the end of 'I Was Made to Love You', one of the doctors tells Buffy in the following episode (5.16: 'The Body'): 'Joyce was aware of the possibility of a rupture, and the effects.' This is a particularly suggestive and intriguing remark in view of all the ways we have been examining in which the narrative fabric of Season Five either is or might have been ruptured: by clashing fictional worlds (Dracula, the Knights of Byzantium, Sunnydale), by the Key opening up portals between dimensions, by Joyce's death, by Buffy's leap from the tower, understandable both as a leap to her death and a leap out of the fictional world, and, finally, by the unrealised possibility of the series coming to an end at the conclusion of the season, as originally planned. In the same episode as the doctor's apt formulation of Joyce's awareness of what might happen to her, which is so resonant across the season as a whole, is Dawn's question about her dead mother – 'Where'd she go?' – mentioned in the first chapter and which may also be given a broader application now. Dawn's question is evocative in terms of her incomprehension of any domain beyond the boundaries of the narrative world in which she finds herself, and her question has obvious relevance to Buffy's post-mortem destination as well.

The series continues to examine itself and its textual strategies in Season Six. For example, relevant issues are raised and discussed in one of Buffy's classes at the University of Sunnydale. The lecturer poses questions about the nature of reality and whether it may best be seen as an individual construction lacking an objective existence of its own, rather than as a given (6.5: 'Life Serial'), such speculations finding their logical culmination in the devastating implications of 'Normal Again'. However, the classroom scene is treated more humorously than the later scenes in the hospital, with Buffy unable to follow the discussion that Willow and the other students are entering into with such enthusiasm. It is instructive to quote the dialogue at some length to demonstrate how such apparently insignificant and casual background details prove to be thematically central.

Lecturer: Social construction of reality. Who can tell me what that is? Rachel.
Rachel: A concept involving a couple of opposing theories: one stressing the externality and independence of social reality from individuals.
Lecturer: And the flip side? Steve.
Steve: That each individual participates fully in the construction of his or her own life.
Lecturer: Good. And who can expand on that? Chuck.
Chuck: Well…
[As Chuck's voice gradually fades into the background, Buffy expresses her bewilderment to Willow, who reassures her while continuing to pay attention to the classroom discussion. The camera stays on the two of them for the rest of the scene in a pattern of shot/reverse-shots which keep them both in the frame as the class carries on around them. Willow raises her hand to respond even as she continues to talk to Buffy.]
Lecturer: Willow.
Willow: Because social phenomena don't have unproblematic objective existences, they have to be interpreted and given meanings by those who encounter them.
Lecturer: Nicely put. So, Ruby, does that mean there are countless realities?

The humour stops well short of parody, the discussion simultaneously making perfect sense as an authentic representation of the sorts of issues that might well be covered in a university class and yet using an academic register which, from Buffy's point of view, is unfamiliar and experienced as excessively obscure. Nevertheless, the topic being debated has direct relevance to themes of central importance to the series. The editing brings the classroom scene to an end on a question which is left unanswered – 'does that mean there are countless realities?' – thus encouraging us to apply it to *Buffy the Vampire Slayer* and to think through its implications for ourselves. The intensely academic tenor of the debate is not held up to ridicule – there is no cheap anti-intellectualism at work here – while, at the same time, it is difficult not to sympathise with Buffy's frustrated incomprehension. Further, what is taken by the eager participating students to be a sort of abstract academic game is given a literalness by the series itself, with very real choices and consequences for Buffy, as we have seen.

Overall, and on many levels, Seasons Five and Six provide immensely rich material bound together in an intimate and complex unity of rhetoric, performance and thematic concerns, and many of the most prominent issues raised throughout this extended stretch of narrative appear to resolve themselves by the end of Season Six. By Season Seven, not only has Buffy committed herself to the Buffy universe for good, but she has freed herself from the sexually addictive and self-loathing relationship with Spike, while Willow is rehabilitated from the abuse of black magic which took her to the dark side in Season Six. Spike himself has a soul in place of the government chip in his head, Faith is no longer a rogue slayer but a reformed and heroic one, and Andrew eventually liberates himself from Warren's bad influence to join up with Buffy and the others. We are back to a much more conventional battle between all of these characters who have redeemed or reformed themselves, on one hand, and an externalised incorporeal manifestation of evil called the First, on the other.

The fact that the First can ony appear in the guise of people who have died (including vampires like Drusilla who are still extant) gives the final season a nostalgic quality knowingly produced by the creators of the series and offered to their audience. Thus, many actors who played characters who died in previous seasons get to return to take a curtain call as the series draws to an end, and their reappearances are like a gift from the series to its fans which both acknowledges their loyalty and anticipates the renewed pleasure to be felt as each of these actors turns up. The return of Faith (who did not die earlier but *has* been absent from the series for a couple of seasons) is a particularly pleasurable bonus for regular viewers. The storylines of some of the characters who now reappear, whether as manifestations of the First or as themselves, have carried on in intervening episodes of *Angel*. Therefore our ability to fill in the gaps is

Fig. 3.10

partially dependent on our familiarity with the composite *Buffy/Angel* text mentioned at the start of this chapter, and not just with *Buffy* itself. This playfulness around the boundaries of the series further contributes to the lighter feel of Season Seven, in contrast with the two very dark seasons which precede it, where the erosion of boundaries has much more serious consequences.

In place of the earlier tension which pulled us towards an emotional commitment to the Buffy universe as a world while, at the same time, impelling us to unravel it intellectually as a text, Season Seven's conflicts are less disturbing, its issues more readily resolved. The earlier concerns persist to a limited extent, but without their previous intensity. Thus, when Andrew makes a video of Buffy and the other characters preparing to go into battle against the First (7.16: 'Storyteller'), there is certainly a lot of play around whether what we see is really happening in the narrative world of Sunnydale precisely in the way it appears, or whether it has been staged for or manipulated by Andrew's camera. For example, we see Spike warning Andrew to stop filming and leave him alone – an apparently genuine moment of disruption to his video-making project – only to then hear Andrew's voice off camera telling Spike that the light was behind him and asking him to do it again. Spike drops the angry manner and agrees at once, looking to either side and adjusting his position: 'Oh, right. Is this better then?'

More openly signalled, rather than being sprung on us as a surprise like the falseness of Spike's enacted anger, are the mediations of Andrew's ongoing commentary and editorial decisions as he films. These include the way he moves his camera away from Buffy during one of her rallying talks to the potential slayers, in order to avoid the boring bits, with Andrew explaining his decision straight to camera in close-up: 'Honestly, gentle viewers, these motivating speeches of hers tend to get a little long.' The introductory scene immediately before the credits is particularly full of such self-conscious rhetoric on Andrew's part as we fade in on a shelf of leather-bound books, with Bach's Brandenburg Concerto No. 3 on the soundtrack. After a dissolve and pan right across various atmospheric artefacts (a skull, some bottles, an hourglass, but also what appears to be a comic book), there is another dissolve to a *Star Wars* poster on the wall, the camera moving down to a roaring fire in the fireplace and to Andrew in a leather chair, looking up from an open book. Wearing a dressing gown and scarf and holding a pipe, Andrew looks furtively up at the camera to check that it is on him, then lowers his eyes and looks up again, as if for the first time, chuckling slightly: 'Oh, hello there, gentle viewers.'

The scene goes on to be a take-off of programmes like *Masterpiece Theatre*, where a narrator gives an intellectual gloss to the story that is to follow, here Andrew's account of Buffy and her world (a version of the series encapsulated within the series itself). Although the set-up seems to be Andrew's, so that we presume he is emulating *Masterpiece Theatre* rather than parodying it, there are details within it that seem to be a parody at Andrew's expense on the part of the series overall. For example, his attempt to convey culture and sophistication is betrayed by details like the comic book,

the *Star Wars* poster, and the coughing fit that follows his pipe-smoking efforts. The most damaging affront to the image he is trying to convey is when he is interrupted by a knock on the door. We cut from a close-up of Andrew surrounded by the rich maroon colours of the chairback and dressing gown to a very different close-up of him in a dark blue shirt against the pale background wall of the bathroom in Buffy's house, where he has sought refuge to record the opening of his film. A reverse-shot makes the

Fig. 3.11

video camera visible as Anya opens the bathroom door and enters, followed by a longer high-angle shot of Andrew which reveals him sitting on the lowered lid of the toilet: 'For God's sakes, Andrew, you've been in here for 30 minutes. What are you doing?' The credits begin, and the tone is set, though it is clearly not a tone of Andrew's choosing or even one of which he is aware.

It is actually rather difficult to describe exactly what it is that we are seeing when Andrew sits in the high-backed leather chair and addresses us. It is not the 'real world' of the Buffy universe or a 'real' film set within it that Andrew inhabits, since he is *actually* sitting in the bathroom as he films, with none of the higher production values of the first part of the scene. However, neither is it a direct representation of Andrew's fantasy version of his film (as he imagines it in his mind), for why would he spoil the effect of his pipe-smoking with the burst of coughing? Or, at least, if it is his fantasy, it is ultimately a fantasy being undermined by details such as this, as well as by its obviously parodic tone. That is, Andrew's fantasised rhetoric of cultured sophistication is itself subject to the parodying rhetoric of the series as a whole, which humorously unmasks the naïveté of the claims to sophistication that he offers us with such apparent sincerity and self-belief.

This strategy of layering the series rhetoric on top of the rhetoric of Andrew's fantasised version of his film extends across a number of scenes in the episode, such as the impossibly glamorous slow-motion shots of Buffy, Spike and Anya in the kitchen (starting with Buffy pouring cereal into a bowl as she tosses her hair and winks provocatively at the camera). Once again, we are presented with Andrew's romantic fantasies and, at the same time, the series' amiable parody of their excess and naïve pretensions. In this case, it is immediately evident to viewers of the episode that this is not a straightforward image of the narrative world, or even such an image distorted by the slow-motion of the mediating camera, since Buffy is unlikely either to toss her hair or to wink in such a way in the midst of her preparations to do battle with the First.

Much more disorientating for the audience, because it initially seems less mediated, is the scene when Anya and Xander are having a serious discussion about their relationship in continuation of one we saw Andrew filming earlier. However, when we then see Andrew watching on his monitor, it seems as if he is still filming them as before. In a further twist, when Andrew goes on to mouth their words along with them, we have to reorientate ourselves a second time. All at once, it looks as if the whole thing has been scripted all along – as was the case with Spike – until the events that we have been watching as if they were unfolding there and then are seen to be rewinding on the monitor. It now finally becomes clear that the entire conversation was filmed earlier, and that Anya and Xander are no longer present in the room. Andrew is able to speak their words along with them not because he scripted them, but because he has watched the tape before. In this case, it is not Andrew who manipulates our responses, as we may have assumed, but rather the producers of Buffy who withhold the knowledge that we are watching an opaque image on Andrew's monitor, rather than looking *through* the monitor as if it were a transparent window onto the actual people being filmed in the spaces of the narrative world that they inhabit. Our access to that world is suddenly blocked as it collapses momentarily into no more than a flat image on a screen.

'Storyteller' is one of the most playfully inventive episodes in the series, though much graver events continue to take place within it, just as was noted in the discussion of 'Real Me' earlier in this chapter, where its predominant tone was also seen to be at odds with some of the themes and events in the episode. These events, in the case of 'Storyteller', centrally concern Andrew himself, and they culminate in Buffy deliberately pushing him to admit his guilty complicity in Jonathan's murder, as Andrew's tears fall upon the mystical seal to the Hellmouth in the high school basement and thereby close it. Thus, serious plot developments unfold in and around the humorous filmmaking plot, with appropriate tonal shifts from one strand to the other, and the two aspects of Andrew which we see – as a figure of fun and as a figure of redemption – exist in reasonably close proximity. So, even in a relatively light episode like this one, the series is able to express both its darker concerns within the narrative world and its purposeful attention to the nature of narrative itself.

Nonetheless, where the 'worldness' and 'textness' of the series were intimately intertwined in Seasons Five and Six, so that our belief in the narrative world was in constant danger of unravelling, now, by Season Seven, the prospect of such a demolition from within has been definitively suppressed. Andrew's filmmaking falls far short of 'unmaking' the Buffy universe in the act of filming it. The sight of Andrew in the bathroom addressing his video camera, while he imagines the scenario in much richer, more accomplished terms, has none of the devastating implications of the final shot of Buffy in her hospital room at the end of 'Normal Again', withdrawn and catatonic as she retreats inside her head. Andrew's fantasies provide an amusing commentary on the Buffy universe, with an affectionate parody of Andrew himself layered on top. Buffy's fantasies, in contrast, may be seen to constitute the Buffy universe itself and to hold the seeds of its undoing.

4. Specialness and *Buffy* fandom: a personal footnote

> **Buffy:** In every generation, one slayer is born … because a bunch of men who died thousands of years ago made up that rule … I say *my* power should be *our* power … From now on, every girl in the world who *might* be a slayer, *will* be a slayer.
>
> – 7.22: 'Chosen'

Buffy the Vampire Slayer is often interested in characters who suffer from their ordinariness or need reassurance that they matter. For example, Marcie, a student at Sunnydale High, becomes invisible as a result of being persistently ignored by everyone else (1.11: 'Out of Mind, Out of Sight'), and Jonathan, having failed at suicide in an earlier episode, conjures up an alternative universe where he is everyone's hero (4.17: 'Superstar'), while even Dawn and Xander experience a shared sense of being on the sidelines in Season Seven (7.12: 'Potential'). As Xander tells her gently, 'They'll never know how tough it is, Dawnie. To be the one who *isn't* chosen. To live so near to the spot-light and never step in it. But *I* know.'

Fig. 4.1

In fact, there are a significant number of characters who, at some point or other, experience the insecurity of their not being special enough for the circles in which they move. Giles, for example, finds it hard to come to terms with the loss of his special status after the Watchers' Council fire him in Season Three (3.12: 'Helpless'). Riley Finn, the boy from Iowa who is the nearest Buffy gets to a 'normal' long-term boyfriend – and who is described by Doug Petrie in the commentary to an episode in Season Four (4.7: 'The Initiative') as 'the Jimmy Stewart of the Buffy universe' – feels hopelessly inadequate to Buffy's needs. Spike drives the point home when he tells Riley he is not the long-haul guy (5.10: 'Into the Woods'): 'The girl needs some monster in her man, and that's not in your nature.' In Season Six, Willow confides to Buffy that she requires the magic she performs as a powerful witch so that she can be special: 'Don't I? I mean, Buffy, who *was* I? Just … some girl' (6.10: 'Wrecked'). Even Anya, a former vengeance demon, muses to Xander, 'What if I'm really nobody?' (7.5: 'Selfless'), further reinforcing just how central these concerns turn out to be.

In contrast, Buffy seems to have her specialness confirmed from the start. During her first meeting with Giles (1.1: 'Welcome to the Hellmouth'), when she wanders into the school library for some books, he recognises her as the Slayer and dramatically slams a weighty ancient volume on the counter in front of her, grinning with obvious self-satisfaction at having anticipated her needs, though she hurriedly runs off, insisting it is not what she wants. Later in the same episode, after a student is killed by a vampire,

Buffy returns to the library to ask Giles why she cannot just be left alone, and he replies, 'Because you are the Slayer', invoking the fundamental principle of slayer lore, which will be repeated at intervals throughout the series, that 'Into each generation a slayer is born. One girl, in all the world, a Chosen One…', to Buffy's evident annoyance. However, when she drowns and is almost immediately revived at the end of Season One (1.12: 'Prophecy Girl'), the brief interval when she is dead is enough to call up the next slayer, Kendra, to take her place (2.9: 'What's My Line?', part 1), though Kendra herself is later killed to more lasting effect than was Buffy (2.21: 'Becoming', part 1), which results in Faith turning up in town four episodes later as replacement slayer for Kendra (3.3: 'Faith, Hope and Trick'). Buffy's uniqueness is blurred by her position as one of a long line of slayers at least two of whom co-exist with her for extended periods. Similarly, her specialness as an only child is unexpectedly cancelled by Dawn's sudden arrival in Season Five (5.1: 'Buffy vs. Dracula') as her teenaged sister.

However, unlike Marcie, Jonathan, Dawn, Xander, Giles and the others, Buffy frequently longs to be unremarkable, experiencing her specialness as more curse than blessing. When Kendra arrives in town, which causes Willow to assume Buffy is feeling undermined and leads her to reassure Buffy that she will always remain Giles' favourite, Buffy wonders wistfully whether Kendra might, in fact, take over altogether so that she herself could lead a normal life. A version of this hope is eventually fulfilled in the final episode of the series, when all the potential slayers in the world are empowered, making Buffy's continuing devotion to her avocation much less critical in future.

The implication that, beyond the final frames, Buffy will finally be free to live the life she seems to want is confirmed in an episode of *Angel* after *Buffy the Vampire Slayer* has come to an end. Spike, who has crossed over to the spin-off series, asks where Buffy is, and Angel tells him that she is off travelling in Europe (A5.2: 'Just Rewards'). This snippet of information is an undeniable encouragement to fans of *Buffy* still recovering from the series having drawn to a close, and now permitted to imagine that the story continues to unfold beyond the edges of *Angel*'s onscreen world. Indeed, the story develops further when Spike and Angel later attempt to look Buffy up in Rome, each vying for her affections yet neither of them managing to catch up with her face to face. Along with the two of them, we catch a tantalising glimpse of Buffy from behind and at a distance (though presumably with Sarah Michelle Gellar no longer in the role) as she dances with her new boyfriend in a Roman club (A5.20: 'The Girl in Question'). The irony of all this, given the ambiguities of 'Normal Again' discussed in the previous chapter, is that the ordinariness she fled from then has now been positively reclaimed, though this time without her being required to sacrifice her friends in the process. She finally seems to have it all: extraordinary powers *and* a normal life (or at least a normal*ish* sort of life, since her boyfriend is an extraordinary and ambiguous being known as 'the Immortal', rather than an ordinary man her own age: however she *is* free of the burdens of being the one and only Slayer).

Thus, the longest story arc of the series, extending from the first episode of Season One all the way to the final episode in Season Seven, involves a movement from Buffy's uniqueness as the Slayer through to a democratising of her power and special status amongst all the girls and women in the world who have the potential to be slayers like her. The series ends with Faith addressing Buffy: 'Yeah, you're not the one-and-only chosen any more. Just gotta live like a person. How's that feel?' Dawn adds a question of her own: 'Yeah, Buffy. What *are* we gonna do now?' No answers are given, leaving us with a lack of any definitive resolution. However, in the very last shot of the series – a long take lasting a minute and thirteen seconds – we get an inkling of good things to come. The camera begins by including Dawn, Buffy, Giles, Willow, Xander, Faith, Andrew and some of the potential slayers in the frame. It then closes in on the first six of these figures in the foreground, their bodies blocking out the others as they hang back by the bus in which they have made their escape. Finally, the camera moves into a close-up of Buffy breaking into a smile, with only Faith visible behind her.

What is intriguing in Season Seven is not just the resultant extension of the film's feminist project from presenting Buffy as an exceptional blonde who fights back to showing a huge range of women as powerful forces for good. For, in addition, and giving an added credibility to the series' values as expressed within the fiction, a similar democratising process is at work in the relationship between the series' creators and their fans.

In a special featurette on the Season Seven DVD entitled '*Buffy*: it's always been about the fans', Janice Pope (identified as the co-host of an internet radio show) points out that '*Buffy* was one of the few shows that we felt never treated their audience like they were idiots.' Joss Whedon later goes on to say, 'We have a connection with the internet fan base … We sort of worship at the same altar. Me and my staff are the biggest Buffy nerds alive. It's kind of a home to us, too,' adding shortly afterwards, 'When we could, we would get together and watch it together as a bunch, as fans…'. James Marsters (who plays Spike) comments appreciatively, 'In the beginning … it was the small and loyal audience that kept it afloat and gave it time to get the critical attention that it needed to reach a wider audience. So we owe a lot to these people.' Alex Jurkat, a *Buffy* fan in the same featurette, next confirms that 'This fan base is so loyal and so intense that I can't imagine that it'll go anywhere soon.' So, even after the end of the series, the community of fans looks set to carry on. Not only are the show's creators aware of and, at the same time, grateful for this loyalty, but distinctions between themselves and the fans may even occasionally become a little smudged around the edges, as Whedon suggests. Another thing worth noting is that the fans of the series have always appreciated not just its stars, but the writers and other creative personnel. Jane Espenson (co-executive producer and writer) points out that 'Every year our fans come out and they throw us this amazing party. And the writers and producers and cast mates all get to come out here, and even the writers are treated like the Beatles for a night.'

Despite the occasional 'star status' given to the writers, however, the relationship of fans to actors is clearly special and needs to be looked at more closely. Once again, the fictional world of *Buffy* dramatises some of these issues. Thus, as we have seen with Jonathan, the fantasised compensation for a character's ordinariness within the narrative world may take the form of an exaggerated achievement of superstardom. Dracula too functions as a star of such dimensions (though he is the real thing, as opposed to

Jonathan's false appropriation of this status) in his one-episode appearance at the start of Season Five, and his fame is so great as to reduce even Buffy to the position of a starstruck admirer, thrilled to discover that he has heard of her. So, the relationship between being special and being ordinary takes one particular shape in the complementary opposition between being a star and a starstruck fan. This thematic preoccupation as it manifests itself amongst characters *within* the narrative world may prove relevant to understanding the equivalent relationship that *Buffy the Vampire Slayer* maintains with its devoted fan base *outside* its world, including its numerous academic admirers.

Unlike movie stars who are household names even for many people who never go to their films or who may not particularly like or admire them, the lead actors of *Buffy the Vampire Slayer* (at least those who have not become well known through appearances in mainstream films and television shows as well) are famous in a much more limited context. Their fame is much more dependent on the fan base for the series, such fans being familiar with the names and faces of a formidable number of actors (a sampling of whom are listed in appendix two at the end of this study). The series actors thus fall short of genuine film stardom, despite some degree of fulfilment of the criterion set forth by John Ellis in *Visible Fictions*, for whom a star is 'a performer in a particular medium whose figure enters into subsidiary forms of circulation, and then feeds back into future performances' (1992: 91). While the images of many of the *Buffy* actors certainly do circulate outside the shows themselves – on posters, T-shirts, mugs, jigsaw puzzles and other merchandise, in the pages of magazines and in the shape of poseable figures, to list only a few examples – such visibility tends to be limited to specialist shops, websites and publications, rather than more general venues and media outlets. Such circulation undoubtedly occurs, as we have seen, but it very much caters for a minority interest, rather than being aimed at the culture at large.

Put most simply, the majority of *Buffy* actors function as *niche stars* whose fame evaporates away from the very specific circle of Buffy fans, though *within* this context, such star status is democratically accorded to a very large number of actors in the series. While their personal appearances at *Buffy* conventions draw large numbers of interested and appreciative fans, many of the same actors could probably walk down the street unrecognised (again, unless they had a significant body of work in mainstream film or television to generate such recognition independently, or unless there happened to be *Buffy* fans nearby). The result is an openly acknowledged two-way appreciation between actors and fans which is much less apparent in the more lopsided relationship of fans with mainstream film stars. This less extreme sense of differentiation between stars and fans is evident at conventions centred on the series and aimed at giving fans the opportunity to meet and mingle with a selection of series actors.

At one such event ('Homecoming', which took place from 31 May to 3 June 2002, in Glasgow), actors and fans intermingled in just such an atmosphere of good-humoured mutual appreciation. At the opening cocktail party, for example, Harry Groener (who plays Sunnydale's Mayor Richard Wilkins), George Hertzberg (Adam) and Robin Sachs (Ethan Rayne) were immediately recognised and applauded when they each slipped into the room unannounced, despite their being what, in the cinema, would be known as character actors, rather than stars. They then circulated casually around the various clusters of fans for friendly chats, rather than being formally presented to everyone at once and from a distance. Such intermingling continued at various social events throughout the convention. Even in the more formal question-and-answer sessions, where the actors sat together at the front, the interchanges were enlivened by humour on both sides. Most questions from the audience were intelligent and well informed, and the actors were consistently addressed and referred to by their own names, rather than those of their characters, with questions being asked about their work outside of *Buffy* as well as within the series. It should be noted that this pulls somewhat against John Ellis's claim that, on television, 'the performer's image is equated with that of the fictional role' (1992: 106), even though that might have been expected in a long-running series like *Buffy*.

The actors themselves, who at various sessions included Charisma Carpenter (Cordelia), Tony Head (Giles) and Danny Strong (Jonathan), as well as Groener, Hertzberg and Sachs, responded to this with what certainly felt like genuine and well-intentioned camaraderie, apparently enjoying themselves rather than merely experiencing themselves as being on show. Danny Strong introduced his sister in the audience, at one point, and her lack of special status as an ordinary member of the audience sitting amongst the fans (and, by extension, the ordinariness of Strong's background) was further confirmation of the democratic mutuality of the occasion (or at least its democratic 'feel'). A shared sense of community seemed to replace any deeply felt schism between 'us' and 'them'. Nevertheless, it remains the case that the *Buffy* stars who attend such events unavoidably retain a specialness and individuality in that context that the mass of fans clearly lack: it is the whole *raison d'être* of the occasion, the reason fans pay to be able to attend while the actors are presumably paid to be there (it was certainly made explicit that they would be paid for signing photographs). The actors, in other words, are recognisable magnets for the fans' attention in ways that the fans can never be for them (short of fans becoming stalkers, for example, or achieving stardom in a niche of their own where the actors would be part of their body of fans, the relative positions of stars and fans flipping over to their opposite poles, as when Buffy becomes starstruck in the presence of Dracula, despite her own status and fame).

Admiring those for whom one can never be more than a face in the crowd, however friendly and down-to-earth they may be, is an uncomfortable position in which to find oneself, since it is hard to imagine how an authentic relationship of equals might develop. However, it could help us understand whatever academic writing may emerge from such fandom as a sort of *compensation* for pronounced feelings of 'ordinariness' which offer no basis to put oneself forward for a genuine interchange with any of the actors and other creators of the work in question. The relationship with them, which would normally remain too skewed, could to some extent be modified if academic fans were able to stand out from the crowd and be noticed in this way. Perhaps more academic writing than we care to imagine is motivated by their authors' desires to carve out niches of their own where they can be recognised and respected not only by their academic peers but by the admired objects of their investigation as well. This is a delicate area which may require a certain amount of self-disclosure in order to pursue it any further.

Buffy the Vampire Slayer is remarkably acute about such issues, and it treats them with the same good-natured acknowledgment within the narrative world as in the broader context of the series' relationship with its fans outside it. Thus, when Spike is interviewed by a woman from the Watchers' Council as part of their investigation into Buffy's competence (5.12: 'Checkpoint'), the following exchange takes place:

> *Watcher:* But we understand that you help the Slayer.
> *Spike:* I pitch in when she pays me.
> *Watcher:* She pays you? She gives you money?
> *Spike:* Money, a little nip of blood outta some stray victim, whatever.
> *Watcher:* Blood?
> *Spike:* Well, if they're gonna die anyway. Come to think of it, though, that's a bit scandalous, innit? Personally, I'm shocked. The girl's slipping.

In this early part of the conversation, Spike appears to be on the defenisve as the Watcher repeatedly challenges what he says.

Although Spike begins this exchange with caution, in the context of a sequence of scenes where Willow, Xander and the others are trying to help Buffy out by showing her in a positive light, his tactlessness, sense of mischief and self-justifying bravado increasingly kick in and threaten to sabotage any similar good intentions on his part. Being Spike, he just cannot seem to help himself, to the undoubted delight of most viewers. The Watcher, for her part, is conscientious in her cross-examination, her manner initially prim and self-confident, even aggressive, as she interrogates Spike, her clipboard at the ready. However, she becomes more and more flustered by Spike's flirty enjoyment of her discomfort as he becomes aware of her vulnerabilities and increasingly takes control. At the same time, Spike manages a bit of personal revenge on Buffy for (at this point) continuing to resist him, suggesting that she 'can't keep a man'. It is worth including some of the performance details to convey the way in which Spike now takes charge:

Fig. 4.2

> *Spike:* A few more disappointments, she'll be crying on my shoulder, mark my words. [He takes a drag on his cigarette.]
> *Watcher:* Is that what you want? I'd think you'd want to kill her. You've killed slayers before. [She frowns, then raises her eyebrows quizzically.]
> *Spike:* Heard of me, have you?' [Spike slowly and deliberately approaches her, ignoring the men in suits just in front of her on either side who attempt to keep him at a distance with crossbow and wooden cross.]

> *Watcher*: I ... wrote my thesis on you. [The Watcher smiles in embarrassment and lowers her eyes for an instant.]
>
> *Spike*: Well, well. Ain't that neat? [Here Spike smiles slyly, eliciting a flustered smile from her in return.]

By the time she admits to having written her thesis on him, their mutual dependency is clear: she is in the invigorating presence of a bad-boy 'star', while he is basking in the admiration of a fan. Although each is responsive to the other's attentions, which provide a kind of two-way affirmation, neither is able to admit unequivocally to such heady pleasures, since to do so would be unseemly for her as a professional Watcher and far too needy for him, given the insolent coolness that is so integral a part of his adopted image as Spike.

The result is her embarrassed confusion and his teasing irony in response. The smirking tones of his 'Well, well. Ain't that neat?' reveal his delight in having found her out even more than any tickling of his vanity. The way Spike reacts to the fact that the Watcher has heard of him contrasts vividly with the complete absence of mischief in Buffy's 'Nah. Really?' when Dracula tells her of her fame, just as Dracula's cool collectedness has none of the flustered star-struckness of Spike's Watcher fan, perhaps because he is a famous 'star' for Buffy even more than she is for him. Thus, the series is consistently character-driven, rather than driven by situations alone, and each new evocation of a familiar theme is given a fresh and memorable treatment. The brief interrogation scene in 'Checkpoint', with its rapid slide from professional detachment and efficiency to guilty pleasures is an indication of just how aware the series is of its symbiotic relationship not only with its fans in general, but its academic fan base in particular. The Watcher's admission that she did her thesis on Spike is a fact she bashfully offers for Spike's gratification and in the hope of a reciprocating nod in her direction. I suppose that I too, as a film studies academic (and thus a 'professional watcher' of sorts), must admit to a similar unseemly fantasy of my own: that if Joss Whedon, say, were to come upon this study, he might not find it excessively wide of the mark.

Appendix one: the episodes

Season one

1. Welcome to the Hellmouth
2. The Harvest
3. The Witch
4. Teacher's Pet
5. Never Kill a Boy on the First Date
6. The Pack
7. Angel
8. I Robot, You Jane
9. The Puppet Show
10. Nightmares
11. Out of Mind, Out of Sight
12. Prophecy Girl

Season two

1. When She Was Bad
2. Some Assembly Required
3. School Hard
4. Inca Mummy Girl
5. Reptile Boy
6. Halloween
7. Lie to Me
8. The Dark Age
9. What's My Line? (part 1)
10. What's My Line? (part 2)
11. Ted
12. Bad Eggs
13. Surprise
14. Innocence
15. Phases
16. Bewitched, Bothered and Bewildered
17. Passion
18. Killed By Death
19. I Only have Eyes For You
20. Go Fish
21. Becoming (part 1)
22. Becoming (part 2)

Season three

1. Anne
2. Dead Man's Party
3. Faith, Hope and Trick
4. Beauty and the Beasts
5. Homecoming
6. Band Candy
7. Revelations
8. Lover's Walk
9. The Wish
10. Amends
11. Gingerbread
12. Helpless
13. The Zeppo
14. Bad Girls
15. Consequences
16. Doppelgangland
17. Enemies
18. Earshot
19. Choices
20. The Prom
21. Graduation Day (part 1)
22. Graduation Day (part 2)

Season four

1. The Freshman
2. Living Conditions
3. The Harsh Light of Day
4. Fear Itself
5. Beer Bad
6. Wild at Heart
7. The Initiative
8. Pangs
9. Something Blue
10. Hush
11. Doomed
12. A New Man
13. The I in Team

14. Goodbye Iowa
15. This Year's Girl
16. Who Are You?
17. Superstar
18. Where the Wild Things Are
19. New Moon Rising
20. The Yoko Factor
21. Primeval
22. Restless

Season five

1. Buffy vs. Dracula
2. Real Me
3. The Replacement
4. Out of My Mind
5. No Place Like Home
6. Family
7. Fool For Love
8. Shadow
9. Listening to Fear
10. Into the Woods
11. Triangle
12. Checkpoint
13. Blood Ties
14. Crush
15. I Was Made to Love You
16. The Body
17. Forever
18. Intervention
19. Tough Love
20. Spiral
21. The Weight of the World
22. The Gift

Season six

1. Bargaining (part 1)
2. Bargaining (part 2)
3. After Life
4. Flooded
5. Life Serial

6. All the Way
7. Once More With Feeling
8. Tabula Rasa
9. Smashed
10. Wrecked
11. Gone
12. Doublemeat Palace
13. Dead Things
14. Older and Far Away
15. As You Were
16. Hell's Bells
17. Normal Again
18. Entropy
19. Seeing Red
20. Villains
21. Two to Go
22. Grave

Season seven

1. Lessons
2. Beneath You
3. Same Time, Same Place
4. Help
5. Selfless
6. Him
7. Conversations with Dead People
8. Sleeper
9. Never Leave Me
10. Bring on the Night
11. Showtime
12. Potential
13. Killer in Me
14. First Date
15. Get It Done
16. Storyteller
17. Lies My Parents Told Me
18. Dirty Girls
19. Empty Places
20. Touched
21. End of Days
22. Chosen

Appendix two: the characters

These are the major characters who are referred to in this study, along with the actors who play them. They are listed in the order in which the characters are first mentioned.

Buffy Summers (Sarah Michelle Gellar)
Darla (Julie Benz)
Angel/Angelus (David Boreanaz)
Rupert Giles (Anthony Stewart Head)
Xander Harris (Nicholas Brendon)
Willow Rosenberg (Alyson Hannigan)
Joyce Summers (Kristine Sutherland)
Jenny Calendar (Robia LaMorte)
Dawn Summers (Michelle Trachtenberg)
Amy (Elizabeth Anne Allen)
Spike (James Marsters)
Anya (Emma Caulfield)
Tara (Amber Benson)
Adam (George Hertzberg)
Professor Maggie Walsh (Lindsay Crouse)
Riley Finn (Marc Blucas)
Cordelia Chase (Charisma Carpenter)
Oz (Seth Green)
Drusilla (Juliet Landau)
Jonathan (Danny Strong)
Faith (Eliza Dushku)
Andrew (Tom Lenk)
April (Shonda Farr)
Harmony (Mercedes McNab)
Warren (Adam Busch)
Glory (Clare Kramer)
Ben (Charlie Weber)
Quentin Travers (Harris Yulin)
Principal Robin Wood (DB Woodside)
Ethan Rayne (Robin Sachs)
Kendra (Bianca Lawson)
Mayor Richard Wilkins III (Harry Groener)

Other more minor characters referred to in the study:

Owen, Marcie, Cecily, Katrina, the First Slayer, a psychiatrist, Dracula, and assorted villains, minions, Knights of Byzantium, Watchers, and students at the University of Sunnydale.

Related titles from Wallflower Press:

MISE-EN-SCÈNE
Film Style and Interpretation

John Gibbs

£12.99 (pbk)
1-903364-06-X

'An admirable job – and positively inspiring in the close readings of John Sayles'
Lone Star (1996) and Douglas Sirk's *Imitation of Life* (1959), where an incredible
array of meanings gets unpacked from the briefest snippets of celluloid.'
– Peter Matthews, *Sight and Sound*

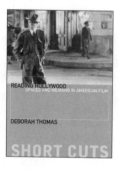

READING HOLLYWOOD
Spaces and Meanings in American Film

Deborah Thomas

£12.99 (pbk)
1-903364-01-9

'It would be difficult to propose, in the context of an introduction to classical
Hollywood, a more precise and rigourous study ... this book deserves to become
essential for undergraduate courses.'
– Professor Reynold Humphries, University of Lille

'Amongst the finest introductions to Hollywood in particular and film studies in
general ... subtler, more complex, yet more readable than most of its rivals, many
of which it will displace.'
– Robin Wood

MUSIC IN FILM
Soundtracks and Synergy

Pauline Reay

£12.99 (pbk)
1-903364-65-5

'A thorough overview of the major developments in mainstream film music, this introduction develops into a welcome and much-needed focus on the pop score and soundtrack with excellent and original choices of case study films and performers.'
– David Butler, University of Manchester

THE MUSICAL
Race, Gender and Performance

Susan Smith

£12.99 (pbk)
1-904764-37-1

'An excellent study of a major and relatively neglected genre. Its welcome focus on race, gender and performance allows for an original discussion of issues all too often treated cursorily in writing on the musical. In her survey of racial and gender stereotypes and key aspects of performance, Susan Smith has produced a theoretically informed and lively, elegantly written volume that will appeal to all students of the formal and social meanings of the musical.'
– Professor Peter Evans, Queen Mary, University of London

Forthcoming in February 2007:

CLOSE-UP #2
Movies and Tone / Reading Rohmer / Voices in Film

Movies and Tone Douglas Pye

Tone is a concept that has had a very limited place in film theory and criticism, but in our experience of movies tone is inescapable, however much we choose to ignore or work around it. This study, the first to focus directly on the concept, argues that tone should be central to film criticism. The emphasis throughout is on exploring through detailed analysis the material decisions which lead to our grasp of tone as a dimension of meaning that is both informing and yet subject to moment by moment modulation. Films discussed include *Partie de Campagne* (1936), Some Came Running (1958), *Strangers on a Train* (1951), *The Deer Hunter* (1978), *Desperately Seeking Susan* (1985) and *Distant Voices Still Lives* (1988).

Reading Rohmer Jacob Leigh

Reading Rohmer studies three of Eric Rohmer's films from the 1980s and 1990s: *Le Beau mariage* (1982), *Le Rayon vert* (1986) and *Conte d'automne* (1998). It examines how decisions about setting and casting connect to decisions about story, themes and structure; in particular, it concentrates on the work of two of Rohmer's most important collaborators, Béatrice Romand and Marie Rivière, the stars of, respectively, *Le Beau mariage* and *Le Rayon vert*, who were re-united in *Conte d'automne*.

Voices in Film Susan Smith

Voices in Film examines some of the creative ways in which the human voice has been deployed in narrative cinema. Focusing on the role that particular stars' voices have played in shaping the distinctive tone and texture of individual films, the study investigates a number of key examples – from the use of Jenny Agutter's voice in *The Railway Children* (1970) to that of James Stewart's in *Mr Smith Goes To Washington* (1939). Notable uses of the singing voice are also analysed, together with instances where the boundary between singing and speaking blurs. The study examines the crucial role that the voice can play in forging relationships between a film and its audience, in directing us to areas of meaning that may otherwise be obscured from view, and in allowing for a deeper exploration and understanding of a character's inner life.